Successful Grants Program Management

Successful

Grants

Program

Management

David G. Bauer

211
BAU
SVC

Jossey-Bass Publishers • San Francisco

Jossey-Bass books and products are available through most bookstores. To contact Jossey-Bass directly, call (888) 378–2537, fax to (800) 605–2665, or visit our Web site at www.josseybass.com.

Substantial discounts on bulk quantities of Jossey-Bass books are available to corporations, professional associations, and other organizations. For details and discount information, contact the special sales department at Jossey-Bass.

Interior design by Bruce Lundquist.

Manufactured in the United States of America.

Library of Congress Cataloging-in-Publication Data

Bauer, David G.
   Successful grants program management / David G. Bauer. — 1st ed.
     p. cm.
   Includes bibliographical references (p.).
   ISBN 0-7879-5039-4
   1. Educational fund raising—United States.   2. Endowments —United States.
I. Title.
LC243.A1B38 2000
371.2'06—dc21   99-44129
                                                      CIP

FIRST EDITION
PB Printing   10 9 8 7 6 5 4 3 2 1

Contents

List of Figures

Introduction

THE CHALLENGES schools face as we move into the twenty-first century are more compelling than at any other time. Solving today's and tomorrow's unknown challenges will require the following:

- Creativity
- Reallocation of resources
- Dedication
- Additional resources

School systems will continue to experience cost-cutting and budget-containment initiatives as our communities search for ways to provide educated citizens for the twenty-first century. But no matter how much we trim down, quality education costs money. Quality education is also a sound investment in our nation's future. This book focuses on helping you develop resources to meet the challenge of providing students with a good education despite pared-down school budgets.

Twenty-two years ago I left public elementary and secondary education to become assistant to the president for governmental affairs at a state university. My first task was to develop a system for seeking grants. Within a year I was also named development director and alumni director, so I could approach funders outside the grants field. I needed a vehicle to handle these nongrant-related resources, so I created a college foundation. I then had to convince my constituency that state tax support and tuition were not providing students with a superior education. The students deserved more, but the cost of providing it caused us to fall further and further behind. I had to get the community excited about paying more to get excellence in education. Eventually I was able to increase the community's understanding that the state university was tax assisted but not tax supported. It was a challenging but extremely rewarding job.

Now I find that our nation's elementary and secondary schools must market the same case to taxpayers, students, alumni, and communities. In addition to the challenges that a decentralized site-based management approach brings to every school district's grants system, our schools also face the challenge of developing resources from outside the tax base or normal budgeting process.

Grantseeking is only one of many strategies that can be employed to raise funds from outside the school's traditional funding mechanism. There are programs, projects, equipment, and staffing needs that grantseeking will not provide. For example, in some cases the grants marketplace will fund the initiation and testing of a model program but will not support the continued operation of the program even when its effectiveness has been proven. Ultimately, your district will be driven to explore the other vehicles for fund development.

These other fund-raising mechanisms are fundamentally different from grantseeking. In other fund-raising strategies the donor is making a contribution to the general purpose, mission, or cause of the organization. The donation is usually unrestricted. It can be used for a variety of programs supported by the organization. In grantseeking a grantor funds a specific project that has designated measurement criteria and budget expenditures. A specific grant amount is awarded to carry out this well-defined project. Thus, grant money is usually restricted.

The challenges in education require that you develop your school district's readiness to build a total school/community resource development program that takes advantage of all forms of fund development.

First—Use the grants marketplace to build community involvement and to incorporate volunteers in your grants system. A successful grantseeking system brings schools and communities together to create solutions and to promote "buying into" the educational mission. The real key to grants success is the involvement and empowerment of the community.

Second—Set goals, objectives, and a direction for growth using extramural resources.

Third—Implement a grants system that disseminates information on how grants coordination is handled in your system.

Fourth—Consider alternative means of developing funds for proposals that do not match funder guidelines and priorities.

Fifth—Organize a fund-raising advisory committee and create a school foundation to handle your fund raising.

Start with grantseeking and then move on to the other forms of fund development because the other vehicles for raising funds are more involved than grantseeking and people are often afraid of them. In grants, someone will get the money. It's as simple as that.

This book provides the school district administrator with a process for analyzing each component of a successful grants system and the knowledge necessary to develop a plan for change and improvement. Assessment tools at the end of each chapter help you evaluate your district's current system and develop a plan for the future. Your existing system may be adequate or even above average in many ways. But some components most likely can be improved. The theme of this book is that constant evaluation and change today promotes excellence tomorrow. The improvements you make in your system will allow your school district to utilize the grants marketplace to meet the mission of your schools.

The Author

DAVID G. BAUER, one of the most highly sought after speakers on grantseeking, is president of David G. Bauer Associates, Inc., a consulting firm created in 1981 to provide educationally based grantseeking and fund-raising seminars and materials. In addition, he has recently served as the Director of Development for the Center for Educational Accountability and Associate Professor at the University of Alabama at Birmingham School of Education. He has also been the Director for Extramural Funding and Grants Management at the University of Rochester School of Medicine, Department of Pediatrics, and Assistant to the President of the State University of New York College of Technology. Bauer, an acknowledged grants expert and lively lecturer, has taught more than 25,000 individuals successful grantseeking and fundraising techniques.

Mr. Bauer is the author of *The How To Grants Manual, The Complete Grants Sourcebook for Higher Education, Administering Grants, Contracts and Funds, The Principal's Guide to Winning Grants, The Fund Raising Primer, Technology Funding for Schools,* and *The Teacher's Guide to Winning Grants.* He is also the coauthor of *The Complete Grants Sourcebook for Nursing and Health* and *Creating Foundations in American Schools.* In addition, he is the developer of three videotape series—*Winning Grants 2, How to Teach Grantseeking to Others,* and *Strategic Fund Raising*—and two software programs—*Winning Links* and *Grant Winner.*

For more information on David Bauer's products and services visit the David G. Bauer Associates, Inc. website at www.dgbauer.com or phone (800) 836-0732.

Chapter 1

The District's Role in Resource Development

NEW THEORIES OF MANAGEMENT will continually influence your school district and its administrative structure. Innovations such as site-based management and total quality management (TQM) have changed education and its administration. Many administrators bemoan these changes, and even parents extol the old days of the "three Rs." The Internet, a global economy, and the need to produce tomorrow's workforce have made change the job of our schools. From evening adult classes to school-based health clinics to after-school programs to curriculum revisions that reflect the latest technological advances, the school district administrator is at the center of change—like it or not! You may yearn for simpler days, but change is inevitable and constant and you must teach your students to accept and profit from it.

The business world's latest theories on organizational development and the reengineering of the workplace all focus on the dynamic process of change and how to understand and utilize it. Many of the strategies and techniques suggested in this book are based on theories for building a learning organization such as the theory described by Peter Senge in his book *The Fifth Discipline.*

As the school district administrator, you are not only faced with promoting a learning organization in your schools, but you also face the challenge of building change and learning into your grants system. One mistake that many administrators make is believing that they have done their job once their grants system is in place. But Senge points out that a system is never done. As the administrator of grants, you must constantly evaluate what you are doing and construct feedback loops to provide your grants system with the analysis necessary to allow for change, improvement, and the incorporation of new information. As you do so you must also recognize that your challenges in the grants area work in parallel with the evaluation and changes that must be implemented in every other aspect of education. Few school districts employ the components of what the corporate world calls a learning organization, but many promote feedback, evaluation, and standardized testing and have embraced the concept of accountability for the funds they accept.

Most educators now believe that parents, teachers, students, and communities must be committed to quality education and must take responsibility for setting educational goals and developing objectives and methods to meet them. The hope is that by transferring this responsibility to individual schools, neighborhoods, and communities, all partners will invest in and accept ownership of the educational interventions necessary to meet the current and future societal and global pressures facing the United States.

The centralization of school services at the district or central-office level was part of a school consolidation movement characterized by a top-down style of management popular in the 1950s and 1960s. This proved expedient and in many ways economical, but current theories of productivity support a decentralized model characterized by a bottom-up style of decision making.

The current decentralization and local-education empowerment movement poses many challenges for school administrators. This book deals with the impact that a changing management style has on a school district's ability to attract and administer resources from outside its normal revenue source. It presents methods to help you develop a tailored grants system for increasing external funding to better meet your district's mission.

In the rush to increase local decision making and to involve schools and communities in taking a responsible and active role in education, we must not overlook the impact these changes will have on the grants system. Of particular concern is the school district's ability to do the following:

- Present a cohesive positive image to outside funding sources and grantors

- Maintain an organized system of control and contact with the district's current grantors

- Coordinate contact with potential grantors

- Ensure that the projects submitted by school units reflect the district's mission and support its priorities

- Increase the quality of the proposals submitted from the district

- Ensure district credibility through compliance with grantors' rules and regulations

How your school district deals with decentralized grantseeking and controls access to grant resources will shape the future of your grants office.

History will record the gains in education that the new theories of local autonomy and control may be responsible for. However, grantors may not be as kind as historians if they are suddenly besieged with a multitude of proposals from every school in the district—particularly if they are accustomed to that district's central office submitting one proposal chosen by the district.

The fact of the matter is that as your district employs site-based management techniques and local budget decisions and responsibility, decentralized grantseeking is bound to result in an increased motivation to attract external funding. In all likelihood you already are or will be overwhelmed with last-minute requests to sign off on proposals that are hastily created and far from your schools' best efforts. Of course, this assumes that your district office is even approached for a final sign-off. Some district grants offices report the receipt of corporate and foundation grant funds that they did not even know their school district had applied for!

School districts are scrambling to deal with these new challenges. Some create elaborate systems of checks and balances, rules, and flow charts that ultimately stifle any creative interest in grantseeking. Others practice denial or the ostrich response. However, ignoring the issue and burying one's head in the sand or in grant money does not address the challenges posed by decentralized grantseeking.

To deal effectively with the issues, you must first review the basis of your proposal development system and determine whether it is proactive or reactive.

Successful systems today are based on a proactive process that promotes the development of proposal ideas related to a predetermined list of priorities that support the district's mission. Proactivity was a key to success even in the 1970s and 1980s, but decentralized or local site-based management has made it a necessity to move into the twenty-first century.

Unfortunately, most school districts employ a reactive grants process. They wait until they locate a grant opportunity, mount a Herculean last-minute effort, and force the proposal through the grant sign-off system and out the door. This is rarely successful. Government reviewers and corporate and foundation board members frown on it.

The empowerment and heightened interest of the community now require the following:

- A change in the way grantseeking is thought about. It should be thought of as a proactive process based on developing projects and programs that are related to the district's mission, not as an entrepreneurial effort employed by a few individuals with the desire to further their own classroom, curriculum, or professional interests.

- An understanding that grantseeking is a resource-development technique utilized to attract external resources *to the school district*. As such, it is a privilege rather than a right to have one's grant request endorsed by the district.

- A cooperative, friendly spirit of grants competition that bases access to potential grantors on how well the proposed project fits the school's strategic plan and matches the granting pattern and interests of the grantor.

The Grants Office Versus the Resource-Development Office

It is a logical, time-efficient, and productive progression to first look for grant money to help your schools move toward their predetermined goals and then to employ other forms of resource development. Interest in other fund-raising strategies has been increasing as schools deal with the need to support educational programs that are not likely to be successful in attracting grants or have operated successfully on a grant and need to move to another source of support for continuation.

As central administration tries to coordinate and increase the district's grants effort and to raise funds from nongrant-related sources, the role of the district grants office may truly become one of *external resource management*, and the office may evolve into a district resource-development office. The role of the district resource-development office would encompass district coordination of all activities aimed at developing extramural funds including, but not limited to, grants.

Coordination and communication are the keys to a successful district resource-development office. The scenario of a grantor being overwhelmed with proposals from your district's schools is not nearly as bad as the disaster created by individual schools operating such diverse fund-raising events as dances, raffles, "thons," telemarketing, balls, and bequests with no coordination or communication with one another. The potential problems resulting from a lack of coordination can have a dramatic effect on your schools' ability to attract outside funding.

If your school district already has a foundation or other fund-raising vehicle, merge or at least coordinate this vehicle with the district grants office. This will ensure that the grants marketplace is approached first for projects and programs that have the potential to attract grant funds before they are funded with unrestricted funds derived from fund raising. In situations where grantseeking and fund raising are not merged or coordinated, many projects that could be funded from grants are supported by the school foundation, leaving limited school foundation funds for the programs that are least likely to be supported by government, corporate, or foundation grantors.

The preceding information lays the groundwork for the development of a proactive resource-development effort that will maintain your school district's image and credibility with grantors. Your constantly developing resource-development system will encourage the most innovative ideas, reward those responsible, and increase your funding.

In a time of educational cutbacks, especially in district administration, there is a critical need for a coordinated and responsive support system for proposal preparation and administration. Schools are in a unique position to capitalize on new and expanded grant opportunities, and a coordinated, responsive support system will ensure that the grants marketplace is approached correctly.

The subsequent chapters will help committed education professionals develop a tailored grants system that works for their districts and avoid the temptation to copy another district's system. Replicating what works in another district may seem expedient, but a system's success is based on many variables, including the personality of the staff and the idiosyncrasies of the district.

The key to developing your system is to encourage responsible action based on a knowledge of the grants marketplace and cooperation among schools. A common cause will place your school system in the best possible light with grantors. Remember, some grantors do not know about or understand the site-based management approach or the current changes in school administration, and few grantors are eager to read twenty proposals from the same school district to determine which one to fund. They want to receive the proposals that reflect each school's highest priority and that are endorsed by each school's district administration because they are an integral part of the district's educational mission.

The assessment tool at the end of each chapter will help you determine your district's need. The final chapter of the book will provide you with techniques to address these needs and develop a comprehensive plan that will result in your district's own personalized grants system.

Remember: the process of developing a constantly changing system makes it work. Education is the key to the process, and motivation is the energy that culminates in a system supported by those you seek to serve. The process of developing the system builds the support necessary to make it work.

Evaluating your current system may provide a starting point for improvement. Consider sending a questionnaire to your schools to evaluate your current efforts and to provide ideas related to the services you could add.

Divide your survey population into two groups: those that have used your office and written grants (group A) and those that have not (group B).

Group A will provide feedback on the services you currently provide. For example, they will be able to rate your office on how well it assists them in researching and locating grantors, making preproposal contact, and writing proposals. They can also provide you with a list of additional services they would like you to offer and can rank the items by preference.

Group B will not be able to complete a survey on your services, as it has never used them. But you can ask its members how they perceive your office, why they have not gotten involved in grantseeking, and what it would take to get them involved.

By evaluating your system before you initiate some of the techniques suggested in this book, you will have reasons to substantiate your changes and baseline data to compare your new strategies to in the evaluation of their success. The assessment tool that follows is a questionnaire that might be distributed to do such an evaluation.

CHAPTER 1 ASSESSMENT TOOL

1. **How many proposals are initiated and submitted by your district's grants office staff? How many are awarded? How many are rejected? What is the percentage of success?**

Year	Submitted No.	Submitted $	Awarded No.	Awarded $	Rejected No.	Rejected $	Success Rate %
20___	___	_____	___	_____	___	_____	___
20___	___	_____	___	_____	___	_____	___
20___	___	_____	___	_____	___	_____	___

2. **How many proposals are initiated by each of your school units? How many are awarded? How many are rejected? What is the percentage of success?**

School	Year	Submitted No.	Submitted $	Awarded No.	Awarded $	Rejected No.	Rejected $	Success Rate %
_____	20___	___	_____	___	_____	___	_____	___
_____	20___	___	_____	___	_____	___	_____	___
_____	20___	___	_____	___	_____	___	_____	___

3. **How are individual schools encouraged to employ local empowerment and involvement strategies and how does this encouragement affect grant proposals?**

_____

_____

4. **How many of your grants are for a consortium of your schools?** _____

5. **How would you rate the attitude of the schools toward your district grants office?** _____

CHAPTER 1 ASSESSMENT TOOL (continued)

6. How have the changes in the management system had an impact on the number of proposals submitted by the school units and the outcome of their proposal efforts (refer to the grants analysis)?

_____

_____

_____

_____

7. How are school priorities and plans made available to other schools?

_____

_____

_____

_____

8. When was the last time you evaluated your grants system and requested feedback from the system users? _____

What did you learn from the evaluation? _____

_____

What did you change based on what you learned? _____

_____

9. Rate your current system in the following areas.
   - Coordination with the District Grants Office
     _____ needs improvement   _____ acceptable   _____ excellent
   - Success rate of proposals sponsored by the District Grants Office
     _____ needs improvement   _____ acceptable   _____ excellent
   - Success rate of proposals initiated by school units
     _____ needs improvement   _____ acceptable   _____ excellent

10. Do you have a school foundation to raise extramural funds from sources other than grants?
    _____ yes   _____ no
    If yes, how much is raised through these other fund-development vehicles? $_____
    If no, is there a need to develop a school foundation to raise funds for projects that are inappropriate for grant funding?   _____ yes   _____ no

11. How can the district central office include extramural funding in the development of strategic plans?

_____

_____

_____

_____

_____

Chapter 2

Coordinating the District's Grantseeking Efforts

THIS BOOK IS ONE in a series of three. Its two companion books are *The Teacher's Guide to Winning Grants* and *The Principal's Guide to Winning Grants.* The first promotes teacher involvement in grantseeking and stresses the importance of coordination with the school principal and the district grants office. The second emphasizes the importance of proposal development and the potential of grant funding to help move schools toward their goals, objectives, and mission.

Both claim that proposal ideas must relate to a school's goals and objectives and that principals must coordinate their school's grants activities with the district grants office.

And this book tells you, the central office administrator, the same thing. This chapter deals with meeting the educational mission of your district by involving district staff in creating and maintaining a cooperative atmosphere that promotes creative problem solving and idea generation that will result in funded proposals.

Creating such an atmosphere may be more difficult than it sounds because of the proliferation of site-based management and the increasing involvement of teachers, principals, and the school/community in the pursuit of grant funding. Grantseeking as a means of gaining access to resources for your schools is a double-edged sword. On one hand, the motivation, involvement, and interest of teachers, principals, and the school/community are welcomed and encouraged. On the other hand, their grantseeking must be coordinated with the school district's philosophy and priorities. The district grants office's role is much greater than seeing that grant funds are administered properly. The central administration must take responsibility for looking at the big picture and the entire district's mission. Even though each school unit may be seeking funds for its particular priority project, each unit must cooperate with district administration so that a cut-throat, overly competitive atmosphere is not created between schools. Some competition is positive, but collaboration and coordination are key to consistent funding.

As a central administrator, you must also be particularly cautious of uncontrolled entrepreneurial grantseeking because it can result in confusing educational outcomes such as:

- Incompatible textbooks, computers, software, and equipment

- Nonendorsed curriculum projects

Site-based management and increased decision making at the school/ community level do not eliminate the need for a strong central grants administration. Charter schools, magnet schools, and schools within schools must be looked at from the grantor's perspective. Does the grantor understand who it is funding? Is the grantor confused? However, from your schools' perspective, the real issue is how to provide the necessary administration without discouraging grass roots involvement and an entrepreneurial spirit at the school/community level. One answer is to develop a district grants support system based on a proactive grantseeking process that matches your schools' priority projects with grantors' needs, uses preproposal contact, and avoids last-minute, chaotic scrambling to meet deadlines and obtain signatures. The mission of the district grants support system should be to serve each of its school units by doing the following:

- Increasing grantseeking knowledge

- Providing a framework for grantseekers to develop grants advisory committees and interest groups

- Assisting grantseekers with research on potential funding sources

- Providing a system to match school priorities to the district's goals and objectives

- Helping each school unit develop and operate its own total quality management (TQM) program or quality circle to improve proposals *before* they are submitted

In addition, the district grants office should operate a preproposal evaluation and endorsement system that prioritizes each school unit's projects and ensures that they relate to the district's mission.

Many offices have not yet exhibited the fortitude required to limit access to their services and resources on a prioritized basis. Most operate according to the myth that they exist to assist *every* grantseeker, when in reality those proposals that fall under federal entitlement programs or are the favorite projects of superintendents and their assistants utilize almost all of the office's resources.

Now, however, the involvement of school units in independent resource development and grantseeking has forced central administrations to consider prioritizing proposed projects. Doing this provides grants administrators with a means of allocating their time and effort.

The process should include the development of a system that directs proposed projects to the grants administrator and ensures that the district endorses a mix of projects, some of which are school unit priorities and some central administration priorities. Under no circumstance should the district grants administrator be allowed to endorse projects based on his or her own personal interests or desire to help particular grantseekers.

One criterion for the performance evaluation of the grants administrator should be his or her effectiveness in attracting funds to prioritized projects. Unfortunately, many grants administrators are evaluated primarily by the total amount of grant funds they help bring into their district. This encourages them to apply their time and skills only to those proposals that will attract significant dollars, which means that mission-related proposals that may result in fewer total dollars or may be harder and more time-consuming to find support for are put aside.

As a central office administrator, encourage the evaluation of your district's grants system based on how well it helps the district move toward accomplishing its predetermined goals and objectives. The grants system must relate the expenditure of its resources to those predetermined ends.

You can use many strategies to identify and prioritize projects. But because of the many interests, personalities, and strong feelings embodied in your district, attempts to reach consensus may be futile. However, by instituting a system that focuses on the areas of greatest concern to the whole district and in which the outcome is determined by vote, you can develop a weighted list that will reduce bickering and provide direction for the entire grants effort.

Your first step should be to ask each school/community unit to develop a prioritized grants wish list. This should be based on the input of teachers, principals, professional staff members, and community advisory groups. Some schools may employ a formal committee structure to generate their list of priority projects. No matter how the list is generated, it must be reconciled with any previously established site-based plans that outline school/community objectives.

Developing District Grants Booklets

To be effective, your districtwide grants system should include a process for explaining to teachers, principals, and community advisory groups how grantseeking is supported in your district. I recommend the development and dissemination of individual booklets describing the major steps involved in grantseeking and the district's role in each. For example:

- Developing Your Proposal Ideas and Securing District Approval

- Researching Grants and Making Contact with Funding Sources

- Writing Your Proposal: Using District Resources to Assist in Preparing the Budget, Writing the Proposal, and Meeting Submittal Requirements

- The Administration of Your Grant

Complete the assessment tool that follows each chapter before you determine what topics will be covered in the booklets and how many booklets will need to be developed. In general, several booklets will be needed; these will usually be better received by grantseekers than one lengthy district grants manual. Remember to look at your grants system from the perspective of your teachers, principals, and community advisory committee members. If you hand them a three-hundred-page document that details each stage of proposal preparation and grants administration, they may become overwhelmed and quit before they even start!

The role grantseeking plays in your school district should be the first topic addressed. Your district administration's endorsement of grantseeking as a district priority and your strong statement of support for the grants procurement system should be a matter of record.

Recent research on the factors contributing to increases in grant acquisition at universities and colleges suggests that the expectations of the chief academic officers have the greatest impact. As in higher education, your system's level of success will depend on your district administration's degree of support and the importance placed on the grants procurement system.

Your grants system should address the need for a coordinated effort and define the process for allocating your grants office's resources. If your district has grants support personnel at the school or subject-area level, this should be understood by all personnel, including new district employees.

The district grants office should be a vehicle for change and provide instructions that outline how the school/community can take part in shaping the district's grants effort.

For example, you may provide your school units with guidelines on how to participate in the development of districtwide grant priorities. Such guidelines could become the basis for a grants booklet. Figure 2.1 provides a sample that you can tailor to your district.

<u>**Figure 2.1**</u>

SAMPLE GUIDELINES FOR DEVELOPING DISTRICTWIDE GRANTS PRIORITIES

Each year the schools that comprise our district will be asked to submit to the district grants office a prioritized list of the areas of need they would like to see addressed as districtwide grants priorities.

The schools may develop their prioritized list by brainstorming areas of need with faculty, staff, advisory groups, and school/community members. Each school's administrator or other designated person will develop the prioritized list through whatever means decided upon (rank ordering, values voting, and so on).

This process is intended to do the following:

1. Focus the efforts of the district grants office

2. Provide a rationale for evaluating the success of the district grants effort

3. Allocate district grants office resources

Each school's participation will have a direct effect on the district grants program and is therefore very important to our entire school system.

Those individuals or groups that choose to pursue grant funding in the prioritized areas of need will receive preference by grants office personnel and will receive help in meeting grantor requirements such as in-kind contributions, matching funds, space needs, and equipment.

The following outlines how the process for developing a prioritized list will be handled in our district. The process for developing a prioritized list of proposal interests will be examined yearly during the month(s) of _____.

Each school unit will be invited to submit a prioritized list of the areas that have the greatest opportunity for improvement in their schools—in other words, those areas with the most compelling needs. School units should be sure to identify areas of need rather than specific solutions. For example, more computer terminals are a solution to a need, not an area of need. The need is to increase computer skills, instruction, and familiarity with computer applications, improve reading and math scores using computer software, etc. (You could even suggest that there are several programs that the district will apply for that year like the Twenty-First Century Learning Grants or other title funds that will require innovative solutions for the proposals due months later.)

To help your school's staff and volunteers develop their list you can suggest that they brainstorm what areas of need they would like to see addressed with an anonymous gift of $_____. After the list of areas that could be improved with the fictitious funds has been developed, request that each person rank order the list. The list, which will be submitted to the district, should include those areas that were consistently ranked as the ones with the greatest need.

The final list will provide the basis for the allocation of matching funds and of support services from the district grants office. It will also be the basis for the measurement of the success of the district grants effort.

A district grants priorities committee could use the prioritized grants list from each school to combine priorities and grant ideas and develop a prioritized district list.

Prioritization should focus on problems or needs that the school wants to address through model projects and other solutions. If, for example, a school says it needs an after-school program it must also explain why, because that is usually the variable that the district committee uses to determine a final priority list. Identification of the problem or need is also necessary to avoid receiving the following:

- The technology committee's list of what it wants but no suggestions of why or by whom the technology will be used

- A playground equipment list without any mention of who will use it for how long and why it is necessary

- A proposal to copy another school's program with no analysis of why it should be done

- Easily developed proposals from sales representatives and corporate marketing groups—replication grants that are not applicable to the school's particular needs

---

CHAPTER TWO ASSESSMENT TOOL

1. **Does your district have a written mission statement?**
   _____ yes   _____ no
   If yes, when was it last revised? _____

2. **Does the district have individual school/community goals and objectives or site-based goals and objectives?**
   _____ yes   _____ no
   If yes, when were they last updated? _____

3. **Does your district have a grants office mission?**
   _____ yes   _____ no
   If yes, how is it related to the district's educational mission? _____
   _____

4. **How does the district grants office allocate time (resources) between districtwide and individual school/community grants efforts?**
   _____
   _____

5. **Are the needs of the district and of individual school units prioritized?**
   _____ yes   _____ no

6. **Is there a clearly defined process for developing districtwide grants priorities?**
   _____ yes   _____ no

Developing Your School's Ability to Create Grant-Winning Solutions

HELP YOUR SCHOOLS articulate their priorities, demonstrate to them how the grants mechanism can meet their needs, and motivate them to further involve themselves in generating proposals.

How? Depending on your schedule and the role you seek to play, you may want to do the following:

- Visit each school to explain how the district grants office can help.

- Conduct in-service classes on documenting need and proposal development.

- Distribute booklets on how to get started in grantseeking at faculty meetings, fall orientation, and new-teacher orientation.

Grant Idea Generation System

Quality ideas developed through the input and sharing of the entire school/community are what an outstanding proposal is all about. It is crucial that the district grants office implement an idea generation system aimed at bringing volunteers and school representatives together to develop ideas to address their prioritized needs. But before they jump in, you must help them do the following:

1. Understand the formula for educational advancement
2. Focus on the needs gap
3. Document the need or problem area
4. Identify the desired outcome or goal

The Formula for Educational Advancement

This formula is a visual aid you can use with grantseekers to illustrate the ingredients necessary to develop strategies to meet the challenges of education (see Figure 3.1).

The main ingredients of the formula are *needs, solutions, commitment,* and *catalyst*. Each is equally important in moving toward the goal of educational advancement.

First, *needs* must be identified. Needs are commonly thought of as problems, but they are actually opportunities to create change. For example, low reading scores provide the opportunity to increase reading levels, and the expansion of an existing successful program provides the opportunity to build on proven achievement.

Second, *solutions* should be generated in response to the district's predetermined needs—not because a grantor has dedicated funding to a specific area.

Third, the *commitment* and extra effort of educators and community leaders are essential to convince grantors that there is a genuine concern for addressing the need. Most grassroots grantseeking is accomplished as a result of this donated effort.

The *catalyst* in the formula is grant money. In this formula the catalyst speeds up the grant reaction. Your schools will move toward their goals irrespective of the availability of grants; but grants will allow them to get there faster.

This formula helps demonstrate to potential grantors that the desired educational advancement is worth their money.

As districts seek to accomplish their mission through increased grants, the central grants office must be sure that all of the components of the formula for educational advancement are present and balanced. A district's

Figure 3.1

FORMULA FOR EDUCATIONAL ADVANCEMENT

Needs +	Solutions +	Commitment =		Educational Advancement
of your students, classroom, community, and society	ideas and strategies to adapt change, strengthen the education system	the extra effort of you, your colleagues, and parents	∞*	new strategies, equipment, and materials to meet the challenges of education

Grantseeking provides the catalyst in this equation and supports change occuring at an increased rate.

long-term credibility and ability to attract grants can be negated by submitting proposals with excellent solutions but no documented needs, or with documented needs and exemplary solutions but no school/community commitment or involvement.

Helping Your Grantseekers Focus on the Needs Gap

This is one of the most critical areas in grantseeking. Unfortunately it also often gets overlooked and minimized in proposal preparation. To focus your grantseekers on a prioritized system, you must help them separate what they want to do from why it needs to be done. For example, the need to upgrade a computer lab or computer classroom capabilities is not documented by providing an inventory of old equipment and a list of the latest computers and software. Grantors may or may not know how beneficial new technology is for the classroom, or whether the potential grantee has a solution that will help with the problem. Even if the grantor knows a lot about the problem, the grantseeker must demonstrate in-depth knowledge of it.

One of the most difficult tasks in grantseeking is to help the proposal developers focus on the problem instead of the solution. If they do, they will clearly see the gap between what is and what ought to be and realize that their proposed solution is just one of many ways to gain the desired outcome.

You can help your grantseekers focus on need by asking them why anyone would care about closing the gap between what is and what ought to be (see Figure 3.2) and by encouraging them to consider what, if anything, would happen if the problem was never addressed.

Documenting the Need

Ask your prospective grantseekers to complete a Needs Worksheet (Figure 3.3) to guide them in collecting the data necessary to convince a grantor that they have the following:

- A command of the most recent literature and of worldwide, national, and regional studies of the problem

Figure 3.2

THE GAP	
What exists now. What is real.	What could be. The goal.
What the present situation is.	The desired state of affairs,
How many students are at this stage.	level of achievement.

- Knowledge of the extent of the local problem (studies, surveys, statistics, and other data that document its existence)

Give your grantseekers a list of the district offices that accumulate data that may help them document the existence of the local problem. This will discourage the collection of unreliable or conflicting data concerning your district and the students and communities you serve. Pertinent district information may include the following:

- Geographical and demographic data
- Achievement scores for reading, math, and science
- Attendance data
- Completion and dropout rates
- Health data
- Job placement statistics
- Financial information

Encourage your grantseekers to compare your district's needs data with studies and articles related to the problem areas they seek to have an impact on. Your state education department and schools of education are

---

Figure 3.3

NEEDS WORKSHEET

Completing this worksheet will help you step back from possible solutions and projects and establish that there is a gap between what is now and what should be.

Problem Area: _____

_____

_____

Documentation of the Need to Address This Problem:

What Exists Now— **The Present State of Affairs**	**Source of Data**
(studies, facts, surveys, case studies, etc.)	(organization)
	(journal, newsletter, newspaper, etc.)
	(date of publication)

Note: *Consider performing a survey of your classroom, school, and/or community to document that the problem exists.*

constantly producing studies and comparisons your grantseekers should have. By placing your schools' data on a website your grantseekers have access to, or on a disk that is circulated to them, you help ensure that false or conflicting data does not appear in the needs section of any proposals put out by your district. The gap that your grantseekers must document between what is and what ought to or could be must demonstrate a clear, compelling, and motivating case for funding their proposal.

The needs statements in your district's proposals will gain credibility when they compare local statistics with regional, national, or international data. Your grantseekers' knowledge of your district's needs data and their command of the national data will add to your district's credibility and hence fundability. The needs section of a proposal may actually be considered more important to reviewers and represent a greater percentage of points when scoring than the objectives and methods section. This is due to the strong relationship needs documentation has to the construction of measurable behavioral objectives and the demonstration of the proposed project's ability to close the gap between what exists and what ought to or could be. The secret is to provide needs documentation that clearly demonstrates what exists in your school and also how your school's problem relates to the problem on a national level or to a particular type of school (such as rural or urban).

When you uncover a particularly interesting study that shows a national need, you could repeat the study in your school to determine if its need is the same, greater, or less. Figure 3.4 is a sample of a needs worksheet based on a national study conducted several years ago surveying twenty-five thousand middle school children. The results of the survey were striking. Your grantseekers could get a small corporate or local foundation grant to see how these findings have changed over time, and particularly since the introduction of the Internet, video games, and other computer-related recreational diversions. In other words, has the level of parental involvement and the constructive use of informal educational experiences changed, and if so, how? A reviewer and ultimately a grantor would be impressed with your up-to-date data and your ability to document the changes called for in your proposal's objectives.

Identifying the Desired Outcome or Goal

A gap requires that there be two end points. With some encouragement and examples, most grantseekers do a good job at documenting the first end point, or what exists now (the left side of Figure 3.2), but have a harder time trying to document what could be or should be (the right side of Figure 3.2).

Figure 3.4

NEEDS WORKSHEET SAMPLE

Completing this worksheet will help you step back from possible solutions and projects and establish that there is a gap between what is now and what should be.

Problem Area: Parents' lack of involvement in their children's formal education and lack of support for constructive informal educational experiences.

_____

Documentation of the Need to Address This Problem:

What Exists Now—
The Present State of Affairs

4 out of 5 parents reported that they regularly discuss schoolwork with their children. Yet two-thirds of the children said their parents rarely or never talked about school with them.

Two-thirds of the parents claimed to place limits on television viewing. Two-thirds of the children said they had no limits on television viewing.

The middle school group (8th graders) reported watching 21.4 hours of television per week, in comparison to spending 5.6 hours per week on homework.

50 percent of the parents reported attending school meetings, but less than one-third had ever visited their child's classroom.

66 percent had never talked to school officials concerning their child's homework.

Source of Data

Department of Education, Office of Educational Research and Improvement, Study reported in the *Wall Street Journal* on January 3, 1992. 25,000 middle school children surveyed.

Note: *You could include findings from surveys of your classroom, school, or community; a consortium of classes; or a comparison to a classroom in Europe or another part of the world.*

The Goals Worksheet (Figure 3.5) will help your grantseekers focus on what the desired outcome would be if we lived in a perfect world and if money and time were not constraints. Although goals are often not achieved, they do help grantors see where projects are headed and understand the gap between what exists and the desired state of affairs. You can also suggest that your grantseekers survey local officials, experts, teachers, or parents to determine what they think ought to be or should be relative to the problem and demonstrated gap.

Figure 3.5

GOALS WORKSHEET

Problem Area:_____

_____

_____

_____

_____

If the needs documented on the Needs Worksheet were fulfilled and the problem was eliminated, what would result? What is the *desired* state of affairs? The ultimate end? The answer to these questions states the goal. The Needs Worksheet documents what exists now. The Goals Worksheet documents what ought to be. The goal provides purpose, direction, and motivation for grantseeking.

Goal: _____

_____

_____

_____

_____

Record studies, quotations, and research findings that document what ought to be. Provide sources and dates.

Studies—Quotations—Research Findings	**Source—Date**

Note: *This is not the place to list solutions. Means of closing gaps are solutions; they are discussed in Chapter Five.*

In the sample worksheet (Figure 3.6), the goal is to have all parents and teachers act as responsible partners who work together to maximize the educational achievement of children. Because there will always be a few parents and teachers who will not act responsibly, the goal is not likely to be attained; however, it is hoped that the proposed solution will reduce the gap and move the school/community closer to the goal.

Developing Fundable Solutions

One role of your district grants office is to provide services to help potential grantseekers develop solutions to the problem areas they have identified. This assistance is a great step toward encouraging high-quality, well-developed proposals. Encourage your grantseekers to brainstorm

Figure 3.6

GOALS WORKSHEET SAMPLE

Problem Area: Parents' lack of involvement in their children's formal education and lack of support for constructive informal educational experiences.

If the needs documented on the Needs Worksheet were fulfilled and the problem was eliminated, what would result? What is the *desired* state of affairs? The ultimate end? The answer to these questions states the goal. The Needs Worksheet documents what exists now. The Goals Worksheet documents what ought to be. The goal provides purpose, direction, and motivation for grantseeking.

Goal: Parents and teachers acting as responsible partners who work together to maximize children's educational achievement.

Record studies, quotations, and research findings that document what ought to be. Provide sources and dates.

Studies—Quotations—Research Findings	Source—Date
Students whose parents discussed their schoolwork recorded higher grades.	Dept. of Education Study, *Wall Street Journal* 1/3/92
Television viewing restrictions tended to boost grades.	Dept. of Education Study, *Wall Street Journal* 1/3/92
"Burden of education should not be on the teachers and schools alone." Education Department study says, "Parents have a major role to play."	Dept. of Education Study, *Wall Street Journal* 1/3/92
Home-based guidance program in Rochester schools demonstrates educational improvement in low-income students. Homeroom teacher acts as liaison between schools and parents. When teacher makes home visits, children do better in school.	Harvard University, 3-year study, Berea, OH, *Democrat & Chronicle* 11/28/91.
Preschool children from single-parent homes have better verbal skills than children from two-parent homes (more one-on-one communication).	Unpublished study 1989–90, Deidre Madden, Baldwin Wallace College, Berea, OH, *Democrat & Chronicle* 11/28/91.
Harrison, Arkansas—Students score in top 10 percent of the nation in test scores, yet Arkansas ranks 272 of 327 in education taxes. One of the lowest tax rates in the U.S. Money may not be the resource that makes the difference. Parents volunteer in their children's classrooms one hour per week. Duties include making copies, grading papers, working with students, listening to students read. Basically, the parents save teachers' time. Parents and teachers meet on school councils and determine the educational goals for next year. Each school reports progress toward goals in a newspaper advertisement. School system received ten new computers donated by civic clubs. Parents made speeches at clubs.	*USA Today* 11/18/91; study identifies good schools through "School Match" of Columbus, Ohio. "School Match" provides information to families moving to new areas.
Frank Newman, President of Education Commission, states, "They're saying parents are important and teachers are important and they should be part of running the schools."	

proposal ideas (solutions) with volunteers, fellow staff members, and professionals in the school/community. Involving others provides a means to do the following:

- Move from a single or self-focused approach

- Incorporate the best components of several approaches into one idea

- Involve others in the project at an early stage of its development, thus increasing commitment and the potential for a consortia proposal

Ask your grantseekers to complete the Worksheet for Developing Solutions and Projects to Reduce the Problem (Figure 3.7). They should record and rank all the proposed solutions. The group leader should tabulate the results and identify the five highest-ranked ideas.

Figure 3.7

WORKSHEET FOR DEVELOPING SOLUTIONS AND PROJECTS TO REDUCE THE PROBLEM

Problem: _____

_____

_____

List any and all proposed solutions. No discussions, please. Discuss the ideas after the time allotted for brainstorming has expired. Then request each participant to rank order the proposed solutions, with 1 being the favorite.

Rank   **Proposed Solutions/Projects to Reduce the Problem**

-
-
-
-
-
-
-
-
-
-
-
-
-
-

The five should then be placed on the Worksheet for Developing the Top Five Suggested Solutions to the Problem (Figure 3.8). Actually, fewer than five solutions may be listed as long as the grantseekers generate more than one solution, maintain a broad view of the problem, and remain flexible when analyzing each solution. Grantseekers should be reminded that being able to locate grantors willing to fund their proposal is in part a function of their flexibility and ingenuity.

The idea generators should use the spaces provided on the worksheet to describe each solution, estimate the cost of each approach and the cost per person served, and list the drawbacks associated with each idea. Note that the worksheet has a place to record whether the problem addressed by the proposed solutions is a district priority. This is the district office's first indication of grants interest and will help the office forecast its potential workload.

Figure 3.8

WORKSHEET FOR DEVELOPING THE TOP FIVE SUGGESTED SOLUTIONS TO THE PROBLEM

Problem: _____

_____

_____

_____

Describe the top five proposed solutions briefly and give a rough estimate of the cost of each. Also provide an estimate of the cost per student or teacher. Include the number of individuals who would benefit directly from each solution and the number who could benefit indirectly through duplication of the approach at other schools. List the drawbacks of each (that is, those things that would impede its success).

Ask the following of each solution. Would you fund this idea with a grant? Will the benefits justify the money expended?

Solution #1:

Solution #2:

Solution #3:

Solution #4:

Solution #5:

Figure 3.9

WORKSHEET FOR DEVELOPING THE TOP FIVE SUGGESTED SOLUTIONS TO THE PROBLEM SAMPLE

Problem: Parents' lack of involvement in their children's education and lack of support for constructive informal educational experience.

Describe the top five proposed solutions briefly and give a rough estimate of the cost of each. Also provide an estimate of the cost per student or teacher. Include the number of individuals who would benefit directly from each solution and the number who could benefit indirectly through duplication of the approach at other schools. List the drawbacks of each (that is, those things that would impede its success).

Ask the following of each solution. Would you fund this idea with a grant? Will the benefits justify the money expended?

Solution #1: Develop a parent-teacher-student education contract that outlines each party's responsibility to support education. Review and renew every month on a three-part carbonless form.

Solution #2: Send a short videotape of classroom and educational techniques to the parents and add a specific segment on the parents' child and her or his progress.

Solution #3: Require teachers to visit every student's home twice per year to report on the child's educational progress.

Solution #4: Allow taxpayers to lower their school taxes by volunteering/working at the school.

Solution #5: Send parents a newsletter each month with articles on how and why they should get involved.

In the sample worksheet provided (Figure 3.9), the grantseekers may decide that combining solutions one and two will result in a greater likelihood that the proposed change will occur.

Your district may decide to develop a booklet comprising selected worksheets to help your individual school units get started in grantseeking. The worksheets listed in the Sample Booklet (Figure 3.10) should be

---

Figure 3.10

SAMPLE BOOKLET OF SUGGESTED WORKSHEETS

How to Get [Name of School] Started in Grantseeking

The following worksheets have been selected and distributed to you by your district grants office to help you attract grant funding. Review and complete each worksheet. Samples have been provided, and our office is available to assist you.

Worksheets
- The Formula for Educational Advancement—Figure 3.1
- Focus on the Needs Gap—Figure 3.2
- Document the Need—Figures 3.3 and 3.4
- Developing Your Goals—Figures 3.5 and 3.6
- Solutions—Figures 3.7, 3.8, and 3.9

tailored to each school unit. Your booklet may include a short narrative describing how to use each of the worksheets.

CHAPTER 3 ASSESSMENT TOOL

Use this assessment tool to rate how effective your district grants office is in involving, interesting, and educating individuals concerning the generation and support of ideas that may lead to grant proposals.

This assessment tool can be revised into a survey to be administered to representatives of your district's various groups. The survey respondents' ratings can then be compared to yours.

1. **Estimate your district's interest in potential grant proposals and idea generation.**
   Five years ago: _____ very low _____ low _____ moderate _____ high _____ very high
   Currently: _____ very low _____ low _____ moderate _____ high _____ very high

2. **Rate the district grants office's current overall efforts to help potential grantseekers develop fundable grant ideas.**
   _____ nonexistent _____ inadequate _____ adequate _____ excellent

3. **Rate the current efforts employed by the district grants office in each of the following areas. (Some of these activities may be nonexistent. In these cases, put a check next to those that you believe should be implemented to increase interest in developing grant ideas.)**
   _____ Meet with faculty and staff at individual school units to discuss the development of grant ideas
   _____ nonexistent _____ inadequate _____ adequate _____ excellent
   _____ Provide grant/proposal idea–generation workshops at school sites
   _____ nonexistent _____ inadequate _____ adequate _____ excellent
   _____ Provide instructional materials (videotapes, software, and so on)
   _____ nonexistent _____ inadequate _____ adequate _____ excellent
   _____ Use a district grants volunteer group to work with individual schools
   _____ nonexistent _____ inadequate _____ adequate _____ excellent
   _____ Sponsor a grantseeking day with a panel consisting of foundation, corporate, and government grantors
   _____ nonexistent _____ existent

4. **List the printed materials that the district grants office distributes to help potential grantseekers. Rate (circle) the quality of each item.**
   _____ poor   adequate   excellent
   _____ poor   adequate   excellent
   _____ poor   adequate   excellent
   _____ poor   adequate   excellent
   _____ poor   adequate   excellent

5. **List suggestions for improvements and/or any additional materials needed (such as a booklet) to help individuals get started in grantseeking.**
   _____
   _____
   _____
   _____

Chapter 4

Promoting Understanding of the Funding Process

SCHOOL DISTRICTS handle the search for grantors in various ways. Variables that determine the district grants office's role in this process include the following:

- The superintendent's and assistant superintendent's interest in and support for grantseeking
- The school district's established grants priorities
- The district grants office's budget and staff resources
- Computer capabilities, access to modems, and funds to support a database search system
- The availability of space for a district grants library and a budget for purchasing resource materials
- The district's location and proximity to a Foundation Center Regional Collection

Impatient generators of proposals want to know where to go fast to get their ideas funded. However, the grants professional knows that fast precludes the importance of selecting prospective grantors carefully and making preproposal contact to verify the grantors' interests and to determine their preference for possible solutions. Your central grants office should strive to develop your district's ability to capitalize on these proven techniques and to help your grantseekers understand why certain types of grantors are recommended for specific types of projects and solutions. This office may actually become involved in teaching inservice grantseeking seminars to your school district personnel and faculty and making grants presentations to community groups.

In an effort to utilize sound educational practices you should ascertain your prospective grantseekers' knowledge about the grants marketplace before the onset of your grants seminars and presentations. Once you have assessed how much they know you can develop and adapt your program content accordingly.

Promotion of knowledge concerning the grants marketplace could be another responsibility of your district grants office. Misconceptions concerning the grants marketplace are rampant and, whether you believe it or not, affect how teachers, administrators, and volunteers view your office's efforts. These same misconceptions also predispose uneducated grantseekers to approach the different segments of the marketplace for inappropriate grant amounts.

After pretesting more than twenty thousand grant seminar participants I can assure you that even those who are successful at grantseeking have misconceptions about the marketplace. If your district's grantseekers do not know where the money is, who has it, and in what amounts, they will not understand your office's strategies. Consider making the improvement of general grants knowledge in your district one of your office's objectives. You do not need to administer the Grants Marketplace Quiz (Figure 4.1) to everyone and you do not need to embarrass anyone by questioning them individually. Instead use any district meeting, from school board to curriculum, as an opportunity to increase grants knowledge. Select one or two questions from the quiz and ask the group members to take a guess at the answers. If you are concerned that the members will be worried about the recognition of their handwriting, pass out small cards with multiple choices listed and ask the members to circle what they think the correct answer is.

Tabulate the responses while the rest of the meeting is going on and at the end of the meeting list the group's responses on the blackboard. Then tell them the correct answers. In a true seminar setting, you may wish to use the entire Grants Marketplace Quiz or a few more questions from it.

The Grants Marketplace Quiz

The Grants Marketplace Quiz (Figure 4.1) is a useful preassessment tool as well as a postevaluation instrument. Correctly answering the questions reflects lower-order cognitive skills such as being aware of specific facts and understanding trends and sequences. If you are going to teach a grants seminar or make a grants presentation that requires higher-order cognitive skills such as analysis, synthesis, and evaluation, you will need to develop additional questions.

Figure 4.1

THE GRANTS MARKETPLACE QUIZ

1. How many 501(c)(3) tax-exempt charitable organizations are recognized by the Internal Revenue Service? _____

2. How many elementary schools, middle schools, and junior high schools are there in the United States? _____

3. How much money will the federal government grant through its 1,300+ granting programs this year? _____

4. What was the total amount of funds distributed to nonprofit groups through foundation grants, corporate grants, bequests, and individuals in the past year? _____

5. What percentage of total funds is granted by each of the following four sources?
   a. Foundations _____%
   b. Corporations _____%
   c. Bequests _____%
   d. Individuals _____%
             100%

Foundations

6. Approximately how many grantmaking foundations are there? _____

7. The business of approximately how many foundations is carried out in offices? _____

8. How many grants of more than $10,000 were awarded in the past year? _____

Corporations

9. Approximately how many corporations are there in the United States? _____

10. What percentage of corporations take a deduction for charitable contributions? _____

11. Which of the following forms of corporate support to nonprofit organizations has experienced the greatest increase in the past five years?
   a. products
   b. cash
   c. securities
   d. loans

Even with its limitations, the Grants Marketplace Quiz will help you, the central grants office administrator, develop a targeted, proactive, success-based, districtwide grantseeking effort. Your district grants strategy must be based on a knowledge of where the grant funds really are.

Present the quiz as an assessment tool in a nonthreatening and relaxed way by asking the members of the group to guess at the answers. Assure them that the quiz does not have to be signed. You may collect the quizzes and correct them or display the correct answers on an overhead screen, board, or flip chart so that the group members can correct their quizzes.

They should then hand in the quizzes so that you can assess the group's level of expertise. It is important for you to explain why the group's overall scores on the quiz may have been low. Point out that newspapers, journals, and newsletters focus on *exceptionally large* grant awards, causing people to believe that all grants are of the million-dollar variety. This is simply not the case.

Emphasize the importance of developing a realistic appraisal of the marketplace. Discuss how inappropriate grants strategies could evolve if grantseekers were to base their grantseeking on overinflated estimates of the grants marketplace.

You may wish to expand your discussion of the correct answers to the quiz by including the background information that follows the answer key (Figure 4.2).

Question #1—The figure of 654,186 is somewhat misleading. There are actually many more 501(c)(3) tax-exempt organizations because some-

---

Figure 4.2

THE GRANTS MARKETPLACE QUIZ ANSWER KEY

1. How many 501(c)(3) tax-exempt charitable organizations are recognized by the IRS?   **654,186**

2. How many elementary schools, middle schools, and junior high schools are there in the United States?   **75,000+**

3. How much money will the federal government grant through its 1,300+ granting programs this year?   **$90 billion**

4. What was the total amount of funds distributed to nonprofit groups through foundation grants, corporate grants, bequests, and individuals in the past year?   **$143.5 billion**

5. What percentage of total funds is granted by each of the following four sources?
   a. Foundations   **9.3%**
   b. Corporations   **5.7%**
   c. Bequests   **8.8%**
   d. Individuals   **76.2%**
                       100%

Foundations

6. Approximately how many grantmaking foundations are there?   **41,588**

7. The business of approximately how many foundations is carried out in offices?   **1,000**

8. How many grants of more than $10,000 were awarded in the past year?   **86,203**

Corporations

9. Approximately how many corporations are there in the United States?   **5 million**

10. What percentage of corporations take a deduction for charitable contributions?   **35%**

11. Which of the following forms of corporate support to nonprofit organizations has experienced the greatest increase in the past five years?   **b. cash**

times several nonprofits operate under one number approved by the IRS. For example, a university may have a center, an institute, and a museum all operating under one number.

Question #2—It is important to focus on how all nonprofit organizations compete for grant funds. It is especially important to note the competition from other school districts. Keep in mind, however, that some of these have *never* applied for a grant, and others have applied for government funding only. Now is the time for the schools in your district to capitalize on the trend in the foundation and corporate grants marketplace to award grants for early intervention to preschools and elementary and middle schools.

Question #3—Although the federal government will grant approximately $90 billion in 1999, far more than this will be appropriated to programs. For example, the Department of Education will not award all of its appropriation in grants, because a large part of it must be used to pay for overhead, office space, and salaries and fringes for the program officers and staff. In other words, the amount *appropriated* to a program is not the same as the amount *awarded* by a program in the form of grants.

Your schools' ability to access federal grant funds is a function of how their projects are defined and whom they are supposed to benefit. The Department of Education is only one source of federal funds. Your district's grantseekers can also apply for federal grant money that is distributed to your state as well as for funds from federal programs that focus on preventing drug and alcohol use, the humanities, science, literacy, health, and many other related areas.

Question #4—The total amount of nongovernment funding for nonprofits is calculated each summer for the previous year. The estimate for 1997 was $143.5 billion, a sum that may startle your district personnel, faculty, and community volunteers. Moreover, most individuals think that the portion of this money granted by foundations and corporations is much greater than it really is.

Once you reveal the correct percentages, some group members may express a strong desire to go after individual giving—76.2 percent or $101.26 billion. That is, until you inform them of the following:

- More than 40 percent of individual giving is to religious organizations.

- That still leaves over $50 billion, but fund-raising techniques must be employed to access these funds, including special events, direct mail, telephone solicitation, and so on.

Seeking grants from foundations and corporations usually consists of preparing a well-targeted two-page letter proposal. Compare this simple process with the stringent proposal requirements of government agencies, and the $13.37 billion in grants from foundations and corporations begins to look very good. Grantseeking in general is a better alternative to securing external resources than other traditional fund-raising techniques.

District personnel, faculty, and community volunteers should be made aware that the federal government has far more financial resources than foundations and corporations. Therefore, private funding sources often prefer that potential grantees look to government sources first. This information will help your prospective grantseekers understand why it is important to pursue federal as well as private grant funds.

Question #6—Highlight the differences between the 1,300-plus federal programs and the 41,588 foundations. Each foundation thinks of itself and the projects it supports as invaluable and unique!

Question #7—No one knows exactly how many federal employees are involved in the grants area. If you include program officers, staff, and auditors, the number must be staggering.

Because foundations often have limited funds, they feel that the more staff they have, the fewer grants they can make. If they do not have an office, they need few if any paid staff. For this reason, fewer than 1,000 foundations occupy offices.

Estimates are that the 41,588 foundations actually employ only slightly more than 3,000 individuals. Keep in mind also that some large foundations have 100 or more employees, whereas thousands of smaller foundations have none.

Armed with these facts, your district personnel, faculty, and community volunteers will clearly understand how important it is to utilize an informal webbing and linkage system in contacting foundation and corporate board members.

Question #8—This information will help prospective grantseekers set realistic expectations based on sound knowledge of the grants marketplace. As only 86,203 grants in excess of $10,000 are reported to the Foundation Center, to receive a $100,000 foundation grant is an admirable achievement.

The positive aspect of this situation is that there are hundreds of thousands of grants of under $10,000. This is good news for the schools in your district that can formulate interesting proposals for small requests to support programs or projects that can influence many students.

Question #9—There are several reasons why many corporations are not deeply involved in philanthropy. The root of their lack of involvement goes back to the late 1930s, when it was actually illegal for corporations to make gifts to nonprofit organizations.

Question #10—In reality, many more corporations make gifts than take deductions. Many do not report deductions for these gifts so as not to invite audits from the IRS. In addition, many owners and executives make contributions from their personal funds. Incorporate the following basic facts of corporate philanthropy into your district's strategy for grantseeking.

1. Corporations do not "give away" money. They "invest" it and expect a return.

2. Corporations invest where they live and where the children of their workers go to school.

3. Corporations value investment. Many will not make a grant unless their employees volunteer time to the nonprofit applicant.

Do not make the mistake of allowing your district personnel, faculty, and community volunteers to think that only large corporations make grants. It often pays to approach smaller corporations. Your prospective grantseekers should especially keep in mind smaller corporations that they have a link with, for example, smaller corporations with employees who are graduates of your school district.

Question #11—Cash is technically the correct answer, according to surveys of corporate contributions taken as tax deductions on corporate tax returns. It is estimated that considerable contributions in the form of products are made by the marketing budgets of corporations and are not recorded or taken as tax deductions. However, the exact figures cannot be verified.

The Grantseekers' Matrix

If your goal is to empower your district grantseekers and reduce their need for your office to assist them in every step of the grantseeking process, then you will find the Grantseekers' Matrix (Figure 4.3) a very helpful tool. To a grants professional, knowing which category of funder prefers what type of project is second nature. The Grantseekers' Matrix will help cultivate this trait in your grantseekers.

Although there are separate matrices for each category of funder, the same column headings are found on each matrix. Column 1 of the Grantseekers' Matrix describes the various types of projects—demonstration, research, equipment, replication, consortium, and international. Columns 2 through 9 provide the grantseeker with insight into how the various categories of grantors view the major variables that determine grants success.

Figure 4.3

GRANTSEEKERS' MATRIX

Type: _____

1 Type of Project	2 Geographic Need	3 Award Size	4 School's Image	5 Credentials of Project Director	6 Preproposal Contact	7 Proposal Content	8 Review & Decision	9 Proposal Information and Administration
Demonstration A								
Research B								
Equipment C								
Replication D								
Consortium E								
International F								

Column 1: Type of Project

There are six basic categories or types of grant proposals listed on the Grantseekers' Matrix. Your task may be to help your district grantseekers focus clearly on a need and on several methods to address it, but this matrix will enable them to look at changes in approaches that would expand the number of potential funders and increase funding opportunities. By altering their focus and methods with slight changes in emphasis, your grantseekers can change the nature of their projects from research to demonstration to international. The secret here is to practice the golden rule of grantseeking—the funder has the gold and therefore makes the rules. Your grantseekers are not going to convince funding sources to change their needs or rules, so they will have to adjust their approach to fit funders' needs.

A. Demonstration—In this category of grants the funder's interest is in developing models for change. The emphasis is on proving what works and on demonstrating change. The funder who awards demonstration grants prefers innovative approaches and ideas. For example, it might be enthused by the idea that a project could become a model for other classrooms, curricula, or schools.

B. Research—At first glance, this category of grants may appear to be out of the question for your district's schools. But give it a second look! By utilizing a link to a college or university, your schools may be able to develop their ability to attract these funds. A demonstration or model project can become a research project if a control group and statistical analysis are incorporated into the project plans. The best part is that to do so your schools do not need to have vast computer systems and experts in statistical design. These resources already exist at your local college or university.

C. Equipment—Sources that fund educational equipment directly are relatively rare. However, grantors want to fund projects that will make a difference. To that end they will allow the purchase of a limited amount of equipment if it plays an integral part in the project.

Even when your district grantseekers solicit a computer-equipment manufacturer, the manufacturer will want to know the following:

- Why they want the equipment

- Who will use it

- How many will benefit from it

- What curriculum changes will occur

- How inservice training will be conducted

By the time your district grantseekers finish writing a proposal for equipment, they will realize that they have really developed a model project and that, in fact, their chance of success in attracting the equipment depends on the quality of their plan or project and on how it will influence change or educational advancement.

D. Replication—Funders of this category of grants do not want to be involved in discovering what works or how and why something works, the rather risky ventures of research and model projects. Rather, they want their grant money to be used to encourage others to use or replicate the techniques that have been proven, usually under someone else's grant funds, to have a positive effect.

E. Consortium—Funders of this type of grant are interested in:

- A partnership of grantseekers, each of whom brings outstanding qualities to the proposal
- An increased likelihood of success
- A sharing rather than a duplication of expensive resources and equipment

Any of the previously mentioned types of grants can be consortia grants. For example, your grantseekers can develop a demonstration, research, equipment, or replication grant that is also a consortium grant. In many cases grantors will encourage consortium grants, and some will even mandate or require them.

Consortium proposals have been around for many years but are just now coming into their own as powerful and cost-effective mechanisms to achieve the outcomes suggested in proposals. Successful grantseekers will enter the year 2000 knowing how to utilize consortium arrangements to maximize cost efficiency and improve their competitive edge. The next few years will be marked by larger problems and fewer resources. Those schools that make the most of the limited resources available to them will win the funding.

Please note that it is very important to make your district grantseekers aware that they must have the endorsement and support of the district administration *before* making contact with any potential consortia partners.

F. International—Many grantors have links to other parts of the world. The political and social changes in Europe and the former Soviet Union, as well as the increasingly international interests of governments and corporations, all point to a marked rise in the success rate for international proposals.

Changes in trade and tariff rules and the growing number of multinational corporations may mean that a local corporation has a vested interest in another country. Including an elementary school from that country in their project plan may dramatically improve your grantseekers' chances for funding. For example, one of the largest U.S.-based manufacturers of blue jeans has just constructed a large manufacturing facility in Poland. A proposal that encourages educational change or that focuses on capitalism or any other of a number of corporate concerns, and that promotes an educated workforce in Poland, might be considered very attractive by that company.

Finding an international partner is not difficult, especially if your grantseekers submit the proposal and initiate the contacts in the United States. Because many of these arrangements require in-kind or matching funds from the school district, coordination through your district grants office is crucial.

Column 2: Geographic Need

In most cases, your schools must demonstrate a considerable local need for the solutions they propose. Some grantors are interested in projects that address that same need in other areas. For example, a school's solution to its need may have a national or an international impact, and highlighting this aspect of the project in the proposal might improve its fundability. In other cases, however, the mention of a national or international focus may have little or no or even a negative impact on the project's fundability because the grantor might be interested only in projects that address local needs.

Column 3: Award Size

The amount of grant funds needed to implement your district grantseekers' solution is a critical factor in determining which type of funding source to approach. It is possible to ask several different types of grantors to fund part of the project, keeping the request within each one's budget, and in so doing obtain funds for a considerably larger project than any one grantor could support.

Column 4: School's Image

What is the image or reputation of the school submitting the proposal? Must it be designated as an outstanding school to attract funding from certain types of grantors?

Column 5: Credentials of Project Director

Each type of funding source has different criteria for what constitutes a credible project director. Local reputation has a positive impact on some grantors; others value doctorate degrees, records of publications, and previous grant awards.

Column 6: Preproposal Contact

The value of preproposal contact (contact before the proposal is written) cannot be overemphasized. However, some types of funding sources will not allow it. The vast differences in this particular area have a lot to do with whether a funding source has a grants staff, program officers, an office, or board members who can be approached through linkages.

Column 7: Proposal Content

This column summarizes the preferred proposal format and the application procedures. Its purpose is not for your prospective grantseekers to ascertain which type of funding source has the shortest application. Just because a grantor does not require a lengthy, detailed proposal does not mean that proposal preparation will be easy. In fact, creating a two-page letter proposal to a foundation or corporation with no guidelines or required format can be much more difficult than preparing a lengthy application to a government funding source.

Column 8: Review & Decision

Who reads and reviews submitted proposals; what their biases, backgrounds, and education are; how much time they will spend reviewing each proposal; and what scoring system they will use are important factors for your district grantseekers to consider in preparing a winning proposal. Naturally, your schools' proposals should be written with the reviewers in mind. The use of educational jargon may be acceptable to one type of reviewer and unacceptable to another.

Having this information before they submit their proposal will enable your grantseekers to perform a preliminary mock review of the proposal and to prepare the best possible proposal.

Column 9: Proposal Information and Administration

It is important to know what the funding source will expect after the grant is awarded. Each type of grantor has different rules, regulations, and guidelines that must be complied with. This column gives you an idea of what will be required of you as a district administrator.

The Government Grantseekers' Matrix

Review the Government Grantseekers' Matrix (Figure 4.4) to determine your district's general strategy for approaching this $90 billion marketplace or to help your grantseekers evaluate a specific project's viability for government funding.

Figure 4.4

GOVERNMENT GRANTSEEKERS' MATRIX

Federal grants to elementary and middle schools come from the Department of Education and other programs that have an interest in children and families. The Department of Agriculture, Health and Human Services, as well as the National Science Foundation and the National Endowment for Arts and Humanities can all be considered as possible grant sources. There are over 1,300 federal programs granting over $90 billion annually.

Type of Project	Geographic Need	Award Size*	School's Image	Credentials of Project Director	Preproposal Contact	Proposal Content	Review & Decision	Proposal Information and Administration
Model/Demonstration—Great variety of areas: Curriculum (math, science, reading, etc.), Learning-disabled, At-risk youth	Local/Regional State National	Medium to large	National/Regional	Being well-known is a plus; published or spoken at conferences, etc.	Write, phone, go see	Long, detailed forms	Peer review by experts	Must follow OMB curricular; long and elaborate forms and financial requirements
Research—Areas: Teaching Learning Vocation Fed. Dropouts Gifted	Local/National	"	National	Experts must be involved—subcontract or consortium or consortium with colleges/universities	"	"	"	"
Equipment—For acquisition (not very common); allowed when integral part of model or research	Local	Small to medium	Regional	Not essential	"	"	"	"
Replication—Not common unless Feds want regional sites or to expand to target population	Local	"	"	Local/Regional expertise	"	"	"	"
Consortium—More common now; allows use of experts and facilities at lower cost	Local/National/ Schools of consortium partners	Medium to large	National/ Regional		"	"	"	"
International—Interested in understanding U.S. language and culture, capitalistic system	Local National International	"	"		"	"	"	"

*Size of award is provided as rough guideline. Small is under $5,000, medium is $5,000–$50,000, and large is $50,000 and up.

As you can see from column two of the matrix, the need must often exist outside of your school district's geographic area. The award sizes are generally well above $10,000 per year, and awards of $50,000 to $250,000 are not uncommon. The school's credibility should be high and the credentials of the project director fairly well established.

The Foundation Grantseekers' Matrix

Large National General-Purpose Foundations

These foundations usually prefer demonstration and model projects. It is estimated that almost 50 percent of their grants are aimed at developing models and projects that promote change in their particular fields of interest. See Figure 4.5.

These larger foundations may look a bit like government grantors because they generally do not fund replication grants, offer larger grants, and prefer to fund well-credentialed project directors. They generally have offices and staff or paid reviewers (consultants) who are experts in the field to critically evaluate proposals.

In some cases your district grantseekers may approach a local foundation or corporation for a small grant to develop preliminary data or to test part of their model, then go to a larger foundation for a grant to develop their project further before they approach a federal grants source for funding the implementation of their program.

Special-Purpose Foundations

Although there are only a few hundred of these, they have a lot of impact on their areas of interest. They are motivated by a strong desire to effect immediate change in their area of special needs. Your grantseekers' ability to improve the problem is paramount in their minds, and the rules and requirements imposed on the special-purpose foundation's grantees are not as stringent as those of government and large foundation funding sources (see Figure 4.6).

When submitting a proposal to these funding sources it is less important to demonstrate an outstanding image and impressive credentials than to captivate and excite them with a novel and cost-effective approach to producing change in the needs area they value.

Community Foundations

These are excellent grant resources for schools. Not every community has one, but they are the fastest-growing area in the foundations marketplace, with over three hundred in existence today. If your area is fortunate

Figure 4.5

FOUNDATION GRANTSEEKERS' MATRIX: Large National General-Purpose Foundations

Examples: Ford, Rockefeller, and MacArthur Foundations

Type: Although there are fewer than 50 members of this group, it has a large percentage of the assets and makes the majority of grants. The members fund both nationally and internationally on a broad area of interests. They have paid staff and offices.

Type of Project	Geographic Need	Award Size	School's Image	Credentials of Project Director	Preproposal Contact	Proposal Content	Review & Decision	Proposal Information and Administration
Model/Demonstration—Variety of interests by subject area and outcomes	Local/Regional/National	Varies, but funds large & medium $50,000+	Regional or national image helps	Expertise in school district very important	Phone, write letter, make a personal visit	Many have guidelines, specific forms and restrictions	Staff are experts in field and hire outside expertise to evaluate	Many have application instructions and forms. Some produce annual reports and newsletters. Many have program specialists and auditors who may make preaward and postaward visits. Administration follows established CPA guidelines. In addition to the above, these grantors may have overseas staff.
Research—Many prefer a systematic research approach with statistical design and evaluation; want to know what works	"	"	Good to include a university	Very important. Utilize higher education linkages to Ed.D., Ph.D., colleges/universities	Critical to proposal acceptance	Length varies but 10–20 pages common. May do a preliminary review of your concept before you are invited to submit	"	
Equipment—Allowable as part of the project methodology; most avoid funding equipment alone	"	"	"	"	"		"	
Replication—Most prefer to fund a model and dissemination of the project, not replication	"	"	"	"	"		"	
Consortium—More interest today than in the past. Look at IRS 990 to assist in choosing a past grantee as a partner	"	Larger sizes	Images of both partner schools important	Need to have experience and degrees in both partners	"		"	
International—Growing interest in the world, but still want to help out at home; discuss a possible foreign site to provide a comparison; look at IRS 990 to locate countries or languages of interest	Local/Regional & International	Larger to accommodate travel expenses	"		May be difficult to get both partners together with funder. Use conference calls & teleconferences	"	"	These grantors may have overseas staff

Figure 4.6

FOUNDATION GRANTSEEKERS' MATRIX: Special-Purpose Foundations

Examples: Exxon Education Trust, Carnegie Foundation

Type: This type of foundation has a narrow, rather specific focus. There are special-purpose foundations for education and for the different levels of education, but don't overlook those that fund subject areas of interest to elementary and middle schools, such as music, art, literacy, literature, health, and so on.

Type of Project	Geographic Need	Award Size	School's Image	Credentials of Project Director	Preproposal Contact	Proposal Content	Review & Decision	Proposal Information and Administration
Model/Demonstration—They prefer project grants that call attention to their field or cause	Special needs population in your area	Large and medium	Not as critical as your ability to make a difference in their special interest	Important but not critical	Contact by phone, write, go see	Varies, usually have a proposal format; some use a concept paper to approve you to submit full proposal	Staff may be experts in target area	Use annual reports and tax returns to learn what they like and what type of organization they prefer as a grantee
Research—Only in their special interest. Usually the larger foundations like some research. On average, 10–20% of grant money awarded for research	"	"	"	Very important	"		Use some outside reviews	"
Equipment—Some will fund equipment; others will allow it if necessary to carry out the project/research	"	"	"	Important but not critical	"			"
Replication—Not usually a priority unless a model was very successful	"	"	"		"		"	"
Consortium—Interested if the alliance will have more impact on the special interest	Special needs population in your area and your partner's	"	"		"		"	"
International—Several are interested in international as well as national	"	"	"		"		"	"

enough to have one or more, your district has a superb source for funding those projects that other sources would not support (such as replication or needs assessment). Such grants are usually small, but the impact they can have on your students and on your ability to make your schools appear more fundable to other grantors is impressive (see Figure 4.7).

If your area does not have a community foundation you would do well to help initiate one. The volunteered services of a community-minded lawyer and banker could get the ball rolling, and your school district could soon have a new and unique source for grant funds. Even if your district has initiated a school foundation, a local community foundation should not be viewed as competition. It is just one more funding source.

Family Foundations

In some ways these resemble community foundations. Built into their board of directors is a strong geographic homing device that is reflected in their granting pattern. They fund what they like, and they like programs that enhance educational opportunities in the geographic regions they care about (see Figure 4.8).

Research is not a top funding priority for them. As they seek to have a more immediate impact, they gravitate toward replication, equipment, and targeted model projects.

Corporate Foundations

For the first time in at least a decade, health and human services received the largest share of 1997 corporate contributions. Although corporate giving to education decreased moderately, it has remained relatively constant through the years because education continues to be a priority for many of the 1,905 corporate foundations. Approximately 30 percent of corporate contributions go to education, and elementary and junior high schools have been the recipients of an increasing percentage of these funds. The key to procuring corporate foundation funds is your school district's proximity to corporate plants or offices, the number of corporate workers who are motivated volunteers at your schools, and the visible return on the corporate foundation's investment (see Figure 4.9).

Corporate Grantseekers' Matrix

Large Corporate Grantors

This group is interested in schools located close to their plants, distribution centers, and stores. Despite what grantseekers are apt to think, these grantors are not particularly motivated by press releases that make them

Figure 4.7

FOUNDATION GRANTSEEKERS' MATRIX: Community Foundations

These are often named after the geographic area of concern. All their grants must benefit the specific area, and boundaries are used to separate the designated area—the Cleveland Foundation, the San Francisco Foundation, and so on. Even smaller cities have them (such as the Utica [New York] Foundation), and some areas have a statewide foundation (such as the North Dakota Foundation). Community foundations exist to support their particular community and are not under political or government sponsorship. They provide an excellent source of funds for elementary and middle school grants, but usually in smaller amounts.

Type of Project	Geographic Need	Award Size	School's Image	Credentials of Project Director	Preproposal Contact	Proposal Content	Review & Decision	Proposal Information and Administrationa
Model/Demonstration—This type of grantor prefers to grant money to projects that are sure to make a difference	Need in the specific geographic area of community	Small; grants up to $10,000, many in the $5,000 range	How well your organization is known in your community and specifically by the board members	The local image of the project director and key individuals involved in the project	Contact with the designated official of the foundation is recommended	Usually a short 2–8 page proposal	Usually a process involving the board. Key factor is that the board is representative of the community	Many with annual reports; their 990 A.R. IRS tax return is very helpful. Most do not have many staff or support personnel, so follow-up is limited
Research—Not usually funded	Only concerned with local need, not field of education		"	"				
Equipment—May fund small purchases that show a lot of use	"	"	"	"	"	"	Greater range in socioeconomic status, more women and minorities on the board	
Replication—A good area; they have proof that it worked someplace else	"	"	"	"	"	"		
Consortium—Interested if all partners are in the same geographic area	"	"	"	"	"	"		
International—Not a good bet; maybe if there is a strong ethnic group in the community								

Figure 4.8

FOUNDATION GRANTSEEKERS' MATRIX: Family Foundations

There are over 38,000 of this type. Most are small, have little or no staff and no office, and meet once or twice per year. They support their families' concerns and values, with an eye to the past and the family member who created the foundation. They represent a valuable resource to elementary and middle school education because you can provide them with a lot of results for a small grant and because you have access to children and thus to the future.

Type of Project	Geographic Need	Award Size	School's Image	Credentials of Project Director	Preproposal Contact	Proposal Content	Review & Decision	Proposal Information and Administration
Model/Demonstration—Of interest to many family foundations. They fear long-range support, so project must show self-sufficiency or other support later	This type of funder has a very specific geographic granting perspective, and the need and your project must be in their area	Small, under $10,000 or even under $5,000	The credibility of your school, the district, and any of your contact people (friends) makes the difference	Project director's image in the school or community is important	Since staff is limited, most state no contact except by letter. Your only opportunity is through "friends" who have contact with the board members	Most want a 1–2 pg letter proposal or letter of inquiry; usually no attachments are allowed. You must submit full proposal	Usually read by board members. You write to the level of expertise of the board. They are often family members and close friends or business associates	Most do not publish an annual report. Information on what they prefer to fund is in their IRS tax return. IRS return found at Foundation Center Regional Collections. Administration should follow standard business practices and established CPA guidelines. Little or no audit, follow-up, or compliance issues
Research—Most want to invest money in what works; not a lot of interest in research	Local. Interest if family had/has a child with educational problem	Some medium-size but relatively rare	Letters of endorsement from community groups help also	Very important				
Equipment—Popular, as tangible things are preferred. Computer is better than teacher's aide	Local							
Replication—Good source for replicating a successful program	Local		Local reputation important					
Consortium—Okay, but only if both partners are in their area of concern	Local							
International—Not best funder unless there is an ethnic relationship								

Figure 4.9

FOUNDATION GRANTSEEKERS' MATRIX: Corporate Foundations

Corporate granting is divided into two major categories: those companies that use a separate private foundation to make grants and corporations that make grants directly from the corporation and have no foundation. Of the five million corporations in the United States, 1,905 corporate foundations are included in the National Directory of Corporate Giving. These represent a significant portion of corporate grants, and the corporate foundation grantseeker has access to IRS Annual Reports so you can verify your approach and the amount you are seeking. In general, this group spends more time reading your proposal than the family foundation.

Type of Project	Geographic Need	Award Size	School's Image	Credentials of Project Director	Preproposal Contact	Proposal Content	Review & Decision	Proposal Information and Administration
Model/Demonstration—Of interest to corporate foundations, especially if it affects their products, profits, or workers	The need must fit the granting perspective. May have a national agenda or a primary focus on needs in their field of corporate interest	Medium, $10,000 to $50,000; and large, over $50,000	The more well-known your school, the better. National rankings, scores, awards, etc., help	Credentials nationally are important as is local image with corporate officials, plant managers, and sales representatives	Phone, write, go see the funder to describe the project. Many have staff	Some have guidelines and even an application form	Review may be done by some staff with knowledge of education. Decision made by the board	Many have annual reports that provide information on grant interests. You can also review IRS tax returns. Administration follows established CPA guidelines; some site visits and audits
Research—Interested if it advances corporate interests								
Equipment—Some support; best chance is for equipment the company produces								
Replication—Some interest if there are proven results								
Consortium—Great approach if your partner is also in same area as corporate interest								
International—Could be a great component if corporation is owned overseas or has a plant there								

appear to be good citizens. Some corporations do not even want their grant awards publicized, as it could result in more requests for grants. They are more usually motivated by projects that position their products with students or teachers, help them develop and improve products, or produce a better-educated workforce (see Figure 4.10).

All Other Corporations

Corporate grantmaking was rarely practiced until a 1953 court case upheld the legality of a corporate grant to a university. Thus the history of corporate support is short and the practice is not as widespread as many believe. But do not let this scare your grantseekers. Smaller corporations are still a very valuable resource for your schools. As they are local, they may have ties and linkages to your schools and they certainly have a vested interest in your community. If your grantseekers approach this group properly, the results may exceed their expectations (see Figure 4.11).

Your community volunteers from the corporate world are your district's key to corporate grants. When a corporate peer approaches a small corporation, explains the project and the direction the school is taking, and then invites the corporation to make a grant, your grantseeker will get results!

Corporations know that voluntary grantmaking to local schools is better than a tax increase. After all, they get recognition and a good feeling from voluntary giving but just a canceled check from the tax collector for nonvoluntary giving.

Service Clubs and Organizations Grantseekers' Matrix

Your grantseekers will get a much better response from service clubs and organizations when they ask them to fund *specific* projects or proposals rather than for money for general purposes. As most of these groups exist to serve the community, they actually *need* projects and causes to get involved in. They sponsor fund-raising events not only to raise money but also to get their members motivated and involved and to demonstrate their community spirit (see Figure 4.12). Naturally, a good public image helps them recruit new members.

Their involvement with your schools provides you with the opportunity to have other citizens tell your district's story to the community. This grassroots involvement of service clubs and organizations will have dramatic effects, but these groups need your district personnel, faculty, and community volunteers to provide them with specific projects for smaller

Figure 4.10

CORPORATE GRANTSEEKERS' MATRIX: Large Corporate Foundations

Of the 5 million corporations, only 1.75 million are reported to make grants to any nonprofit organization. Those grants total less than $8.2 billion. The large corporate grantors have such good public relations that most grantseekers think that there are billions more in corporate grants than there are. From the perspective of education, this type of grantor offers a large resource because estimates are that 30 percent of corporate grants go toward education. Although higher education has traditionally received the greatest portion, elementary and middle schools are attracting increasing interest.

Type of Project	Geographic Need	Award Size	School's Image	Credentials of Project Director	Preproposal Contact	Proposal Content	Review & Decision	Proposal Information and Administration
Model/Demonstration— Interest if there is a direct or indirect benefit to the company	The need for the project must be prevalent locally, but must correspond to the values of the corporation	Medium, $10,000 to $50,000; some large, $50,000 and over	Your school should have a relationship with the company, not necessarily a record of grant support. Should have company support in the form of loaned executives and employees as volunteers	Should have regional image and credentials	Contact sales people, plant managers, regional supervisors by phone and personal contact. Involve them in the project and work through them unless application has different instructions	Some have an application form. Many prefer a 2–5 page letter	Several have staff and a few employ one outside reviewer	Little or no verifiable information available. Most entries in published directories are not verified. Some site visits and very few audits
Research— If the research will contribute to the field of interest and enhance product development								
Replication— Some interest if there are proven results								
Equipment— Will grant company products, especially if the grant will put them in a position to sell more products to school, students, or parents								
Consortium and International— Depends on where the company has other plants, facilities								

Figure 4.11

CORPORATE GRANTSEEKERS' MATRIX: All Other Corporations

This group includes small- and medium-sized companies. They have great concern for the communities in which they live and work. They listen because of their concern for their workers and the education of their workers' children. Most are not planning on opening a business in another country and want quality education in their community. Get a list of local corporations from your Chamber of Commerce. Try to involve them in your advisory committee. How many of their workers' children are in your school? Remember, these companies are still concerned about their products and profits. They are not as motivated by a burning desire to do good things as you may think. They want something back for their investment.

Type of Project	Geographic Need	Award Size	School's Image	Credentials of Project Director	Preproposal Contact	Proposal Content	Review & Decision	Proposal Information and Administration
Model/Demonstration—Some interest, but concern is for what works **Research**—Little or no interest unless a product could benefit **Equipment**—May donate used equipment or the equipment they sell **Consortium**—Sharing with other schools, public and private, would look good, maximize resources **National/International**—Not interested unless they have investments other places	Basic concern is where the company is located and how the project will affect its workers, children, and community	Most are small, up to $10,000; some medium, $10,000 to $50,000	Your record in receiving grants is not very important. Involvement and familiarity with your school is greatest asset	Being known locally is what matters. No need for regional or national image; that could even detract from what you do locally	Definitely make contact with corporate decision maker by phone and in person. Cold proposals have little success. Involve the corporation's employees on your committees and use your "friends"	Few have application forms or formats. Most instruct you to write a letter	Most have no full-time staff and few have part-time. They meet a few times per year and may not even read all the proposals—unless they are looking for yours	Little or no verifiable data available. Use "friends" to perform a credit check through Dunn and Bradstreet or another reviewer. More profitable the better. Few rules, almost never an audit. Follow CPA guidelines

Figure 4.12

SERVICE CLUBS AND ORGANIZATIONS GRANTSEEKERS' MATRIX

These nonprofits include service organizations, Hellenic groups, and business and professional organizations. They are ready and willing grantmakers, providing the linkages to friends that you need, and in many cases raising money to grant to your school's projects, programs, and needs. Members of these organizations understand that by donating computers, for example, they increase the quality of education locally but do not increase taxes. Many schools have used them to involve the community in its schools. NOTE: Make a list of your school/community's service clubs and organizations. When and where they meet is often listed on a sign as you enter your community.

Type of Project	Geographic Need	Award Size	School's Image	Credentials of Project Director	Preproposal Contact	Proposal Content	Review & Decision	Proposal Information and Administration
Model/Demonstration—Not much interest in developing and discovering what works	Primary concern of this type of funder is local need: How will the grant change things in the community?	Most are small; up to $10,000	Local perception of your school's ability to serve the community and how the school has implemented other grants is critical	Local credibility is essential. Credibility based on caring about education and kids is more important than publishing	Essential to phone, go see individuals. For many groups the entree is to speak at their meeting to inform them of what you are doing. Remember, a volunteer from your grants advisory committee can do this	Most have a simple 3–4 page application or suggest a letter proposal	Some service clubs have a grants committee or a committee for education of youth that recommends the proposal to the main group for approval	Some organizations produce an annual report that states what activities and groups they have supported. Best source is a linkage or friend who belongs to the group. Follow-up is usually not formal. You can ask to give a result speech one year later, etc.
Research—Little or no interest in studying why something works		"						
Equipment—Interested when it shows good cost-benefit ratio and is used by teachers and students	"	"		"		"		"
Replication—Interested in implementing what worked in another school	"	"	Concerned about image regarding access to programs and equipment.	"	"	"	"	
Consortium—Some interest, but the larger the project the more the cost goes up	"	"	Concerned with record of theft and maintenance					
National/International—Some groups have strong international ties to other countries. German, Polish, African groups might like to sponsor a second site	"	"		"	"	"	"	"

amounts of money that they can take on as challenge. However, coordination with the district grants office is still imperative because it is crucial that your school district does the following:

- Present an organized and credible image to these local funders
- Avoid the embarrassment of making multiple requests to the same service club or organization

---

CHAPTER 4 ASSESSMENT TOOL

1. **How knowledgeable are the various groups in your district concerning the grants marketplace? (Your response can be based on your opinion or educated guess, or you can administer an unsigned pretest to random members from each group to obtain a more accurate assessment.)**

	Very Knowledgeable	Somewhat Knowledgeable	Not Knowledgeable
School Board Members	_____	_____	_____
Administrators	_____	_____	_____
Principals	_____	_____	_____
Teachers	_____	_____	_____
Staff	_____	_____	_____
Volunteers	_____	_____	_____
School Foundation Members	_____	_____	_____

2. **How can you better assess the knowledge level of each of these groups?**

_____

_____

_____

_____

3. **How can you determine whether there has been a change in knowledge levels after you implement the educational interventions you plan for your district? For example, what measurement tools can you use?**

_____

_____

_____

_____

Chapter 5

Helping Your Grantseekers Search the Grants Marketplace

THE ROLES AND SERVICES of the district central office are undergoing dramatic changes. Even with site-based management, school units continue to expect the district office to provide them with support services. Naturally, the school units do not want to pay for these services, including grantseeking support services. However, because grantseeking is a revenue-generating strategy the district is more likely to provide support for it and to view that support as worth the investment.

To be effective, a district grants office must consider various techniques to serve the grants-research needs of their district's grantseekers, including the development or expansion of a district grants library and access to computer-based grants search services. No technique should be dismissed solely on the basis of cost. Chapter 14 outlines a plan for grants success that actually includes seeking a grant to support the expansion of your grants program.

Developing Your District's Grants Library

During this computer age it may seem that there would be little demand for a district grants library that is a print-based collection of grantseeking materials. But many people are still more comfortable with a book than with a computer. This chapter describes many of the resource books and computer-based searching services that are commonly found in grants libraries; the bibliography gives addresses for ordering these materials.

If your district already has a grants library, consider the following questions.

1. What is the purpose of the library?

2. Who uses it and how often?

3. What does it cost to stock the library, and what does it cost to search for a potential funder?

4. Can a medium other than print provide the necessary functions more efficiently and at a more reasonable cost? (For example, would moving from a print-based to a computer-based medium save time and money? Could online tutorials or videotape training programs be used to increase user skills and use?)

If the library's materials must be used in a specific place and may not be borrowed or sent to individual schools, consider the following:

- How the distance between the potential user and the grants library affects the library's use

- If it is possible to implement an easy and inexpensive sign-out system for the materials

- How an on-line system could solve access problems

One of the most efficient services that a district grants office can provide through its grants library is the search for potential grantors. Most grants offices already have the necessary resource books to conduct these searches. However, as you are already evaluating your district's grants system you may want to consider more efficient ones, such as a computer-assisted grantor search system.

Computer-Assisted Grantor Search Systems

Many school districts are increasing their use of computer databases to help match grantors with prospective grantees. The databases contain the same information available in print but are faster in locating matches and require less dedication of office staff. You can purchase on-line search services or grants research data that can be directly loaded onto your computer.

There are two major factors to consider when deciding whether to use on-line services or to purchase grants research. The first is the number of searches to be performed; the second is who will perform the searches—the individual grantseeker, each school or district unit, or the district grants office.

If the district office is to perform the searches, you may decide to use an on-line system because you can control access to computer time. If you decide on that, you will need to purchase the service. Be sure to check with the database provider to make sure that your computer equipment is compatible. Also, check the cost, which will depend on the time you are on-line or the number of searches you request. Check the Computer Research Services section in the bibliography of this book for providers, costs, and ordering information.

On-line charges can mount up quickly. Therefore your grants office may instead decide to purchase grants research data and load it onto your computer. One advantage of this is that the time spent searching for appropriate funders is not billed by the minute. Searches can be performed by grantseekers who may not be as fast as your staff but who are searching on their own time, thereby reducing the demand on your staff's time. In fact, you could encourage each of your school units to hire and train an individual to act as a grants representative.

One database purchased by many school districts is the computerized version of the Federal Assistance Program Retrieval System (FAPRS). If you do not want to buy it, you can initiate a FAPRS search by contacting the agency designated to provide such searches in your state. You may or may not be asked to pay a small fee for this service. To locate your nearest access point, write or call to:

The Federal Domestic Assistance Catalog Staff (MVS)
Reporters Building, Room 101
300 7th Street S.W.
Washington, DC 20407
Telephone 202-708-5126
Toll-Free Answering Service 1-800-669-8331

The FAPRS disks are relatively inexpensive, but by paying slightly more you may get a more user-friendly version. For instance, GrantScape CFDA is available from Aspen Publications, 7201 McKinney Circle, Frederick, MD 21704, telephone 1-800-638-8437.

Most school districts do not take advantage of what their local colleges and universities have to offer. Contact the grants office at your nearest college or university that has a school of education. Ask to set up a meeting with the school of education and the grants office to explore the possibility of providing your district with access to their grants database. Many colleges and universities have elaborate databases for their professors' use. Some of them allow for off-campus connection so that professors can search for grant opportunities at home. Many even come with an e-mail alert service that notifies grantseekers immediately of any new funding opportunities within their area of interest.

Because most grantors encourage consortia approaches, look to your local schools of education for possible collaboration. Professors and undergraduate and graduate education students alike need experience with P–12 schools. You have the problems to solve, and they the expertise, inexpensive labor (graduate students), and credibility. With a little creativity your school district can benefit from their degrees, publications, and desire to relate their work to the real world of education. Instead of worrying that they will tell you what to do, tell them what you would like from them—searching services, consortia arrangements, and assistance in evaluation.

As an associate professor at the school of education at the University of Alabama–Birmingham, I worked with the local schools to move beyond the problems of the past and to develop new approaches for the future. Because I was also the director of Development for the Center of Educational Accountability, my expertise in helping the schools evaluate what they accomplished with a grantor's money was not just tolerated, it was welcomed.

Remember the marketplace quiz in Chapter Four? Well, professors, students, and university staff also have a lot of misconceptions about the grants marketplace. Perhaps you could teach them the realities about it as part of your consortium effort.

Developing a List of Key Search Words

Whether your grants research system is based on printed materials or electronic retrieval, the ability to search for appropriate grantors is a function of how the grantseekers define their project. Projects can be defined in terms of key search words. For example, a project to improve the math skills of fourth graders in an inner-city school could be defined in various ways. In a search for potential grantors you might look for those that have expressed an interest in elementary education, math skills, urban education, disadvantaged youth, and so on.

The first task of grantseekers or members of a school grants advisory committee should be to relate their project to as many key search words, constituency groups, types of support, and geographic parameters as possible. The worksheets in Figures 5.1 and 5.2 should help them.

Expanding the Universe of Grantors Worksheet

By increasing the number of key search words, your grantseekers will expand their universe of potential funders. At first glance, this may seem counterproductive because they are trying to narrow their list of potential funding sources to the "best" five or six. But your ultimate goal is to help them locate the grantor who is most likely to fund their project. By altering their project slightly, they can do the following:

- Expand their list of key search words

- Increase their list of potential funding sources

- Have a greater appeal to a particular funding source's values

- Dramatically increase their grants success rate

<u>**Figure 5.1**</u>

EXPANDING THE UNIVERSE OF GRANTORS WORKSHEET

1. **What subject areas will the project have an impact on?**

    _____ Preschool education   _____ Music education

    _____ Elementary education   _____ Art education

    _____ Middle school education   _____ Social studies education

    _____ Health education   _____

    _____ Reading education   _____

    _____ Science education   _____

    _____ Humanities education

2. **What problem areas could your project be aimed at affecting?**

    _____ Alcohol   _____ Handicapped

    _____ Computer literacy   _____ Homeless

    _____ Disadvantaged   _____ Immigrants

    _____ Drugs   _____

    _____ Dropouts   _____

    _____ Gifted and talented   _____

3. **How does your project currently relate to the problem areas identified in question 2?**

    _____

    _____

    _____

4. **How could the project be changed to relate to other problem areas?**

    _____

    _____

    _____

5. **Geographic Considerations—How could the project be altered to appeal to funders who value the following:**

    • Local problems/solutions?

    • Statewide problems/solutions?

    • Regional problems/solutions?

    • National problems/solutions?

    • International problems/solutions?

Key Words Worksheet for Government, Foundation, and Corporate Grantseeking

This worksheet lists some of the key words that can be used to search for government and private funding sources. Before your district grantseekers begin their search, they should review this list and put a check mark next to the words that relate to their project. They should also review the lists of potential constituency groups, geographic parameters, corporate considerations, and types of support, and list any potential partners.

Figure 5.2

KEY WORDS WORKSHEET FOR GOVERNMENT, FOUNDATION, AND CORPORATE GRANTSEEKING
Elementary and Secondary Education

Subcategories: Review this list and place a check mark next to those that relate to your project.

____ Early childhood education	____ Secondary/high school
____ Preschool education	_____
____ Middle school/junior high	_____

Key Words: Many of the following key words are used in electronic data retrieval systems and printed reference books. Review the list and place a check mark next to the key words that relate to your project. When necessary, make a brief notation of any significant changes that must be made to your solution in order to relate your project to other key words.

____ ESL	____ Bilingual
____ Drop out prevention	____ Gifted/talented
____ Truancy	____ Math
____ Science	____ Technology
____ Ethics	____ Faculty/staff development
____ Program evaluation	____ Public education
____ Private education	____ School reform
____ Health education	____ Charter schools
____ Administration/regulation	____ Community involvement
____ Management/technical aid	____ Special education
____ Information services	____ Management development
____ Testing/measurement	____ Accountability
____ Crime	____ Alcohol
____ Drug abuse	____ Literacy
____ Vocational	____ Neglected
____ Delinquent	____ Physical fitness
____ Film/video/radio	____ Aging
____ Child development	____ Learning disorders
____ Computer systems/equipment/software	____ Dispute resolution
____ Domestic violence	____ Music
____ Parks/playgrounds	____ Poverty
____ Religion	____ Social services
____ Telecommunications	____ Voluntarism
____ Cognition/information processing	____ Learning disorders
____ Computer-assisted instruction	____ Counseling/guidance
____ Parental involvement	____ Rural education
____ Urban education	____ Teacher education
____ Mental health	____ Health
____ Human services	____ Recreation
____ After-school programs	____ Art
____ Nutrition	____ Day care
____ Substance abuse	____ Culture
____ Family	____ Library services
____ Reading	

Figure 5.2 (continued)

Constituency Groups: Review the following list of constituency groups and place a check mark next to the groups related to your project. When necessary, make a brief notation of any significant ways you could change your solution to relate it to other constituency groups.

____ Children	____ Youth
____ Teachers	____ Parents
____ Grandparents	____ Teenagers
____ Hispanics	____ Homeless
____ Immigrants/refugees	____ Mentally disabled
____ Minorities	____ Deaf
____ Economically disadvantaged	____ Blind
____ Boys and young men	____ Gifted
____ Girls and young women	____ Native Americans
____ Physically disabled	____ Single parents
____ Abuse victims	____ Migrant workers
____ Asian	_____
____ Pregnant adolescents	_____

Corporate Considerations: Review the corporate considerations and place a check mark next to those that could relate to your project. When necessary, make a brief notation of any significant ways you could change your solution to relate it to other corporate considerations.

____ Employee benefits	____ Company sales, product positioning
____ Employee productivity, motivation, quality of future employees	____ Company expansion, product expansion, patents
____ Employee training	____ Corporate profits
____ Company products, product development	_____

Geographic Parameters: Place a check mark next to the areas on which your project could have an impact. When necessary, make a brief notation of any significant ways you could change your solution to relate it to other geographic parameters.

____ City/town/community	____ Nation
____ County/borough/parish	____ International
____ State	_____
____ Region	_____

Types of Support/Types of Grants: Review your project in relation to the different types of grant funds and support. Place a check mark next to the types your project could relate to. When necessary, make a brief notation of any significant ways you could change your solution to relate it to other types of support/grants.

____ Endowments	____ Emergency funds
____ Seed money	____ Planning grant
____ Model/demonstration project	____ Research
____ Capital campaign	____ Publications
____ Training grant	____ Building/renovation
____ Discretionary	____ Equipment grant
____ Collections acquisition	____ Conferences/seminars
____ Performance/productions	_____

Searching for Government Grants

State Grant Funds

Many of the state grant funds for education come from the federal government. And though the federal government has an organized, easy-to-track grants system, the states do not. Your grantseekers can find out about federal money available to your state by using their key search words to uncover related federal grant programs and then checking to see if state education agencies are eligible recipients under the federal regulations. They should also check with your district grants office to determine if your school district is already receiving those funds distributed to your state in a block grant or according to a formula. If it is not, your office may be able to provide the grantseeker with the name and phone number of a contact person in your state's education department. You may also want to check out the following websites to help you locate state and government local resources:

- http://lcweb.loc.gov/global/state/stategov.html
- http://www.nasire.org/ss/index.html
- http://www.piperinfo.com/state/states.html

Federal Grant Funds

These funds come from taxes and are therefore subject to freedom of information laws. Using their key search words, your grantseekers can use several systems to locate government grant opportunities.

Most grantseekers fear the federal grants process because they do not act proactively. They do not realize that grantseeking does not have to be last-minute, chaotic, and reactive. Your job is to teach them that the best way to develop successful federal proposals and to deal effectively with the pressure of deadlines is to be knowledgeable about the federal grants process and to start early. Grantseekers can note several federal deadlines a year in advance and take advantage of all available resources to meet deadlines and even submit proposals early. You can help your district's grantseekers learn to develop a controlled approach to federal grantseeking that will allow them to carry out their regular responsibilities and still apply for federal funds.

The federal government grants over $90 billion each year in a strictly organized yearly cycle. I refer to this cycle as the federal grants clock (Figure 5.3).

Most federal grantseekers know that application packages are normally sent to prospective grantees four to eight weeks before the completed applications are due and that the grants are usually awarded four to

Figure 5.3

THE $90 BILLION FEDERAL GRANTS CLOCK™

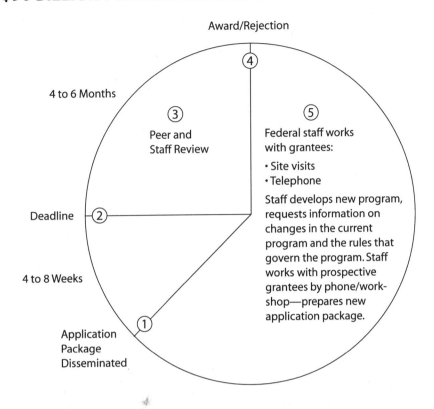

The clock operates Monday through Friday (except federal holidays) 52 weeks per year. The federal government's year begins on October 1 and ends September 30.

six months after submission. The key to proactive government grantseeking is knowing what else occurs during this time and how grantseekers' actions can dramatically increase their success rate and decrease the madness associated with trying to meet deadlines at the last minute.

Your district's grantseekers should not wait until they receive an application package before they learn about grant opportunities and begin developing their schools' proposals. They should start early! To do so, they need to have a working knowledge of how the federal grants clock works:

1. The application package is disseminated.

2. Deadline—Most grantseekers do not begin their grants work until they receive the application package. This leaves only a short time to work on the proposal before the deadline. The inflexible federal grants clock chimes the hour proposals are due, and submitting a proposal five minutes late delays consideration of it for one year!

3. Peer and Staff Review—Proposals are read, scored, and ranked.

4. Award and rejection notices are sent out.

5. During the final phase of the clock, the federal grants staff begins to get ready for another grants cycle and works with the current grantees.

If your district's grantseekers understand the predictable and programmed nature of the federal grants clock they will be able to get to work long before the application packages are mailed. To start early, they will also need a working knowledge of the basic federal grant information publications—the *Catalog of Federal Domestic Assistance* and the *Federal Register*.

The Catalog of Federal Domestic Assistance (CFDA)

The search for federal grants begins with the CFDA. Produced in the fall of each year, this catalogue lists the 1,300-plus programs that disseminate approximately $90 billion in grants annually and provides all sorts of valuable information, including deadlines.

Where can you get the CFDA? You may purchase one from the Superintendent of Documents, P.O. Box 371954, Pittsburgh PA, 15250-7954 (telephone 202-512-1800). The CFDA is also provided free to at least two libraries in each congressional district. Your congressperson should know which libraries have been designated as Federal Depositor Libraries. In addition to these designated libraries, most public libraries have a copy, as do college and university libraries and grants offices. The CFDA is also available free on the Internet at www.gsa.gov/fdac/default.htm. I suggest that your office maintain its own printed copies of the CFDA for your grantseekers' use or make it available to them on the World Wide Web.

Why should district grantseekers use the CFDA? First and foremost, the CFDA gives you access to $90 billion in grant funds. But even if your grantseekers are planning to pursue only foundation or corporate grants, they should be knowledgeable about federal programs in their project areas. So armed, they will be able to explain to prospective private grantors why they are approaching these grantors instead of a federal agency. For instance, if your grantseekers know for certain that no federal funds are designated for their project area or that federal funding is limited to three projects in their field across the entire country, it will be easier for them to demonstrate why private grant support is so necessary.

How do you use the CFDA? If using the printed copy of the CFDA, the most efficient way to locate the granting agencies that are your grantseekers' best opportunities is to compare the key search words they circled on their Key Words Worksheets to the CFDA indexes, of which there are five:

- *Deadline Index*—This is not very useful when searching for education-related grants because the Department of Education does not publish many program deadlines early in the federal year.

- *Applicant Eligibility Index*—This allows your grantseekers to determine which granting programs are restricted to state applicants and which are designated for local education agencies (LEAs), such as your school district. If your grantseekers' projects fall under granting programs restricted to state recipients, have them check with your state education department to determine how the previous year's funds were allocated.

- *Agency Program Index*—This lists all programs in numerical order by five-digit codes.

- *Functional Index*—There are twenty basic functional categories of federal support and 176 subgroupings.

- *Subject Index*—This is the most useful index for locating both Department of Education grant opportunities and those in other federal departments with an interest in education or a related area.

If using the electronic version of the CFDA, the most efficient way to locate potential funding sources is to query the catalogue to perform a search. For example, assume that one of your school units has a project related to parent-teacher-student involvement. Go to the website (www.gsa.gov/fdac/default.htm), click on "Query the Catalog" and then follow the instructions on-screen, entering search terms in the space provided. Using "parents and students" as the search term could match your schools' interests with several federal programs, including CFDA 84.310: Goals 2000: Parental Assistance Program. Using "school improvement" or "parental involvement" could bring up programs such as CFDA 84.298: Innovative Education Program Strategies. "Student achievement" could result in a match with CFDA 84.305: National Institute on Student Achievement, Curriculum, and Assessment.

If a school changed its grant idea slightly to focus solely on drugs and violence and parent-teacher-student involvement, that would result in other matches such as 84.814: Safe Drug-Free School and Communities. If the focus were on improving educational opportunities of migrant children they would want to consider CFDA 84.214: Even Start Migrant Education. If charter schools were the searchers' thing they could relate their project to the objectives of CFDA 84.282: Charter Schools. If they were interested in building a parent-teacher-student involvement component into a larger community center–based program aimed at expanding the overall learning opportunities for children in a safe environment, they would want to investigate CFDA 84.287: Twenty-First Century Community Learning Centers. The possibilities are endless and really depend on what area or field the school wants to focus on, its ability to define and redefine its project, and the search terms it uses to locate potential funding sources.

Figures 5.4 and 5.5 are reproductions of the electronic versions of CFDA 84.310 (Goals 2000: Parental Assistance Program) and CFDA 84.287 (Twenty-First Century Community Learning Centers). They have been included to help you and your grantseekers understand the federal grants system. The information contained in CFDA entries is crucial to sustaining a proactive grantseeking system that enables grantseekers to start the process early and make preproposal contact with appropriate funding agencies.

CFDA 84.310 Goals 2000: Parental Assistance Program—In this example, the numbers that appear next to the left margin can be used as reader aids. These are the numbers that appear in the actual CFDA document (Figure 5.4).

:030 *Federal Agency:* This informs grantseekers of the arm of the government that handles the program. Although many grant programs are sponsored by the Department of Education, your grantseekers may also apply to the National Science Foundation, the National Endowment for the Arts, and so on.

:040 *Authorization:* This tells grantseekers the source of the funding.

:050 *Objectives:* This section provides grantseekers with the first indication of the appropriateness of their idea in relationship to the funding program.

:060 *Types of Assistance:* Grantseekers must know what types of assistance are provided to determine if the federal program is interested in funding projects or research or if it funds on a formula basis that allocates the funds to eligible recipients through predetermined criteria.

:070 *Uses and Use Restrictions:* Uses and use restrictions help grantseekers further determine if the program is an appropriate source of funds for their project.

:080 *Eligibility Requirements:*

- Applicant Eligibility—This section tells your grantseekers if their school is an eligible recipient. Your district's schools are designated as Local Education Agencies (LEAs). If your schools are not eligible for funding under this program, this section will give your grantseekers the information they need to determine whom they should develop a relationship with so that they can submit their proposal through another organization.

Figure 5.4

84.310 GOALS 2000: PARENTAL ASSISTANCE PROGRAM

:030 FEDERAL AGENCY: OFFICE OF ELEMENTARY AND SECONDARY EDUCATION, DEPARTMENT OF EDUCATION

:040 AUTHORIZATION: Goals 2000: Educate America Act, Title IV, Public Law 103-227.

:050 OBJECTIVES: To provide grants to nonprofit organizations and nonprofit organizations in consortia with local education agencies (LEAs) to assist them in establishing parental information and resource centers. These centers strive to: (1) increase **parents'** knowledge of and confidence in child-rearing activities such as teaching and nurturing their young children; (2) strengthen partnerships between **parents** and professionals in meeting the educational needs of preschool and school-aged children and the working relationships between home and school; and (3) enhance the developmental progress of the children assisted under this program.

:060 TYPES OF ASSISTANCE: Project Grants.

:070 USES AND USE RESTRICTIONS: Each grantee receiving funds under this program must use at least 50 percent of the funds provided to serve areas with high concentrations of low-income families in order to serve **parents** that are severely educationally or economically disadvantaged. Other requirements include the establishment of a special advisory committee and design requirements. For funding in subsequent years, grantees must demonstrate that a portion of the services provided under this project is supported through nonfederal contributions.

:080 ELIGIBILITY REQUIREMENTS:

:081 Applicant Eligibility: Nonprofit organizations and nonprofit organizations in consortia with LEAs may apply.

:082 Beneficiary Eligibility: Preschool and school-aged children and their **parents** will benefit.

:083 Credentials/Documentation: None.

:090 APPLICATION AND AWARD PROCESS:

:091 Preapplication Coordination: This program is eligible for coverage under E.O. 12372, "Intergovernmental Review of Federal Programs." An applicant should consult the office or official designated as the single point of contact in his or her State for more information on the process the State requires to be followed in applying for assistance, if the State has selected the program for review.

:092 Application Procedure: Applications must be prepared and submitted in accordance with the notice published in the Federal Register. Contact the program office for more information.

:093 Award Procedure: Applications are reviewed by panels of field readers. Points are awarded according to the selection criteria for discretionary grants contained in the Education Department General Administrative Regulations (EDGAR). Applications are ranked based on the number of points awarded and are selected for funding based on their rank order and geographic location in order to satisfy statutory provisions. Grants are distributed, to the greatest extent possible, to all geographic regions of the country.

:094 Deadlines: Contact the program office for application deadlines and information.

:095 Range of Approval/Disapproval Time: The range of approval/disapproval time is approximately 60 through 90 days following the application deadline.

:096 Appeals: None.

(continued)

Figure 5.4 (continued)

:097 Renewals: Renewals are based on the review of annual performance reports and the recommendation of the project officer. All renewals are subject to the availability of funds.

:100 ASSISTANCE CONSIDERATIONS:

:101 Formula and Matching Requirements: Grantees are required to contribute, from nonfederal sources, a portion of the services provided under the project after the first year.

:102 Length and Time Phasing of Assistance: Projects generally may be supported for 1 to 4 years. Funds are granted on a 12 month basis.

:110 POST ASSISTANCE REQUIREMENTS:

:111 Reports: Annual financial and progress reports must be submitted as required by grant award terms and conditions.

:112 Audits: In accordance with the Education Department General Administration Regulations (EDGAR), 34 CFR 74, nonprofit organizations are subject to the audit requirements in OMB Circular No. A-133, "Audits of States, Local Governments, and Non-Profit Organizations."

:113 Records: As required by the Education Department General Administrative Regulations.

:120 FINANCIAL INFORMATION:

:121 Account Identification: 91-0500-0-1-501.

:122 Obligations: (Grants) FY 97 $15,000,000; FY 98 est $25,000,000; and FY 99 est $25,000,000.

:123 Range and Average of Financial Assistance: $50,000 to $500,000; $350,000.

:130 PROGRAM ACCOMPLISHMENTS: Awards have been made for parent information and resource centers in 40 States to help link families and schools to support children's learning. The nonprofit organizations conduct training activities, referral networks, and other projects to support **parents** and schools.

:140 REGULATIONS, GUIDELINES, AND LITERATURE: Education Department General Administrative Regulations (EDGAR). For more information contact the program office.

:150 INFORMATION CONTACTS:

:151 Regional or Local Office: None.

:152 Headquarters Office: Goals 2000, Office of Elementary and Secondary Education, Department of Education, 600 Independence Ave., SW., Portals Bldg., Room 4000, Washington, DC 20202. Contact: Daisy Greenfield. Telephone: (202) 401-0039.

:160 RELATED PROGRAMS: None.

:170 EXAMPLES OF FUNDED PROJECTS: No examples are available.

:180 CRITERIA FOR SELECTING PROPOSALS: The selection criteria contained in the Education Department General Administrative Regulations are used to evaluate this program. For more information contact the program office.

- Beneficiary Eligibility—This section tells grantseekers the type of individual or organization that is intended to benefit from the project.

- Credentials/Documentation—The Office of Management and Budget (OMB) publishes several management booklets that outline the rules for requesting, spending, and documenting expenditures under a federal grant.

:090 *Application and Award Process*:

- Preapplication Coordination—This section outlines the OMB requirements related to your state's review and knowledge of your grantseeker's proposal. You, as district office grants administrator, should know whom to contact in your state office concerning this matter.

- Application Procedure—This describes the rules for submitting applications.

- Award Procedure—This tells who will review and approve proposals. Proposals submitted to this particular program will be reviewed by program staff based on the published criteria. Although experts will also read the proposals and assist the staff members, your grantseeker's writing style and level should be in accordance with the background of the staff.

- Deadlines—Deadlines are published in *The Federal Register*. This publication is explained immediately following the CFDA example. In CFDA 84.310 they ask that you contact the program office for application deadlines. You can also go to the Department of Education's homepage at http://ocfo.ed.gov/, click on "grants info," then click on "grants forecast." "Grants forecast" identifies programs under which the department has invited or expects to invite proposals. It also announces estimated and actual deadline dates. In this example the application notice is to be published in the Federal Register on March 15, 1999, and the deadline is April 29, 1999.

  - Range of Approval/Disapproval Time—This is the period between submittal and notification of approval or disapproval.

  - Appeals—In CFDA 84.310 there is no procedure for appealing the grantor's decision. Some federal programs have a specific appeal procedure.

  - Renewals—This information is important when grantseekers are planning a project that may take several years.

:100 *Assistance Considerations:*

- Formula and Matching Requirements—This section outlines what portion of the project's costs will be borne by your school district. It is vital that your grantseekers have a plan for the match and the district's endorsement that it will commit this share. In CFDA 84.310, the recipient needs to contribute an undisclosed portion of the services after the first year.

- Length and Time Phasing of Assistance—The length of the project period in CFDA 84.310 is approximately twelve months.

:110 *Post-Assistance Requirements:* Your district will be required to make reports and maintain records and may be subject to audits.

:120 *Financial Information:*

- Account Identification—Account Identification Number

- Obligations—By reviewing this section your grantseekers can determine if the program is slated to increase or decrease its funding level. Note: It is estimated that the future budget for this program will be $27,214,000, but Congress could drastically change this figure. In this example, program funds went up, then down.

- Range and Average of Financial Assistance—In CFDA 84.310, the range is $50,000 to $500,000, with the average award being $350,000. This should tell your grantseekers that this program is not their best choice if their project request is $25,000 per year.

:130 *Program Accomplishments:* This section provides grantseekers with important information on previously selected grantees. It also says if the program is being phased out. For example, it may say "no new awards."

:140 *Regulations, Guidelines, and Literature:* This section outlines the rules and guidelines. Most of the rules mentioned pertain to your district personnel and business office.

:150 *Information Contacts:*

- Regional or Local Office—Most regional offices have been closed.

- Headquarters Office—This section provides the contact name, address, and phone number grantseekers will need if they select this funder as a possible source.

:160 *Related Programs:* This section lists the CFDA names and codes of other sources of funds that have similar target populations or objectives.

:170 *Examples of Funded Projects:* This section provides a sample of the solutions that the grantor valued highly enough to fund.

:180 *Criteria for Selecting Proposals:* This section lists the types of criteria that the agency will follow in its evaluation procedures. Each agency has its own criteria, and criteria may differ between programs. The criteria used in CFDA 84.310 is EDGAR (see Chapter Ten).

Review the second example, CFDA 84.287: Twenty-First Century Community Learning Centers (Figure 5.5).

After reviewing both examples you will realize that the CFDA provides the basic information that your district's grantseekers must have in order to "play the grants game."

Figure 5.5

84.287 TWENTY-FIRST CENTURY COMMUNITY LEARNING CENTERS

:030 FEDERAL AGENCY: ASSISTANT SECRETARY FOR EDUCATION RESEARCH, STATISTICS, AND IMPROVEMENT, DEPARTMENT OF EDUCATION

:040 AUTHORIZATION: Elementary and Secondary Education Act of 1965, Title X, Part I, Section 10901, Public Law 103-382, 108 Stat. 3844, 20 U.S.C. 8241.

:050 OBJECTIVES: To enable rural and inner-city public elementary and secondary schools or consortia of such schools to plan, implement, or expand projects that benefit the educational, health, social service, cultural, and recreational needs of their **community**.

:060 TYPES OF ASSISTANCE: Project Grants.

:070 USES AND USE RESTRICTIONS: Projects funded under this program must be for the purpose of meeting the needs of the residents of rural and inner city communities, through the creation or expansion of **community learning** centers. Centers must include not less than four of the activities listed in Section 10905 of Elementary and Secondary Education Act of 1965 (ESEA). Priority will be given to those applications that provide expanded **learning** opportunities for children and youth in a safe and drug-free environment and engage the support of citizens in those efforts.

:080 ELIGIBILITY REQUIREMENTS:

:081 Applicant Eligibility: Rural and inner city public elementary and secondary schools or consortia of such schools.

:082 Beneficiary Eligibility: Residents of all ages within the communities served by the **learning** centers will benefit.

:083 Credentials/Documentation: None.

:090 APPLICATION AND AWARD PROCESS:

:091 Preapplication Coordination: This program is eligible for coverage under E.O. 12372, "Intergovernmental Review of Federal Programs." An applicant should consult the office or the official designated as the single point of contact in his or her State for more information on the process the State requires to be followed in applying for assistance, if the State has selected the program for review.

:092 Application Procedure: Procedures are described in an application notice published in the Federal Register if awards are to be made during that fiscal year. Contact the headquarters office listed below for application packages containing the announcement, application, and other forms.

(continued)

Figure 5.5 (continued)

:093 Award Procedure: Applications are reviewed and evaluated by outside experts and program staff annually, in accordance with the procedures set out in the Education Department General Administrative Regulations (EDGAR) 34 CFR 74, 75. The Assistant Secretary for Educational Research and Improvement approves the selection.

:094 Deadlines: Deadlines will be announced in application notices published in the Federal Register. Contact the headquarters office listed below for application deadlines.

:095 Range of Approval/Disapproval Time: The approval time is approximately 2 to 4 months.

:096 Appeals: None.

:097 Renewals: None.

:100 ASSISTANCE CONSIDERATIONS:

:101 Formula and Matching Requirements: None.

:102 Length and Time Phasing of Assistance: Awards are made annually. Following the initial, competitively selected award of up to 12 months, two additional 1-year, non-competing continuation awards may be made, for a total maximum term of 3 years.

:110 POST ASSISTANCE REQUIREMENTS:

:111 Reports: Annual progress and financial reports as required by EDGAR 34 CFR 75, unless otherwise required in the award document, are necessary.

:112 Audits: In accordance with the EDGAR, Appendix to 34 CFR 80, State and local governments that receive financial assistance of $100,000 or more within the State's fiscal year shall have an audit made for that year. State and local governments that receive between $25,000 and $100,000 within the State's fiscal year shall have an audit made in accordance with the Appendix to Part 80, or in accordance with Federal laws and regulations governing the programs in which they participate.

:113 Records: As required by the provisions in EDGAR for direct grant programs. Records related to grant funds, compliance, and performance must be maintained for a period of 5 years after completion, subject to the exceptions listed in EDGAR 34 CFR 34.

:120 FINANCIAL INFORMATION:

:121 Account Identification: 91-1100-0-1-503

:122 Obligations: (Grants) FY 97 $1,000,000; FY 98 est $40,000,000; and FY 99 est $200,000,000.

:123 Range and Average of Financial Assistance: The average award was $143,000 in 1997.

:130 PROGRAM ACCOMPLISHMENTS: Seven projects were funded in 1997.

:140 REGULATIONS, GUIDELINES, AND LITERATURE: The regulations applicable to this program are in the Education Department General Administrative Regulations, 34 CFR 74, 75, 77, 79, 80, 81, 82, 85, and 86.

:150 INFORMATION CONTACTS:

:151 Regional or Local Office: Not applicable.

:52 Headquarters Office: Carol Mitchell, Office of Reform Assistance and Dissemination, State and Local Service Division, office of Educational Research and Improvement, Department of Education, Washington, DC 20208-5524. Telephone: (202) 219-2128.

:160 RELATED PROGRAMS: None.

Figure 5.5 (continued)

:170 EXAMPLES OF FUNDED PROJECTS: Funded projects include one center which expanded an existing **community** center to provide education and support services to at-risk families, in order to empower these families to become economically self-sufficient. Another created a **learning** center and six "satellite" centers, which provide information about employment, education, and social service opportunities. A third center provides services in the areas of literacy, technology, parenting skills, and employment. All of these centers are located in economically depressed areas.

:180 CRITERIA FOR SELECTING PROPOSALS: The criteria for selecting proposals under this program include how well the project meets the purposes of the authorizing statute, the extent of need for the project, Quality of Project Services, management plan, project and evaluation plan. (See 34 CFR 75.210 for details.)

The Federal Register

The *Federal Register* can be described as the federal government's daily newspaper. A free copy can be found in your congressionally designated federal depository library. However, your district grants office should either subscribe to it or make it available through the Internet at www.nara.gov/fedreg/ because you should take responsibility for reviewing it. Your district's grantseekers do not need to read this publication every day. They only need to know its purpose as it relates to federal grantseeking and how to use it to increase their knowledge of the grants cycle.

The *Federal Register* provides the government with a mechanism to announce new opportunities for federal funding and to invite comments on what the rules should be. If Congress and the president establish new grant programs for elementary and junior high schools, the first announcement will be in the *Federal Register* to invite comments on the rules that will govern the programs.

In addition, the *Federal Register* is used to announce deadlines and to solicit feedback on the grant rules that governed the previous year's grant solicitation and award process. It is not unusual for a federal agency to print last year's rules for granting funds in the *Federal Register* six months before the next deadline to solicit the public's opinions on the way the grants were awarded the previous year.

The public is usually given thirty days to comment on the rules. The agency reviews the comments and based on them may make changes in the rules. The public is then allowed another thirty days to comment on the changes before the final rules are printed. Because these rules govern the program's priorities and the scoring or review system, they provide valuable insight into exactly what the agency is looking for. The important point is that the proactive grantseeker needs to have advance knowledge of the information in the *Federal Register*.

Now that you are aware of this process, you know that there is no need for your grantseekers to wait around until they receive a formal application package. The point is that it is not necessary to wait until four weeks before the deadline to get started. The information your grantseekers obtained from the CFDA and the *Federal Register* will give them enough data to decide on the appropriateness of that grant program opportunity for their project ideas. If they decide that it is appropriate, they can begin to position themselves to receive a grant.

With information from the CFDA and the *Federal Register,* grantseekers are placed in the grants information loop. However, they should still always check with your district grants office before they begin to write or telephone federal grants program officers.

Your grantseekers can use their knowledge concerning the two most basic federal grants publications, the CFDA and the *Federal Register,* to look like grants pros. For example, assume that they have used their key search words and the CFDA indexes to determine that CFDA 84.287, Twenty-First Century Community Learning Centers, looks to be a likely funding source for their school's project. They could contact Carol Mitchell, the information contact listed in the CFDA, to ask if the deadline has been announced yet, and if it hasn't, when she thinks it will appear in the *Federal Register.* They could also ask if any relevant notices have been published in the *Register,* such as comments on the rules and so on.

For example, suppose one of your grantseekers contacted Ms. Mitchell in November and was told that the invitation to apply was to be printed in December and that the application deadline was expected to be March. Clearly, your grantseeker would gain both an advantage over your competitors and significant insight by consulting the December *Federal Register.* Review the following sample notice from the *Federal Register* shown in Figure 5.6 and use the guide numbers on the left to help you understand this important publication.

1. *CFDA No.:* You now know that all 1,300-plus federal programs are referred to by a CFDA number.

2. *Program Title and Purpose of the Notice:* This section states the title of the program and whether the purpose of the notice is to invite applications, solicit comments, publish final rules, and so on.

3. *Purpose of Program:* This section gives a brief description of the aim of the program.

4. *Eligible Applicants:* This section lists any changes that may have occurred since the comments on the rules were made. For example, if funding community organizations has proven disastrous in the past, the rules regarding eligibility may have changed, and in this granting cycle only local educational agencies may be eligible.

Figure 5.6

FEDERAL REGISTER ENTRY SAMPLE

(1) [CFDA No. 84.287]

(2) 21st Century **Community Learning Centers**; Notice Inviting Applications for New Awards for Fiscal Year 1999

(3) **Purpose of Program:** The 21st Century **Community Learning Centers** Program was established by Congress to award grants to rural and inner-city public schools, or consortia of such schools, to enable them to plan, implement, or expand projects that benefit the educational, health, social services, cultural and recreational needs of the **community.** School-based **community learning centers** can provide a safe, drug-free, supervised and cost-effective after-school, weekend or summer haven for children, youth and their families.

(4) **Eligible Applicants:** Only rural or inner-city public elementary or secondary schools, consortia of those schools, or LEAs applying on their behalf, are eligible to receive a grant under the 21st Century **Community Learning Centers** Program. An LEA considering serving more than one school is encouraged to submit a consortium application on their behalf. Applicants must demonstrate that they meet the statutory program purpose as being either a "rural" or "inner-city" school or a consortium of such schools.

(5) **Applications available:** December 3, 1998.

(6) **Deadline for Transmittal of Applications:** March 1, 1999.

(7) **Deadline for Intergovernmental review:** May 1, 1999.

(8) **Available funds:** $100 million.

(9) **Estimated range of awards:** $35,000–$2,000,000, depending on the number of **Centers** included in each grant application.

(10) **Estimated average size of awards:** $375,000, for a grant that will support 3 **Centers.** The average funding for a single Center is $125,000.

(11) **Estimated number of awards:** 275–300, but the actual number will depend on how many awards will assist multiple **Centers.**

(12) **Project period:** Up to 36 months. Please note that all applicants for multi-year awards are required to provide detailed budget information for the total grant period requested. The Department will negotiate at the time of the initial award the funding levels for each year of the grant award.

Note: The Department is not bound by any estimates in this notice.

(13) **Applicable regulations:** (a) The Education Department General Administrative Regulations (EDGAR) in 34 CFR parts 75, 77, 79, 80, 81, 82, 85, and 86, and (b) the regulations in 34 CFR part 299.

(14) **Priorities**
The Absolute Priority and Competitive Priority 1 in the notice of final priorities for this program published in the Federal Register on December 2, 1997 (62 FR 63773) and repeated below, apply to this competition. In addition, the Secretary gives preference to applications that meet Competitive Priority 2 (34 CFR 75.105(c)(2)(ii) and 34 CFR 299.3(a)). The Secretary selects an application that meets Competitive Priority 2 over an application of comparable merit that does not meet this competitive priority.

(continued)

Figure 5.6 (continued)

Absolute Priority: Under 34 CFR 75.105(c)(3), the Secretary gives an absolute preference to applications that meet the absolute priority in the next paragraph. The Secretary funds under this competition only applications that meet this absolute priority.

Activities To Expand Learning Opportunities: The Secretary funds only those applications for 21st Century **Community Learning Centers** grants that include, among the array of services required and authorized by the statute, activities that offer significant expanded **learning** opportunities for children and youth in the **community** and that contribute to reduced drug use and violence.

Competitive Priorities
Under 34 CFR 75.105(c)(2)(i), the Secretary gives preference to applications that meet one or both of the two competitive priorities in the next two paragraphs.
Competitive Priority 1: Projects designed to assist students to meet or exceed State and local standards in core academic subjects such as reading, mathematics or science, as appropriate to the needs of the participating children. The Secretary awards up to five (5) points for the 100 points an application may earn under the selection criteria that will be included in the application package.
Competitive Priority 2: Projects that will use a significant portion of the program funds to address substantial problems in an Empowerment Zone, including a Supplemental Empowerment Zone, or an Enterprise **Community** designated by the United States Department of Housing and Urban Development or the United States Department of Agriculture.
Note: A list of areas that have been designated as Empowerment Zones and Enterprise Communities is published as an appendix to this notice.

⑮ **Supplementary Information:** The 21st Century **Community Learning Centers** Program is authorized under Title X, Part I (20 U.S.C. 8241) of the Elementary and Secondary Education Act. Grantees under this program are required to carry out at least four of the activities listed in section 1905 of the Elementary and Secondary Education Act (20 U.S.C. 8245), as listed below:

(1) Literacy education programs; (2) Senior citizen programs; (3) Children's day care services; (4) Integrated education, health, social service, recreational, or cultural programs; (5) Summer and weekend school programs in conjunction with recreation programs; (6) Nutrition and health programs; (7) Expanded library service hours to serve **community** needs; (8) Telecommunications and technology education programs for individuals of all ages; (9 Parenting skills education programs; (10) Support and training for child day care providers; (11) Employment counseling, training, and placement; (12) Services for individuals who leave school before graduating from secondary school, regardless of the age of such individual; and (13) Services for individuals with disabilities.

Applicants should propose an array of inclusive and supervised services that include extended **learning** opportunities (such as instructional enrichment programs, tutoring, or homework assistance) but may also include recreational, musical and artistic activities; opportunities to use advanced technology, particularly for those children who do not have access to computers or telecommunications at home, or safety and substance-abuse prevention programs. Grants awarded under this program may be used to plan, implement, or expand **community learning centers.**

⑯ **Geographic distribution:** In awarding grants, the Secretary assures an equitable distribution of assistance among the States, among urban and rural areas of a State, and among urban and rural areas of the United States.

⑰ To **Obtain an Application Package:** Written requests should be mailed to: Adria White, U.S. Department of Education, Office of Educational Research and Improvement, 555 New Jersey Avenue, NW, Washington, DC 20208-5644, Attn: 21st Century Center **Learning Centers.** Requests may also be

Figure 5.6 (continued)

e-mailed to 21stCCLC@ed.gov or faxed to (202) 219-2198. Applications may also be requested by calling 1-800-USA-LEARN.   **For Further Information Contact:** Amanda Clyburn (202-219-2180) or Steve Balkcom (202-219-2089), U.S. Department of Education, Office of Educational Research and Improvement, 555 New Jersey Avenue, NW., Washington, DC 20208-5644. E-mail inquiries should be sent to: 21stCCLC@ed.gov. Faxed inquiries should be sent to: (202) 219-2198.

Individuals who use a telecommunications device for the deaf (TDD) may call the Federal Information Relay Service (FIRS) at 1-800-877-8339 between 8 a.m. and 8 p.m., Eastern time, Monday through Friday.

Individuals with disabilities may obtain this document in an alternate format (e.g., Braille, large print, audiotape, or computer diskette) on request to the contact persons identified in this notice.

Individuals with disabilities may obtain a copy of the application in an alternate format, also, by contacting that person. However, the Department is not able to reproduce in an alternate format the standard forms included in the application package.

⑱ Electronic Access to This Document

Anyone may view this document, as well as all other Department of Education documents published in the Federal Register, in text or portable document format (pdf) via Internet at either of the following sites:

http://ocfo.ed.gov/fedreg.htm

http://www.ed.gov/news.html

To use the pdf you must have the Adobe Acrobat Reader Program with Search, which is available free at either of the previous sites. If you have questions about using the pdf, call the U.S. Government Printing Office at (202) 512-1530 or, toll free, at 1-888-293-6498.

Anyone may also view these documents in text copy only on an electronic bulletin board of the Department. Telephone: (202) 219-1511 or, toll free, 1-800-222-4922. The documents are located under Option G-Files/Announcements, Bulletins and Press Releases.

Note: The official version of a document is the document published in the Federal Register.

Program Authority: 20 U.S.C. 8241–8246.

Dated: December 2, 1998.

C. Kent McGuire, Assistant Secretary for Educational Research and Improvement.

⑲ Appendix: Empowerment Zones and Enterprise Communities

Empowerment Zones (Listed Alphabetically by State): California: Oakland; Georgia: Atlanta; Illinois: Chicago; Kansas: Kansas City; Kentucky: Kentucky Highlands Area (Clinton, Jackson, and Wayne Counties); Maryland: Baltimore; Massachusetts: Boston; Michigan: Detroit; Mississippi: Mid-Delta Area (Bolivar, Holmes, Humphreys, and LeFlore Counties); Missouri: Kansas City; New Jersey: Camden; New York: Harlem, Bronx; Pennsylvania: Philadelphia; Texas: Houston, Rio Grande Valley Area (Cameron, Hidalgo, Starr, and Willacy Counties).

Supplemental Empowerment Zones (Listed Alphabetically by State): California: Los Angeles; Ohio: Cleveland: Enterprise Communities (Listed Alphabetically by State); Alabama: Birmingham, Chambers County, Greene County, Sumter County; Arizona: Arizona Border Area (Cochise, Santa Cruz, and Yuma Counties), Phoenix; Arkansas: East Central Area (Cross, Lee, Monroe, and St. Francis Counties), Mississippi County, Pulaski County; California: Imperial County, Los Angeles (Huntington Park), San Diego, San Francisco (Bayview, Hunter's Point), Watsonville; Colorado: Denver; Connecticut: Bridgeport, New Haven; Delaware: Wilmington; District of Columbia: Washington; Florida: Jackson County; Georgia: Central Savannah River Area (Burke, Hancock, Jefferson, McDuffie, Tallaferro, and Warrent Counties), Crisp County, Dooley County; Illinois: East St. Louis, Springfield; Indiana: Indianapolis; Iowa: Des Moines; Kentucky: Louisville, McCreary County;   Louisiana: Macon Ridge Area (Catahouis, Concordia, Franklin, Morehouse, and Tensas Parishes), New Orleans, Northeast Delta Area

(continued)

Figure 5.6 (continued)

(Madison Parish), Quachita Parish; Massachusetts: Lowell, Springfield; Michigan: Five Cap, Flint, Muskegon; Minnesota: Minneapolis, St. Paul; Mississippi: Jackson, North Delta Area (Panola, Quitman, and Tallahatchie Counties); Missouri: East Prairie, St. Louis; Nebraska: Omaha; Nevada: Clarke County, Las Vegas; New Hampshire: Manchester; New Jersey: Newark; New Mexico: Albuquerque, Moro County, Rio Arriba County, Taos County; New York: Albany, Buffalo, Kingston, Newburgh, Rochester, Schenectady, Troy; North Carolina: Charlotte, Edgecombe County, Halifax County, Robeson County, Wilson County; Ohio: Akron, Columbus, Greater Portsmouth Area (Scioto County); Oklahoma: Choctaw County, McCurtain County, Oklahoma City; Pennsylvania: Harrisburg, Lock Haven, Pittsburgh; Rhode Island: Providence; South Carolina: Charleston, Williamsburg County; South Dakota: Beadle County, Spink County; Tennessee: Fayette County, Haywood County, Memphis, Nashville, Scott County; Texas: Dallas, El Paso, San Antonio, Waco; Utah: Ogden; Vermont: Accomack County, Norfolk; Washington: Lower Yakima County, Seattle, Tacoma; West Virginia: Huntington, McDowell County, West Central Areas (Braxton, Clay, Fayette, Nichols, and Roane Counties); Wisconsin: Milwaukee

[FR Doc. 98-32455 Filed 12-3-98; 10:56 am]

BILLING CODE 4000-01-P

---

5. *Applications Available:* This is the date when the application package will be available. Your grantseekers will already be ahead of the game at this point, and the following chapters will provide you with more suggestions for getting them even further ahead.

6. *Deadline for Transmittal of Applications:* This is the last date on which the current year's applications will be accepted.

7. *Deadline for Intergovernmental Review:* After your district's grantseekers submit their schools' applications to the federal government, copies must be sent to your state's "single point of contact" with a request that this agency send comments to the federal agency by the deadline for intergovernmental review.

8. *Available Funds:* This is not a final figure, but it will give you a good estimate of the total amount of funding available. If the figure is significantly different from the one in the CFDA, you will know that the program is either in favor or falling out of favor. You can help your grantseekers adjust their grants strategy accordingly.

9. *Estimated Range of Awards:* These high and low figures enable you to help your grantseekers select which of their solutions best matches the size of the expected award.

10. *Estimated Average Size of Awards:* This information gives you more focus on the average size of awards. If your grantseekers envision securing $25,000 for their project and the program's estimated average award is $375,000, they need to discuss the appropriateness of their project with the program officer.

11. *Estimated Number of Awards:* This figure gives you insight into how intense the competition for funding might be. In the sample entry, twenty awards throughout the entire United States is not very many, but your grantseekers will discover that other programs expect to make even fewer awards!

12. *Project Period:* This is the time allotted for support. In the sample entry, the project period is up to thirty-six months. Therefore, your grantseekers would have to project their objectives and measurement indicators for a three-year period.

13. *Applicable Regulations:* This refers to the Department of Education's grant policies that must be followed. (Note: Items 14 through 19 are usually repeated in the application package. But by having access to this information early, your grantseekers can increase their ability to control their time and to use the federal grants clock efficiently. The data contained here are more detailed and more timely than those in the CFDA.)

14. *Priorities—Absolute and Competitive:* Review these priorities. They will enable you to help your district's grantseekers select the solution that will obtain the highest ranking. In the sample notice, projects that offer significant expanded learning opportunities for children and youth in the community and that contribute to reduced drug use and violence will receive preference.

15. *Supplementary Information:* In the sample, grantees are required to carry out at least four of the activities listed in this section.

16. *Geographic Distribution:* This section outlines how the program's grants will be distributed geographically.

17. *Application Package:* Here you will find out how to obtain an application package and who to contact for further information.

18. *Electronic Access to This Document:* This section provides information on how to access the document via the Internet.

19. *Appendix:* The sample includes an appendix listing the areas that have been designated as Empowerment Zones and Enterprise Communities.

Foundation Research Tools

The U.S. Justice Department investigated foundations in the late 1960s and raised many questions concerning information on their granting patterns and the public's access to this information. One of the results of these investigations was a renewed effort on the part of the foundations to provide timely and accurate data on their granting programs. In fact, foundation grants were utilized to initiate and are now utilized to support a network of library collections on foundation information. The Foundation Center's National Collections now offer the best available selection of information on foundation and corporate grants. The national collections are located in New York City; Washington, D.C.; Cleveland; San Francisco; and Atlanta. To assist nonprofit organizations without access to the national collections, cooperating collections have been established in libraries, community foundations, and even some nonprofit agencies throughout the United States. The organizations that house the cooperating collections do not get paid to do so, although they do receive the publications for free. Use the list shown in Figure 5.7 to locate the collection closest to you.

The Foundation Center publishes several popular reference materials on foundations, including *The Foundation Directory.* Available at your Foundation Center Regional Library, *The Foundation Directory,* published each year, is the most important single reference work available on grant-making foundations in the United States. To be included in the directory, a foundation must either have assets of over $2 million or make grants in excess of $200,000 annually. Over 10,000 foundations have met one or both of these criteria and are included in the 1999 edition of the directory.

The Foundation Directory, Part 2: A Guide to Grant Programs $50,000 to $20,000 is another very important publication. The 1999 edition lists over 5,700 foundations.

Both *The Foundation Directory* and *The Foundation Directory, Part 2* are indexed according to foundation name, subject area, geographic region, type of support, and key officials:

- *Foundation Name*—If you know the name of a foundation that may be interested in elementary or middle school education, you can locate it in the directories using this index. The index entry itself will provide you with one crucial piece of information—the state in which the foundation is registered. You need to know this to locate the foundation in the directories, because the entries are in alphabetical order by state.

- *Subject Area*—Your grantseekers' Key Words Worksheets will provide them with the words they need to access this index and find the foundations interested in their particular area. Remember that elementary education is becoming an increasingly popular target of funding.

- *Geographic Region*—This index will help you find foundations in your area that share your school district's interests.

Figure 5.7

FOUNDATION CENTER COOPERATING COLLECTIONS

The Foundation Center is an independent national service organization established by foundations to provide an authoritative source of information on foundation and corporate giving. The New York, Washington, D.C., Atlanta, Cleveland, and San Francisco reference collections operated by the Foundation Center offer a wide variety of services and comprehensive collections of information on foundations and grants. Cooperating Collections are libraries, community foundations, and other nonprofit agencies that provide a core collection of Foundation Center publications and a variety of supplementary materials and services in areas useful to grantseekers. The core collection consists of:

THE FOUNDATION DIRECTORY 1 AND 2, AND
   SUPPLEMENT
THE FOUNDATION 1000
FOUNDATION FUNDAMENTALS
FOUNDATION GIVING
THE FOUNDATION GRANTS INDEX

THE FOUNDATION GRANTS INDEX
   QUARTERLY
FOUNDATION GRANTS TO INDIVIDUALS
GUIDE TO U.S. FOUNDATIONS, THEIR TRUSTEES,
   OFFICERS, AND DONORS
THE FOUNDATION CENTER'S GUIDE TO
   PROPOSAL WRITING

NATIONAL DIRECTORY OF CORPORATE
   GIVING
NATIONAL DIRECTORY OF GRANTMAKING
   PUBLIC CHARITIES
NATIONAL GUIDE TO FUNDING IN ... (SERIES)
USER-FRIENDLY GUIDE

All five Center libraries have FC Search, The Foundation Center's Database on CD-ROM available for patron use, and most Cooperating Collections have it as well, as noted by the symbol (+). Also, many of the network members make available for public use sets of private foundation information returns (IRS Form 99-PF) for their state and/or neighboring states noted by the symbol (*). A complete set of U.S. foundation returns can be found at the New York and Washington, D.C., offices of the Foundation Center. The Atlanta, Cleveland, and San Francisco offices contain IRS Form 990-PF returns for the southeastern, midwestern, and western states respectively. Because the collections vary in their hours, materials, and services, it's recommended that you call the collection in advance. To check on new locations or current holdings, call toll-free 1-800-424-9836, or visit our Web site at http://fdncenter.org/library/library.html.

Participants in the Foundation Center's Cooperating Collections network are libraries or nonprofit information centers that provide fundraising information and other funding-related technical assistance in their communities. Cooperating Collections agree to provide free public access to a basic collection of Foundation Center publications during a regular schedule of hours, offering free funding research guidance to all visitors. Many also provide a variety of services for local nonprofit organizations, using staff or volunteers to prepare special materials, organize workshops, or conduct orientations.

The Foundation Center welcomes inquiries from libraries or information centers in the U.S. interested in providing this type of public information service. If you are interested in establishing a funding information library for the use of nonprofit organizations in your area or in learning more about the program, please write to: Rich Romeo, Coordinator of Cooperating Collections, The Foundation Center, 79 Fifth Avenue, New York, NY 10003-3076.

REFERENCE COLLECTIONS OPERATED BY THE FOUNDATION CENTER

THE FOUNDATION CENTER 8th Floor 79 Fifth Ave. New York, NY 10003 (212) 620-4230	THE FOUNDATION CENTER 312 Sutter St., Rm. 312 San Francisco, CA 94108 (415) 397-0902	THE FOUNDATION CENTER 1001 Connecticut Ave., NW Washington, DC 20036 (202) 331-1400	THE FOUNDATION CENTER Kent H. Smith Library 1422 Euclid, Suite 1356 Cleveland, OH 44115 (216) 861-1933	THE FOUNDATION CENTER Suite 150, Grand Lobby Hurt Bldg., 50 Hurt Plaza Atlanta, GA 30303 (404) 880-0094

ALABAMA

BIRMINGHAM PUBLIC LIBRARY*
Government Documents
2100 Park Place
Birmingham 35203
(205) 226-3620

HUNTSVILLE PUBLIC LIBRARY+
915 Monroe St.
Huntsville 35801
(256) 532-5940

UNIVERSITY OF SOUTH ALABAMA*
Library Building
Mobile 36688
(334) 460-7025

AUBURN UNIVERSITY AT
MONTGOMERY LIBRARY*+
7300 University Drive
Montgomery 36124-4023
(334) 244-3200

ALASKA

UNIVERSITY OF ALASKA AT
ANCHORAGE LIBRARY*+
3211 Providence Drive
Anchorage 99508
(907) 786-1846

JUNEAU PUBLIC LIBRARY+
292 Marine Way
Juneau 99801
(907) 586-5267

ARIZONA

FLAGSTAFF CITY–COCONINO
COUNTY PUBLIC LIBRARY
300 West Aspen Ave.
Flagstaff 86001
(520) 779-7670

PHOENIX PUBLIC LIBRARY*+
Information Services Dept.
1221 N. Central
Phoenix 85004
(602) 262-4636

TUCSON-PIMA LIBRARY*+
101 N. Stone Ave.
Tucson 87501
(520) 791-4010

ARKANSAS

WESTARK COMMUNITY COLLEGE -
BORHAM LIBRARY*+
5210 Grand Avenue
Ft. Smith 72913
(501) 788-7200

CENTRAL ARKANSAS LIBRARY
SYSTEM*+
100 Rock St.
Little Rock 72201
(501) 918-3000

PINE BLUFF–JEFFERSON COUNTY
LIBRARY SYSTEM
200 E. Eighth
Pine Bluff 71601
(870) 534-2159

CALIFORNIA

HUMBOLDT AREA FOUNDATION*+
P.O. Box 99
Bayside 95524
(707) 442-2993

VENTURA COUNTY COMMUNITY
FOUNDATION*+
Resource Center for Nonprofit
Organizations
1317 Del Norte Road, Suite 150
Camarillo 93010-8504
(805) 988-0196

FRESNO REGIONAL FOUNDATION+
Nonprofit Advancement Center
1999 Tuolumne Street, Suite 650
Fresno 93720
(559) 498-3929

(continued)

Figure 5.7 (continued)

CENTER FOR NONPROFIT
MANAGEMENT IN SOUTHERN
CALIFORNIA
Nonprofit Resource Library
315 West 9th Street, Suite 1100
Los Angeles 90015
(213) 623-7080

FLINTRIDGE FOUNDATION
Philanthropy Resource Library
1040 Lincoln Avenue, Suite 100
Pasadena 91103
(626) 449-0839

GRANT & RESOURCE CENTER OF
NORTHERN CALIFORNIA*+
Building C, Suite A
2280 Benton Dr.
Redding 96003
(530) 244-1219

LOS ANGELES PUBLIC LIBRARY
West Valley Regional Branch
Library
19036 Van Owen St.
Reseda 91335
(818) 345-4393

RIVERSIDE PUBLIC LIBRARY
3581 Mission Inn Ave.
Riverside 92501
(909) 782-5202

NONPROFIT RESOURCE CENTER*+
Sacramento Public Library
828 I Street, 2nd Floor
Sacramento 95814
(916) 264-2772

SAN DIEGO FOUNDATION
Funding Information Center
1420 Kettner Boulevard, Suite 500
San Diego 92101
(619) 239-8815

SAN FRANCISCO FIELD OFFICE
AND LIBRARY+
312 Sutter Street, Rm. 312
San Francisco 94108
(415) 397-0902

NONPROFIT DEVELOPMENT
CENTER*+
Library
1922 The Alameda, Suite 212
San Jose 95126
(408) 248-9505

PENINSULA COMMUNITY
FOUNDATION*+
Peninsula Nonprofit Center
1700 S. El Camino Real, #300
San Mateo 94402-3049
(650) 358-9392

LOS ANGELES PUBLIC LIBRARY
San Pedro Regional Branch
9131 S. Gaffey St.
San Pedro 90731
(310) 548-7779

VOLUNTEER CENTER OF ORANGE
COUNTY*+
Nonprofit Management Assistance
Center
1901 East 4th Street, Suite 100
Santa Ana 92705
(714) 953-5757

SANTA BARBARA PUBLIC LIBRARY+
40 E. Anapamu St.
Santa Barbara 93101-1019
(805) 564-5633

SANTA MONICA PUBLIC LIBRARY+
1343 Sixth St.
Santa Monica 90401-1603
(310) 458-8600

SONOMA COUNTY LIBRARY+
3rd & E Streets
Santa Rosa 95404
(707) 545-0831

SEASIDE BRANCH LIBRARY+
550 Harcourt St.
Seaside 93955
(831) 899-8131

SONORA AREA FOUNDATION+
20100 Cedar Road, N.
Sonora 95370
(209) 533-2596

COLORADO

EL POMAR NONPROFIT RESOURCE
LIBRARY+
1661 Mesa Ave.
Colorado Springs 80906
(719) 577-7000

DENVER PUBLIC LIBRARY*+
General Reference
10 West 14th Avenue Parkway
Denver 80204
(303) 640-6200

CONNECTICUT

DANBURY PUBLIC LIBRARY+
170 Main St.
Danbury 06810
(203) 797-4527

GREENWICH PUBLIC LIBRARY*+
101 West Putnam Ave.
Greenwich 06830
(203) 622-7900

HARTFORD PUBLIC LIBRARY*+
500 Main St.
Hartford 06103
(860) 543-8656

NEW HAVEN FREE PUBLIC
LIBRARY*+
Reference Dept.
133 Elm St.
New Haven 06510-2057
(203) 946-8130

DELAWARE

UNIVERSITY OF DELAWARE*+
Hugh Morris Library
Newark 19717-5267
(302) 831-2432

FLORIDA

VOLUSIA COUNTY LIBRARY
CENTER+
City Island
105 E. Magnolia Ave.
Daytona Beach 32114-4484
(904) 257-6036

NOVA SOUTHEASTERN
UNIVERSITY*+
Einstein Library
3301 College Ave.
Fort Lauderdale 33314
(954) 262-4601

INDIAN RIVER COMMUNITY
COLLEGE+
Learning Resources Center
3209 Virginia Ave.
Fort Pierce 34981-5596
(561) 462-4757

JACKSONVILLE PUBLIC LIBRARIES*+
Grants Resource Center
122 N. Ocean St.
Jacksonville 32202
(904) 630-2665

MIAMI-DADE PUBLIC LIBRARY*+
Humanities/Social Science
101 W. Flagler St.
Miami 33130
(305) 375-5575

ORANGE COUNTY LIBRARY
SYSTEM
Social Sciences Department
101 E. Central Blvd.
Orlando 32801
(407) 425-4694

SELBY PUBLIC LIBRARY
Reference
1331 First St.
Sarasota 34236
(941) 316-1183

TAMPA-HILLSBOROUGH COUNTY
PUBLIC LIBRARY*+
900 N. Ashley Drive
Tampa 33602
(813) 273-3652

COMMUNITY FDN. OF PALM
BEACH & MARTIN COUNTIES*+
324 Datura St., Suite 340
West Palm Beach 33401
(561) 659-6800

GEORGIA

ATLANTA FIELD OFFICE & LIBRARY
Suite 150, Grand Lobby
Hurt Building, 50 Hurt Plaza
Atlanta 30303-2914
(404) 880-0094

ATLANTA-FULTON PUBLIC
LIBRARY*+
Foundation Collection
Ivan Allen Department
1 Margaret Mitchell Square
Atlanta 30303-1089
(404) 730-1900

UNITED WAY OF CENTRAL
GEORGIA*+
Community Resource Center
277 Martin Luther King Jr. Blvd.,
Suite 301
Macon 31201
(912) 745-4732

SAVANNAH STATE UNIVERSITY+
Asa Gordon Library
P.O. Box 20394
Savannah 31404
(912) 356-2185

THOMAS CTY PUBLIC LIBRARY*+
201 N. Madison St.
Thomasville 31792
(912) 225-5252

HAWAII

UNIVERSITY OF HAWAII*+
Hamilton Library
2550 The Mall
Honolulu 96822
(808) 956-7214

HAWAII COMMUNITY
FOUNDATION FUNDING
RESOURCE LIBRARY+
900 Fort St., Suite 1300
Honolulu 96813
(808) 537-6333

IDAHO

BOISE PUBLIC LIBRARY*+
715 S. Capitol Blvd.
Boise 83702
(208) 384-4024

CALDWELL PUBLIC LIBRARY*+
1010 Dearborn St.
Caldwell 83605
(208) 459-3242

ILLINOIS

DONORS FORUM OF CHICAGO*+
208 South LaSalle, Suite 735
Chicago 60604
(312) 578-0175

Figure 5.7 (continued)

EVANSTON PUBLIC LIBRARY*+
1703 Orrington Ave.
Evanston 60201
(847) 866-0305

ROCK ISLAND PUBLIC LIBRARY+
401 - 19th St.
Rock Island 61201
(309) 788-7627

UNIVERSITY OF ILLINOIS AT
SPRINGFIELD*+
Brookens Library
P.O. Box 19243
Springfield 62794-9243
(217) 206-6633

INDIANA

EVANSVILLE–VANDERBURGH
COUNTY PUBLIC LIBRARY*+
22 Southeast Fifth St.
Evansville 47708
(812) 428-8200

ALLEN COUNTY PUBLIC LIBRARY*+
900 Webster St.
Ft. Wayne 46802
(219) 421-1200

INDIANAPOLIS–MARION COUNTY
PUBLIC LIBRARY*+
Social Sciences
P.O. Box 211
40 E. St. Clair
Indianapolis 46206
(317) 269-1733

VIGO COUNTY PUBLIC LIBRARY*+
1 Library Square
Terre Haute 47807
(812) 232-1113

IOWA

CEDAR RAPIDS PUBLIC LIBRARY
Foundation Center Collection
500 First St., SE
Cedar Rapids 52401
(319) 398-5123

SOUTHWESTERN COMMUNITY
COLLEGE*+
Learning Resource Center
1501 W. Townline Rd.
Creston 50801
(515) 782-7081

PUBLIC LIBRARY OF DES
MOINES*+
100 Locust
Des Moines 50309-1791
(515) 283-4295

SIOUX CITY PUBLIC LIBRARY*+
529 Pierce St.
Sioux City 51101-1202
(712) 252-5669

KANSAS

DODGE CITY PUBLIC LIBRARY*+
1001 2nd Ave.
Dodge City 67801
(316) 225-0248

TOPEKA AND SHAWNEE COUNTY
PUBLIC LIBRARY*+
1515 SW 10th Ave.
Topeka 66604-1374
(785) 233-2040

WICHITA PUBLIC LIBRARY*+
223 S. Main St.
Wichita 67202
(316) 261-8500

KENTUCKY

WESTERN KENTUCKY UNIVERSITY+
Helm-Cravens Library
Bowling Green 42101-3576
(502) 745-6125

LEXINGTON PUBLIC LIBRARY*
140 East Main Street
Lexington 40507-1376
(606) 231-5520

LOUISVILLE FREE PUBLIC
LIBRARY*+
301 York Street
Louisville 40203
(502) 574-1611

LOUISIANA

EAST BATON ROUGE PARISH
LIBRARY*+
Centroplex Branch Grants
Collection
120 St. Louis
Baton Rouge 70802
(225) 389-4967

BEAUREGARD PARISH LIBRARY*+
205 S. Washington Ave.
De Ridder 70634
(318) 463-6217

OUACHITA PARISH PUBLIC LIBRARY
1800 Stubbs Avenue
Monroe 71201
(318) 327-1490

NEW ORLEANS PUBLIC LIBRARY*+
Business & Science Division
219 Loyola Ave.
New Orleans 70140
(504) 596-2580

SHREVE MEMORIAL LIBRARY*
424 Texas St.
Shreveport 71120-1523
(318) 226-5894

MAINE

MAINE GRANTS INFORMATION
CENTER*+
University of So. Maine Library
314 Forrest Ave.
Portland 04104-9301
(207) 780-5039

MARYLAND

ENOCH PRATT FREE LIBRARY*+
Social Science & History
400 Cathedral St.
Baltimore 21201
(410) 396-5430

MASSACHUSETTS

ASSOCIATED GRANTMAKERS OF
MASSACHUSETTS*+
294 Washington St., Suite 840
Boston 02108
(617) 426-2606

BOSTON PUBLIC LIBRARY*+
Soc. Sci. Reference
700 Boylston Street
Boston 02117
(617) 536-5400

WESTERN MASSACHUSETTS
FUNDING RESOURCE CENTER+
65 Elliot St.
Springfield 01101-1730
(413) 452-0615

WORCESTER PUBLIC LIBRARY*+
Grants Resource Center
60 Fremont St.
Worcester 01603
(508) 799-1655

MICHIGAN

ALPENA COUNTY LIBRARY*+
211 N. First St.
Alpena 49707
(517) 356-6188

UNIVERSITY OF MICHIGAN–
ANN ARBOR*+
Graduate Library
Reference & Research Services
Ann Arbor 48109-1205
(313) 764-9373

WILLARD PUBLIC LIBRARY*+
Nonprofit and Funding Resource
Collections
7 West Van Buren St.
Battle Creek 49017
(616) 968-8166

HENRY FORD CENTENNIAL
LIBRARY*+
Adult Services
16301 Michigan Ave.
Dearborn 48124
(313) 943-2330

WAYNE STATE UNIVERSITY*+
Purdy/Kresge Library
5265 Cass Avenue
Detroit 48202
(313) 577-6424

MICHIGAN STATE UNIVERSITY
LIBRARIES*+
Reference
100 Library
East Lansing 48824-1048
(517) 355-2344

FARMINGTON COMMUNITY
LIBRARY*+
32737 West 12 Mile Rd.
Farmington Hills 48334
(248) 553-0300

UNIVERSITY OF MICHIGAN–FLINT
Library*
Flint 48502-2186
(810) 762-3408

GRAND RAPIDS PUBLIC LIBRARY*+
Business Dept., 3rd Floor
60 Library Plaza NE
Grand Rapids 49503-3093
(616) 456-3600

MICHIGAN TECHNOLOGICAL
UNIVERSITY+
Van Pelt Library
1400 Townsend Dr.
Houghton 49931
(906) 487-2507

MAUD PRESTON PALENSKE
MEMORIAL LIBRARY+
500 Market St.
St. Joseph 49085
(616) 983-7167

NORTHWESTERN MICHIGAN
COLLEGE*+
Mark & Helen Osterin Library
1701 E. Front St.
Traverse City 49684
(616) 922-1060

MINNESOTA

DULUTH PUBLIC LIBRARY*+
520 W. Superior St.
Duluth 55802
(218) 723-3802

SOUTHWEST STATE UNIVERSITY*+
University Library
North Highway 23
Marshall 56253
(507) 537-6176

MINNEAPOLIS PUBLIC LIBRARY*+
Sociology Department
300 Nicollet Mall
Minneapolis 55401
(612) 630-6300

(continued)

Figure 5.7 (continued)

ROCHESTER PUBLIC LIBRARY
101 2nd Street, SE
Rochester 55904-3777
(507) 285-8002

ST. PAUL PUBLIC LIBRARY+
90 W. Fourth St.
St. Paul 55102
(651) 266-7000

MISSISSIPPI

JACKSON/HINDS LIBRARY
SYSTEM*+
300 N. State St.
Jackson 39201
(601) 968-5803

MISSOURI

CLEARINGHOUSE FOR
MIDCONTINENT FOUNDATIONS*+
University of Missouri
5110 Cherry, Suite 310
Kansas City 64110
(816) 235-1176

KANSAS CITY PUBLIC LIBRARY*+
311 E. 12th St.
Kansas City 64106
(816) 701-3541

METROPOLITAN ASSOCIATION FOR
PHILANTHROPY, INC.*+
One Metropolitan Square, Ste 1295
211 North Broadway, Suite 1200
St. Louis 63102
(314) 621-6220

SPRINGFIELD–GREENE COUNTY
LIBRARY*+
397 E. Central
Springfield 65802
(417) 837-5000

MONTANA

MONTANA STATE
UNIVERSITY–BILLINGS*+
Library - Special Collections
1500 North 30th St.
Billings 59101-0298
(406) 657-2046

BOZEMAN PUBLIC LIBRARY*+
220 E. Lamme
Bozeman 59715
(406) 582-2402

MONTANA STATE LIBRARY*+
Library Services
1515 E. 6th Ave.
Helena 59620
(406) 444-3004

UNIVERSITY OF MONTANA*+
Maureen & Mike Mansfield Library
Missoula 59812-1195
(406) 243-6800

NEBRASKA

UNIVERSITY OF NEBRASKA-
LINCOLN*+
Love Library
14th & R Streets
Lincoln 68588-0410
(402) 472-2848

W. DALE CLARK LIBRARY*+
Social Sciences Department
215 S. 15th St.
Omaha 68102
(402) 444-4826

NEVADA

CLARK COUNTY LIBRARY*+
1401 E. Flamingo
Las Vegas 89119
(702) 733-3642

WASHOE COUNTY LIBRARY*+
301 S. Center St.
Reno 89505
(775) 785-4190

NEW HAMPSHIRE

CONCORD PUBLIC LIBRARY
45 Green Street
Concord 03301
(603) 225-8670

PLYMOUTH STATE COLLEGE*+
Herbert H. Lamson Library
Plymouth 03264
(603) 535-2258

NEW JERSEY

CUMBERLAND COUNTY LIBRARY+
800 E. Commerce St.
Bridgeton 08302
(609) 453-2210

FREE PUBLIC LIBRARY OF
ELIZABETH*+
11 S. Broad St.
Elizabeth 07202
(908) 354-6060

NEW JERSEY STATE LIBRARY*+
Governmental Reference Services
185 West State St.
Trenton 08625-0520
(609) 292-6220

NEW MEXICO

ALBUQUERQUE COMMUNITY FDN*
3301 Menaul NE, Suite 30
Albuquerque 87176-6960
(505) 883-6240

NEW MEXICO STATE LIBRARY*+
Information Services
1209 Camino Carlos Rey
Santa Fe 87505-9860
(505) 476-9714

NEW YORK

NEW YORK STATE LIBRARY*+
Humanities Reference
Cultural Education Center, 6th floor
Empire State Plaza
Albany 12230
(518) 474-5355

SUFFOLK COOPERATIVE LIBRARY
SYSTEM+
627 N. Sunrise Service Rd.
Bellport 11713
(516) 286-1600

NEW YORK PUBLIC LIBRARY+
Bronx Reference Center
2556 Bainbridge Ave.
Bronx 10458-4698
(718) 579-4257

NONPROFIT CONNECTION, INC.+
One Hanson Place, Room 2504
Brooklyn 11243
(718) 230-3200

BROOKLYN PUBLIC LIBRARY+
Social Sciences/Philosophy
Division
Grand Army Plaza
Brooklyn 11238
(718) 230-2100

BUFFALO & ERIE COUNTY PUBLIC
LIBRARY*+
Business, Science, and Technology
Dept.
1 Lafayette Square
Buffalo 14203
(716) 858-7097

HUNTINGTON PUBLIC LIBRARY+
338 Main St.
Huntington 11743
(516) 427-5165

QUEENS BOROUGH PUBLIC
LIBRARY+
Social Sciences Division
89-11 Merrick Blvd.
Jamaica 11432
(718) 990-0700

LEVITTOWN PUBLIC LIBRARY*+
1 Bluegrass Lane
Levittown 11756
(516) 731-5728

FOUNDATION CENTER OFFICE AND
LIBRARY+
79 Fifth Avenue
2nd Floor New York 10003-3076
(212) 620-4230

NEW YORK PUBLIC LIBRARY+
Countee Cullen Branch Library
104 W. 136th St.
New York 10030
(212) 491-2070

ADRIANCE MEMORIAL LIBRARY+
Special Services Department
93 Market St.
Poughkeepsie 12601
(914) 485-3445

ROCHESTER PUBLIC LIBRARY*+
Social Sciences
115 South Avenue
Rochester 14604
(716) 428-8120

ONONDAGA COUNTY PUBLIC
LIBRARY+
447 S. Salina St.
Syracuse 13202-2494
(315) 435-1818

UTICA PUBLIC LIBRARY
303 Genesee St.
Utica 13501
(315) 735-2279

WHITE PLAINS PUBLIC LIBRARY*+
100 Martine Ave.
White Plains 10601
(914) 422-1480

YONKERS PUBLIC LIBRARY
Reference Department, Getty
Square Branch
7 Main St.
Yonkers, NY 10701
(914) 476-1255

NORTH CAROLINA

COMMUNITY FDN. OF WESTERN
NORTH CAROLINA*+
Nonprofit Resources Center
16 Biltmore Avenue, Suite 201
P.O. Box 1888
Asheville 28802
(828) 254-4960

THE DUKE ENDOWMENT*+
100 N. Tryon St., Suite 3500
Charlotte 28202
(704) 376-0291

DURHAM COUNTY PUBLIC
LIBRARY+
301 North Roxboro
Durham 27702
(919) 560-0110

STATE LIBRARY OF NORTH
CAROLINA*+
Government and Business Services
Archives Bldg., 109 E. Jones St.
Raleigh 27601
(919) 733-3270

FORSYTH COUNTY PUBLIC
LIBRARY*+
660 W. 5th St.
Winston-Salem 27101
(336) 727-2680

Figure 5.7 (continued)

NORTH DAKOTA

BISMARCK PUBLIC LIBRARY
515 North Fifth St.
Bismarck 58501
(701) 222-6410

FARGO PUBLIC LIBRARY*+
102 N. 3rd St.
Fargo 58102
(701) 241-1491

OHIO

STARK COUNTY DISTRICT LIBRARY+
715 Market Ave. N.
Canton 44702
(330) 452-0665

FOUNDATION CENTER OFFICE AND
LIBRARY+
Kent H. Smith Library
1422 Euclid Avenue, Suite 1356
Cleveland, OH 44115
(216) 861-1933

PUBLIC LIBRARY OF CINCINNATI &
HAMILTON COUNTY*+
Grants Resource Center
800 Vine St., Library Square
Cincinnati 45202-2071
(513) 369-6940

COLUMBUS METROPOLITAN
LIBRARY+
Business and Technology Dept.
96 S. Grant Ave.
Columbus 43215
(614) 645-2590

DAYTON & MONTGOMERY
COUNTY PUBLIC LIBRARY*+
Grants Resource Center
215 E. Third St.
Dayton 45402
(937) 227-9500 x211

MANSFIELD/RICHLAND COUNTY
PUBLIC LIBRARY*+
42 West 3rd Street
Mansfield 44902
(419) 521-3110

TOLEDO–LUCAS COUNTY PUBLIC
LIBRARY*+
Social Sciences Department
325 Michigan St.
Toledo 43624-1614
(419) 259-5245

PUBLIC LIBRARY OF YOUNGSTOWN
& MAHONING COUNTY*+
305 Wick Ave.
Youngstown 44503
(330) 744-8636

MUSKINGUM COUNTY LIBRARY+
220 N. 5th St.
Zanesville 43701
(614) 453-0391

OKLAHOMA

OKLAHOMA CITY UNIVERSITY*+
Dulaney Browne Library
2501 N. Blackwelder
Oklahoma City 73106
(405) 521-5822

TULSA CITY–COUNTY LIBRARY*+
400 Civic Center
Tulsa 74103
(918) 596-7940

OREGON

OREGON INSTITUTE OF
TECHNOLOGY+
Library, 3201 Campus Dr.
Klamath Falls 97601-8801
(541) 885-1780

PACIFIC NONPROFIT NETWORK*+
Grantsmanship Resource Library
33 N. Central, Suite 211
Medford 97501
(541) 779-6044

MULTNOMAH COUNTY LIBRARY+
Government Documents
801 SW Tenth Ave.
Portland 97205
(503) 248-5123

OREGON STATE LIBRARY*+
State Library Building
Salem 97310
(503) 378-4277

PENNSYLVANIA

NORTHAMPTON COMMUNITY
COLLEGE+
Learning Resources Center
3835 Green Pond Rd.
Bethlehem 18017
(610) 861-5360

ERIE COUNTY LIBRARY+
160 East Front St.
Erie 16507
(814) 451-6927

DAUPHIN COUNTY LIBRARY
SYSTEM+
Central Library
101 Walnut St.
Harrisburg 17101
(717) 234-4976

LANCASTER COUNTY PUBLIC
LIBRARY+
125 N. Duke St.
Lancaster 17602
(717) 394-2651

FREE LIBRARY OF PHILADELPHIA*+
Regional Foundation Center
Logan Square
Philadelphia 19103
(215) 686-5423

CARNEGIE LIBRARY OF
PITTSBURGH*+
Foundation Collection
4400 Forbes Ave.
Pittsburgh 15213-4080
(412) 622-1917

POCONO NORTHEAST
DEVELOPMENT FUND+
James Pettinger Memorial Library
1151 Oak St.
Pittston 18640-3795
(570) 655-5581

READING PUBLIC LIBRARY+
100 South Fifth St.
Reading 19475
(610) 655-6355

MARTIN LIBRARY*+
159 Market St.
York 17401
(717) 846-5300

RHODE ISLAND

PROVIDENCE PUBLIC LIBRARY*+
225 Washington St.
Providence 02903
(401) 455-8000

SOUTH CAROLINA

ANDERSON COUNTY LIBRARY*+
202 East Greenville St.
Anderson 29621
(864) 260-4500

CHARLESTON COUNTY LIBRARY*+
68 Calhoun St.
Charleston 29401
(843) 805-6950

SOUTH CAROLINA STATE
LIBRARY*+
1500 Senate St.
Columbia 29211-1469
(803) 734-8666

COMMUNITY FOUNDATION OF
GREATER GREENVILLE
27 Cleveland Street, Suite 101
P.O. Box 6909
Greenville 29606
(864) 233-5925

SOUTH DAKOTA

SOUTH DAKOTA STATE LIBRARY*+
800 Governors Drive
Pierre 57501-5070
(605) 773-3131
(800) 592-1841 (SD residents)

DAKOTA STATE UNIVERSITY
Nonprofit Grants Assistance
132 S. Dakota Ave.
Sioux Falls 57104
(605) 367-5380

SIOUXLAND LIBRARIES*+
201 N. Main Ave.
Sioux Falls 57104
(605) 367-7081

TENNESSEE

KNOX COUNTY PUBLIC LIBRARY*+
500 W. Church Ave.
Knoxville 37902
(423) 544-5750

MEMPHIS & SHELBY COUNTY
PUBLIC LIBRARY*+
1850 Peabody Ave.
Memphis 38104
(901) 725-8877

NASHVILLE PUBLIC LIBRARY*+
Business Information Division
225 Polk Ave.
Nashville 37203
(615) 862-5842

TEXAS

NONPROFIT RESOURCE CENTER+
Funding Information Library
500 N. Chestnut, Suite 1511
P.O. Box 3322
Abilene 79604
(915) 677-8166

AMARILLO AREA FOUNDATION*+
Funding Research and Nonprofit
Management Library
Nonprofit Services Center
700 First National Place, Ste. 700
801 S. Fillmore
Amarillo 79101
(806) 376-4521

HOGG FOUNDATION FOR MENTAL
HEALTH*+
3001 Lake Austin Blvd.
Austin 78703
(512) 471-5041

BEAUMONT PUBLIC LIBRARY*+
801 Pearl Street
Beaumont 77704-3827
(409) 838-6606

CORPUS CHRISTI PUBLIC
LIBRARY*+
Funding Information Center
805 Comanche Street
Corpus Christi 78401
(361) 880-7000

DALLAS PUBLIC LIBRARY*+
Urban Information
1515 Young St.
Dallas 75201
(214) 670-1487

(continued)

Figure 5.7 (continued)

SOUTHWEST BORDER NONPROFIT
RESOURCE CENTER+
1201 W. University Drive
Edinburgh 78539
(956) 384-5900

CENTER FOR VOLUNTEERISM &
NONPROFIT MANAGEMENT+
1918 Texas Avenue
El Paso 79901
(915) 532-5377

FUNDING INFORMATION CENTER
OF FORT WORTH*+
329 S. Henderson
Fort Worth 76104
(817) 334-0228

HOUSTON PUBLIC LIBRARY*+
Bibliographic Information Center
500 McKinney
Houston 77002
(713) 236-1313

NONPROFIT MANAGEMENT AND
VOLUNTEER CENTER
Laredo Public Library
1120 East Calton Road
Laredo 78041
(956) 795-2400

LONGVIEW PUBLIC LIBRARY*
222 W. Cotton St.
Longview 75601
(903) 237-1352

LUBBOCK AREA FOUNDATION,
INC.+
1655 Main St., Suite 209
Lubbock 79401
(806) 762-8061

NONPROFIT RESOURCE CENTER OF
TEXAS*+
111 Soledad, Suite 200
San Antonio 78205
(210) 227-4333

WACO–McLENNAN COUNTY
LIBRARY*+
1717 Austin Ave.
Waco 76701
(254) 750-5975

NORTH TEXAS CENTER FOR
NONPROFIT MANAGEMENT*+
624 Indiana, Suite 307
Wichita Falls 76301
(940) 322-4961

UTAH

SALT LAKE CITY PUBLIC LIBRARY*
209 East 500 South
Salt Lake City 84111
(801) 524-8200

VERMONT

VERMONT DEPT. OF LIBRARIES*+
Reference & Law Info. Services
109 State St.
Montpelier 05609
(802) 828-3268

VIRGINIA

HAMPTON PUBLIC LIBRARY+
4207 Victoria Blvd.
Hampton 23669
(757) 727-1312

RICHMOND PUBLIC LIBRARY*+
Business, Science & Technology
101 East Franklin St.
Richmond 23219
(804) 780-8223

ROANOKE CITY PUBLIC LIBRARY
SYSTEM*
Main Library
706 S. Jefferson St.
Roanoke 24016
(540) 853-2477

WASHINGTON

MID-COLUMBIA LIBRARY*
405 South Dayton
Kennewick 99336
(509) 586-3156

SEATTLE PUBLIC LIBRARY*+
Fundraising Resource Center
1000 Fourth Ave.
Seattle 98104-1193
(206) 386-4620

SPOKANE PUBLIC LIBRARY*
Funding Information Center
West 811 Main Ave.
Spokane 99201
(509) 444-5336

UNITED WAY OF PIERCE COUNTY*+
Center for Nonprofit Development
1501 Pacific Ave., Suite 400
P.O. Box 2215
Tacoma 98401
(253) 597-7496

GREATER WENATCHEE
COMMUNITY FOUNDATION AT THE
WENATCHEE PUBLIC LIBRARY
310 Douglas St.
Wenatchee 98807
(509) 662-5021

WASHINGTON, D.C.

FOUNDATION CENTER OFFICE AND
LIBRARY*
1001 Connecticut Avenue, NW
Suite 938
Washington, DC 20036
(202) 331-1400

WEST VIRGINIA

KANAWHA COUNTY PUBLIC
LIBRARY*+
123 Capitol St.
Charleston 25301
(304) 343-4646

WISCONSIN

UNIVERSITY OF WISCONSIN-
MADISON*+
Memorial Library, Grants
Information Center
728 State St., Room 276
Madison 53706
(608) 262-3242

MARQUETTE UNIVERSITY
MEMORIAL LIBRARY*+
Funding Information Center
1415 W. Wisconsin Ave.
Milwaukee 53201-3141
(414) 288-1515

UNIVERSITY OF WISCONSIN-
STEVENS POINT*+
Library–Foundation Collection
900 Reserve St.
Stevens Point 54481-3897
(715) 346-4204

WYOMING

NATRONA COUNTY PUBLIC
LIBRARY*+
307 E. 2nd St.
Casper 82601-2598
(307) 237-4935

LARAMIE COUNTY COMMUNITY
COLLEGE*+
Instructional Resource Center
1400 E. College Dr.
Cheyenne 82007-3299
(307) 778-1206

CAMPBELL COUNTY PUBLIC
LIBRARY*+
2101 4-J Road
Gillette 82718
(307) 687-0115

TETON COUNTY LIBRARY*+
125 Virginia Lane
Jackson 83001
(307) 733-2164

ROCK SPRINGS LIBRARY+
400 C St.
Rock Springs 82901
(307) 362-6669

PUERTO RICO

UNIVERSIDAD DEL SAGRADO
CORAZON+
M.M.T. Guevara Library
Santurce 00914
(809) 728-1515 x 4357

- *Type of Support*—Many foundations have severe restrictions on the types of funding they will provide. This index allows your grantseekers to quickly discover this important information.

- *Donor, Trustees, and Officers (Key Officials)*—This index provides you with information that may be useful in developing linkages with foundations.

All of the indexes refer to the foundations by a four-digit number that appears above each foundation's name. As already mentioned, the foundations are arranged in alphabetical order according to the state in which they are incorporated. *The Foundation Directory* also has an international giving index and an index of foundations new to the edition.

The following fictitious sample is set up like a real entry in *The Foundation Directory*.

The Foundation Directory: Sample Entry

2762

The Sebastian Jessica Foundation

2604 Northstar

Chicago 60604   (312) 896-8630

Incorporated in 1926 in IL

Donor(s): *Vastell Jessica, Mrs. Sebastian Jessica*

Foundation type: *Independent*

Financial data *(yr. ending 6/30/99): Assets, $150,444,176 (M); expenditures, $6,488,200; qualifying distributions, $6,400,200 including $4,488,200 for 126 grants (high: $300,000; low: $200; average $10,000–$50,000).*

Purpose and activities: *Dedicated to enhancing the humane dimensions of life through activities that emphasize the theme of improving the quality of teaching and learning. Serves precollegiate education through grantmaking and program activities in elementary and secondary public education.*

Types of support: *Consulting services, technical assistance, special projects.*

Limitations: *No support for colleges and universities (except for projects in elementary and secondary education). No grants to individuals or for building or endowment funds or operating budgets; no loans.*

Publications: *Annual report, informational brochure (including application guidelines), financial statement, grants list.*

Application information: *Grant proposals for higher education not accepted; fellowship applications available only through participating universities. Application form not required.*

> *Initial approach: Letter*
> *Copies of proposal: 1*
> *Deadline(s): None*
> *Board meeting date(s): May and Nov. and as required*
> *Final notification: 4 weeks*
> *Write: Dr. Stefan Ross, Pres.*

Officers: Vastell Jessica, Chair; Ann Jessica, Vice-Chair and Secy.; Stefan Ross, Pres.; Winifred L. Boser, V.P.; Franz Kirshbauer, Treas.; Bilal Ali, Prog. Dir.

Trustees: John R. Bige; Alice S. Romana; Donald C. Crown, Jr.; Charles Power; George Gaylin; P. John Passitty.

Number of staff: 4 full-time professionals; 1 part-time professional; 4 full-time support.

Employer Identification Number: 679014579

Selected grants: The following grants were reported in 1998.

$15,000 to Towan School District. For innovative reform.

$20,000 to Dade County Schools. For the development of effective classroom tools.

$10,000 to Wiler Foundation. For computers for school program.

In an effort to find a funder for our example project involving parents, teachers, and students in responsible education, we turn to our key words and the subject index in *The Foundation Directory*. We were able to determine that the (fictitious) Sebastian Jessica Foundation has an expressed interest in elementary education. From the entry, we were also able to ascertain that our request will fall within the foundation's average grant size of $10,000 to $50,000. However, we are still not ready to write a proposal or even to telephone the foundation.

We need to learn more about the Sebastian Jessica Foundation. For example, what do they really value? What types of organizations did they make their awards to? Because the entry in *The Foundation Directory* does not state that the foundation limits its giving to any one geographic area, we are also interested in knowing where it has awarded its grants in the past.

Another popular Foundation Center publication, *The Foundation Grants Index*, can provide us with much of this information. *The Foundation Grants Index*, published annually, lists approximately 86,000 grants of $10,000 or more made by one thousand of the largest independent, corporate, and community foundations. *The Foundation Grants Index* is divided into seven sections.

Section I—Grants Listing This is an alphabetical listing by state of the foundations included in the publication. Each grant of $10,000 or more awarded by the foundation is listed under the foundation's name. Each grant has a grant identification number. In our example, to locate a listing of the grants awarded by the Sebastian Jessica Foundation we would go to the Section I index, locate Illinois (the state of incorporation), and find Jessica in the alphabetical listing.

Section II—Grant Recipients This is an alphabetical listing of the names of grant recipients (grantees). The recipient's name, state, and grant identification number are provided in each entry. This information allows you to trace the entry to the grantor by locating the grant identification number in Section I.

Section III—Subject Index This index lists subject areas (key words) in alphabetical order. Under each subject area is a list of grant identification numbers. These numbers identify the grants that were awarded in that particular subject area. Again, the grants in Section I can be located by using their identification numbers.

Section IV—Type of Support/Geographic Area This section is an alphabetical index by type of support (such as education, science/social science, youth development, and so on). The grants in each subject area are listed by state and identification number. This enables analysis of geographic granting patterns as related to types of support and subject areas.

Section V—Recipient Category Index This index provides an alphabetical listing by type of recipient organization (e.g., schools, youth development organizations, and so on). Each recipient category is further broken down by type of support awarded and the state where the recipient organization is located.

Section VI—Grants by Foundation This section lists all the grants found in Section I alphabetically by foundation state, then by foundation name.

Section VII—Foundations This is an alphabetical listing of the foundations along with their addresses, telephone numbers, and limitations, including geographic, program, and type of support restrictions.

The following shows a fictitious entry as it might appear in Section I of *The Foundation Grants Index*.

The Foundation Grants Index: Section I Sample Entry
The Sebastian Jessica Foundation
No support for colleges and universities (except for projects in elementary and secondary education). No grants to individuals or for building or endowment funds or operating budgets; no loans.
2713 Association of Indiana School Administrators, South Bend, IN. $25,000, 1999. For Reorganization of Schools Project. 9/14/98.

2714 Association of Michigan School Administrators, Detroit, MI. $14,000, 1999. For Consortium for Schools of the Future. 10/21/98.
2715 Association of California School Administrators, Fresno, CA. $15,000, 1999. For Reorganization of Schools Project. 10/10/98.
2716 Hazelnut School District, Hazelnut, MO. $12,500, 1999. For individualized alternative program for at-risk students. 7/9/98.
2717 Kids in Between, Agnes Middle School, Alexandria, VA. $13,000, 1999. For educational program for teachers working with children of divorce and their parents. 10/15/98.
2718 Platterton School District, Agnes Middle School, Alexandria, VA. $13,000, 1999. For staff development activities related to Marginal Learners/Responsive School Project. 7/15/98.

From this list we can see that the Sebastian Jessica Foundation appears to exhibit values compatible with those of our example project. It appears that a grant of $25,000 would be the foundation's upper limit and that a proposal for $10,000 to $15,000 might stand a better chance of being funded.

Besides having many excellent books on foundation funding, your Foundation Center Regional Library has two other references you and your grantseekers should be familiar with—Internal Revenue Service Foundation Tax Returns and Grant Guides.

- **The 990 Internal Revenue Service Foundation Tax Returns**—The Internal Revenue Service requires private foundations to file income tax returns each year. The 990-PF returns provide fiscal details of receipts and expenditures, compensation of officers, capital gains or losses, and other financial matters. Form 990-AR provides information on foundation managers, assets, and grants paid and/or committed for future payment. The Foundation Center's National Collections in New York City, San Francisco, Washington, D.C., Cleveland, and Atlanta have the past three years' tax returns of all private foundations on microfiche. Each of the Cooperating Collections has returns of private foundations located in its state and sometimes in surrounding states. IRS tax returns of private foundations may also be obtained by writing to the Ogden IRS Service Center, P.O. Box 9953, Mail Stop 6734, Ogden, Utah 84409. See the bibliography at the end of this book for more information.

- **Grant Guides**—Published by the Foundation Center, these computer-produced, customized guides to foundation giving provide descriptions of hundreds of foundation grants of $10,000 or more recently awarded in specific subject areas. There are currently thirty-five guides available in subject areas ranging from aging to women and girls, including guides in the subject areas of children and youth, elementary and secondary education, health programs for children and youth, information technology, and science and technology programs.

State foundation books, which many states compile, are also useful research tools. These are publications describing the granting patterns of foundations located in a particular state. These books derive their data from the annual reports of foundations and from Internal Revenue Service tax returns. They are usually available at Foundation Center Cooperating Collections. Also, you can visit the Rural Information Center on the Internet at www.nal.usda.gov/ric/ricpubs/funding/funding1.htm for a comprehensive listing of available state directories.

Corporate Research Tools

If a corporation has a foundation, you will be able to locate its 990-AR IRS tax return. However, many corporations that have foundations also make grants directly through the corporation. Because grants made through a corporate foundation are subject to public scrutiny (the 990-AR) and non-foundation corporate grants are not, many corporations make grants that they do not wish to be publicized through their corporate giving program.

The current federal IRS rules allow a corporation to take up to 10 percent of its gross profits as a tax deduction when this amount is given as grants to nonprofit organizations—501(c)(3)s. However, few if any corporations give this much. The national average is approximately 2 percent of gross profits.

Corporate stockholders have strong opinions concerning who should and should not receive their hard-earned grant dollars. This is another reason why many corporations make grants through both a corporate foundation and a corporate giving program. When grants are made through a corporate giving program, the data are confidential, because not even a stockholder can get a copy of the corporation's tax return. In addition, when a corporation perceives that a potential project will bring it commercial benefit (such as by enhancing marketplace positioning or product testing), it will often make the grant through its marketing department and usually will not take a write-off against taxable profits. Again, this type of grant will not show up in any grant list or research tools unless the company voluntarily supplies the information. The inability to verify corporate support accounts for the inaccuracy and lack of specificity that characterize the corporate grants marketplace.

What motivates corporations to make grants? What benefits can they receive by funding the schools in your district? By reviewing the values of corporate funders, we can see that their motivation comes from a concern for the following:

- Their workers and the children of their workers
- Product development
- Product positioning

Corporations know that they cannot keep pace in the global economy without educated workers. This includes education of their future workforce. Schools that actively involve corporations and their workers as volunteers do a lot better at grant time. Do your schools seek out corporations for in-service education, cooperative work experiences, teacher-worker exchange programs, adopt-a-school programs, or any other programs to keep themselves and their educational concerns in the minds of the local corporations?

It is imperative that the schools in the vicinity of the corporations are exemplary in performance. One of the first places a corporate recruiter takes a prospective new employee or a transfer employee with children is to the local school. If they do not actually visit the school, they will at least point out how well the school performs on state and national tests. Even when the prospective new employee or transferee does not have or plan to have children, he or she will ask about schools because of the impact they have on the resale of homes.

Once you start looking at corporations outside of your geographic area as potential grantors, you must relate your proposals to other corporate motivations such as product development and positioning. The simple fact is that companies are very motivated by sales and profits.

In the example project to increase responsible educational behavior in parents, students, and teachers, the solution calls for the possible use of computers to provide a link between parent and teacher and between the student's level of performance and responsible educational practices. Companies in the area with employees whose children attend the local school may be interested in the project. Companies out of the area might be interested in funding a model project if it could help to position their products with parents, teachers, and students—their future consumers. If the model project were to result in an educational change, not only would education benefit, but so would the companies.

So there are many reasons for companies to support grant projects. But remember, they are not simply interested in doing nice things for education and your school. They want and expect a return.

How can your grantseekers locate the companies that will be most interested in their school's project and its potential benefits? In addition to the records your school district may maintain on local corporations, your public library or local college library should have several helpful resources. If you are near a Foundation Center National Collection or a Regional Cooperating Collection you and your grantseekers will have access to many resources, including two of the Foundation Center's primary corporate research tools—*The National Directory of Corporate Giving* and *Corporate Foundation Profiles.*

- *The National Directory of Corporate Giving*—The fifth edition of this directory provides information on 2,895 corporate foundations and direct corporate giving programs. It also has an extensive bibliography and seven indexes to help you target funding prospects.

- *Corporate Foundation Profiles*—The tenth edition of this publication contains detailed analyses of 195 of the largest corporate foundations—grantmakers who give at least $1.2 million annually. An appendix lists financial data on 1,000 additional smaller corporate grantmakers.

Because companies define themselves in terms of markets and products, it would be helpful for your grantseekers to look at those funding prospects that might value their school's project because of its potential impact in the marketplace. *The North American Industry Classification (NAICS) Manual* is an excellent tool for finding out who makes what products. It is available at your public library. Once your grantseekers have determined the companies that manufacture the products incorporated in their school's grant, they can call the local sales representative or phone or write the company's corporate offices to ascertain their level of interest in the project.

One crucial fact to remember is that corporate grants decrease as profits go down. A look at Dun and Bradstreet's *Million Dollar Directory* will tell your grantseekers how the largest U.S. businesses stand financially. A company that is financially weak is not a prime target for a grant request.

Obtaining Corporate Grants from Companies in Your Community

Corporations in your area are another good bet for grant support. Identify them and find out if the schools in your district serve the children of their workers. If they do, your grantseekers are more likely to receive a positive response, because some of the company's future workers may attend these schools.

Corporations give where they live, but they nonetheless expect a professional approach from potential grantees. Just as companies are judged by the quality of their sales representatives, your school district will be judged by the quality of the individual who approaches the company. Grantseekers should always check with the district grants office before approaching a company for grant support. As many elementary and middle schools do not have a formal grants system, many classroom leaders have taken their proposals to corporations themselves. They may have been quite successful too, but uncoordinated access to grantors can pose major hazards to the district's overall image as a unified organization.

Chambers of commerce usually produce an annual list of all the companies in their area. The list ranks the companies by number of employees and payroll and often gives product information. This is an excellent research tool. Your schools should have several members from the corporate world on their grants advisory groups, one of whom should be able to procure this invaluable list.

Because most corporations make grants out of their profits, knowing which local companies are profitable will be a big help. If there are stockbrokers on your schools' grants advisory committees they can find out which companies in your area are paying increasing stock dividends because of increased profits. Another advantage to including business leaders in grants advisory groups has to do with corporations' concern with their customers' credit ratings. How companies pay their bills is a reflection of their fiscal situation and profitability. Hence, companies subscribe to several services that keep close tabs on their customers. Grantseekers can request information on what services the corporate members of the grants advisory group subscribe to and ask them to get a report of the companies the school is planning to approach. The more grantseekers know about these companies, the more respect the companies will have for them.

Obtaining Grants from Service Clubs and Organizations

The service clubs and organizations that are closest to your school district are most likely to make a grant to your schools. This grant will not be a donation of cash for general use. These groups need a proposal and a project that they can see themselves sponsoring.

As an example, one of my seminar participants from a nonprofit organization in Alaska raised over $2,000 from service clubs and organizations to sponsor her attendance at a grants workshop of mine held in Washington, D.C. She reported that she actually had fun seeking funds for the seminar and that contact with her local service clubs and organizations allowed her to develop lasting relationships with them. The clubs and organizations that sponsored her saw the benefits of sending her to a grants workshop. They realized that once she developed expertise in grantseeking, her organization's clientele would begin to benefit from improved and expanded programs made possible through her acquisition of external resources.

Your district's grantseekers should check with the district grants office before contacting service clubs and organizations because your office should maintain a list of district administrators and other personnel with membership in these groups.

Following the step-by-step system outlined on the next few pages and completing the accompanying worksheets will enable you to help your grantseekers match their schools' projects to the "best" service clubs and organizations in your community. A service club's or organization's funding interests can be determined from the areas of support and espoused values they describe in their statement of purpose and from the projects and groups they have supported in the past.

The Foot-in-the-Door Worksheet in Chapter 6 requests information on links with service clubs and organizations. This information will be of great help to your grantseekers when they are soliciting support from these groups. Most service clubs and organizations have a contact person or corresponding secretary. Your grantseekers should make direct contact or use any links they may have to these individuals.

In general, service clubs and organizations prefer to support projects that require smaller amounts of grant funds. In addition, they are motivated by a tight focus on the target population. A grant for equipment that will be used by many students in your district and be available to parents or other members of the community is a good example. Whether they are financing after-school programs or computer equipment, service clubs and organizations want to feel that they are making a difference in the community.

The pragmatic nature of these organizations and the fact that many of the members are businesspeople lead them to analyze information about the number of students or beneficiaries who will be affected, what they will be able to do, and at what price or cost per student beneficiary. Your office can help your district's grantseekers complete the Target Population Worksheet in Figure 5.8. This worksheet will help grantseekers focus on the types of data your local service groups will respond to.

Figure 5.8

TARGET POPULATION WORKSHEET

What school/youth population do you currently serve?

- Target age group(s)
- Number of youth currently served (by age, grade level, special needs population, and so on)
- Geographic area served (school boundaries, open enrollment, population, daily attendance)
- Number of programs currently provided by your school (you may choose to focus your response on the target population)

From your Needs Worksheet (Figure 3.3), list those studies, examples, and articles that document the local need for this project and the target population that will benefit from it.

_____

_____

_____

Select an affordable ($1,000 to $10,000) solution from the Solutions Worksheet (Figure 3.7) and describe how it would change the local situation. (Remember your Service Clubs and Organizations Matrix [Figure 4.12] here. These funding sources are not usually interested in research. They want to fund what works.)

_____

_____

_____

As your district's grantseekers intensify their search for these potential grantors, remind them that these groups will make grants and adopt and support projects based on their perception of and past experiences with the grantee. It is important to realize that the members of clubs and organizations may have a totally different view of education than your school district and component schools. I was once rebuffed by a local service club dedicated to supporting projects related to literacy and at-risk students, even though I was asking for a grant to support library resources. Why? Because the individuals I met with from the club never used the research section of our public school library. In fact, one member of the service club's education committee had never used the library at all because he had been thrown out of it as an eighth grader. Changing our grant to request funding for a conversational library and including books and manuals on everything from herb gardening to snowmobile and motorcycle repair resulted in our project being met with much greater enthusiasm and financial support.

Service Clubs and Organizations Worksheet

Review the Service Clubs and Organizations Worksheet (Figure 5.9) and help your district's grantseekers identify those groups that are in your

Figure 5.9

SERVICE CLUBS AND ORGANIZATIONS WORKSHEET

Place a check mark next to those service clubs and organizations that may be interested in sponsoring your project. Record contact's name and phone number and the club's/organization's areas of interest and values. Add to the list of clubs and organizations.

Check	Club/Organization	Contact/Phone	Areas of Interest/Values
_____	Rotary Club	_____	_____
_____	Junior League	_____	_____
_____	Kiwanis Club	_____	_____
_____	Zonta Club	_____	_____
_____	Jaycees	_____	_____
	Hellenic groups:		
_____	_____	_____	_____
_____	_____	_____	_____
_____	_____	_____	_____
	Fraternal groups:		
_____	_____	_____	_____
_____	_____	_____	_____
_____	_____	_____	_____
_____	Masons	_____	_____
_____	Knights of Columbus	_____	_____
	Church groups:		
_____	_____	_____	_____
_____	_____	_____	_____
_____	_____	_____	_____
	Other:		
_____	_____	_____	_____
_____	_____	_____	_____

area. Your public library may have a list of local service clubs and organizations, and the telephone book can be of great help. There may even be a sign as you enter your city, town, or village that lists the service organizations and the places and times of their meetings.

The Service Clubs and Organizations Worksheet is not intended to be a complete list. Feel free to add more groups to it and to have your grantseekers add more groups. For example, there are many Hellenic, fraternal, and social groups and societies that will help the schools in your district.

Approaching Service Clubs and Organizations

Figures 5.10, 5.11, 5.12, and 5.13 provide you with sample letters and a checklist that will enable you to help your district's grantseekers tailor

---

Figure 5.10

OUTLINE FOR CONSTRUCTING A LETTER TO SERVICE CLUBS OR ORGANIZATIONS

Tailor Your Letter

1.   What information do you have on the service club or organization's purpose and values and the programs it has supported in the past? (Focus on this in the letter.)

   _____

   _____

   _____

   _____

2.   What contacts or friends do you have in the service club or organization? Mention these in the letter so that the club or organization can confirm your legitimacy through them.

   _____

   _____

   _____

   _____

3.   List any past positive experiences that your school or educational programs have had that the service club or organization may have knowledge of (awards, commendations, and so on). Consider reminding them of these; also, thank them for past support, if any.

   _____

   _____

   _____

   _____

---

their approach to service clubs and organizations. Types of contact include letters to introduce your schools and their needs, telephone calls, and personal visits.

The standard approach is to write, telephone, and make personal contact, but any combination may be appropriate. However, the most effective approach is personal contact. A study published in *Grants Magazine* substantiates the importance of personal contact in appealing to foundations, corporations, and government agencies by citing a 500 percent increase in success if the funding source is contacted before the proposal is written. This positive effect also results from personal contact with a service club or organization that your grantseekers want to sponsor their project. Personal contact works because it enables your grantseekers to gather valuable information about the service club or organization face-to-face, information that allows them to tailor their approach to the funding source's values as well as to the size of its pocketbook. If personal contact cannot be made, then your grantseekers must find information about prospective funding sources through other means before writing to them.

Figure 5.11

SAMPLE LETTER TO SERVICE CLUBS OR ORGANIZATIONS

Dear _____:

The work of the [name of club or organization] and your concern for _____ lead me to contact you with an important project. Your support of [an organization, program, or project they have funded in the past] indicates your care and concern for _____.

The [school, school district, etc.] shares your concern and is dedicated to [statement of your purpose; be brief]. The need for our program here in [geographic area] is demonstrated by [cite studies, statistics, case studies, etc.].

Just as your club [or organization] is faced with many requests for assistance, we too face the reality of continuing a program for _____, as well as relentlessly seeking funds to add more programs to serve _____.

I am asking you, as business and community leaders, to consider this request of $_____ to _____.

I have enclosed detailed information on our project and our budgeted costs. [Number] groups and organizations have already contributed to this project, including _____. [If your project has partial support from your school district, or other grant funds, mention them here.] I will be happy to report back to your club [or organization] on the benefits of the project.

I will telephone you to discuss this opportunity to maximize your club's [or organization's] investment in our school, our children, and our community.

Sincerely,

Figure 5.12

TELEPHONE CHECKLIST

Most communities have a directory of service clubs and organizations. Telephone the individuals listed as contact people in your community's directory.

1. If you have written to their organization, ask if they received your letter. Tell them you know of the good work they do and why you selected them to contact.

2. Ask if they are interested in having you or one of your grants advisory committee members speak or present your request at a meeting.

3. Ask for their thoughts regarding your request.

4. Inform them of the time frame under which you are operating.

5. If appropriate, ask for an appointment to meet with them or their committee to discuss the project.

6. Ask them what other information you could provide to help the organization make a decision.

Keep an accurate log of your phone calls to the organization and their responses.

Organization	Contact Person	Phone #	Response	Follow-Up
_____	_____	_____	_____	_____
_____	_____	_____	_____	_____
_____	_____	_____	_____	_____

Figure 5.13

PERSONAL CONTACT/VISIT CHECKLIST

1. Dress in the same style as the group or individual you will be meeting with.

2. Never bring more than two people to represent your school. A grants advisory committee member or other volunteer is better than a paid staff person.

3. Start the conversation with a comment about the service club/organization, not with your school's need. For example, you could begin by commenting on community projects the club/organization has sponsored in the past. This will break the ice and also show that you have done some research on the club/organization.

4. Be brief and to the point.

5. Use photographs or examples (such as case studies) of your students and programs to educate them about the need.

6. Record your personal contacts. Keep a record of thank you letters sent, follow-ups, and results.

Date	Individual Contacted	Results/Follow-Ups	Thank You
_____	_____	_____	_____
_____	_____	_____	_____
_____	_____	_____	_____
_____	_____	_____	_____

Other Research Tools

This chapter provides information on grantseeking materials. Many of these materials are inexpensive or free. In addition to the resources already mentioned, you and your district's grantseekers may be interested in newsletters in the education/grants field. There are many, including these: *Education Grants Alert, Education Daily, Foundation and Corporate Grants Alert,* and *Federal Grants and Contracts Weekly.* All are published by Aspen Publishers, Inc., 7201 McKinney Circle, Frederick MD 21704, (800)-638-8437. Contact the publishers for a free sample and subscription information. The bibliography notes other resources, including a variety of computer research services and databases.

CHAPTER 5 ASSESSMENT TOOL

1. a. **How would you rate your district's grant library?**
   _____ nonexistent _____ inadequate _____ adequate _____ excellent
   b. **Where is the grants library located?**
   c. **How much is the grants library used?**
   d. **What is the relationship between the use of the library and the grants success rate of the users?**

2. **List the materials your office provides to district grantseekers. Include the location of the material and the date of publication.**

FEDERAL GRANTS SUPPORT MATERIALS	Location	Date
Catalog of Federal Domestic Assistance	_____	_____
The Federal Register	_____	_____
FOUNDATION GRANTS SUPPORT MATERIALS	Location	Date
Foundation Directory	_____	_____
Foundation Grants Index	_____	_____
State Foundation Directory (Resource)	_____	_____
CORPORATE GRANTS SUPPORT MATERIALS	Location	Date
List of corporations from Chamber of Commerce	_____	_____
National Directory of Corporate Giving	_____	_____
SERVICE CLUBS/COMMUNITY SERVICES GROUPS	Location	Date
List of clubs in your geographic area and the projects they support	_____	_____

3. a. **How effective are your grants searching services?**
   _____ ineffective _____ effective _____ very effective
   b. **Are the searches done manually (hands-on searching through printed source materials) or by computer?**
   _____ manual _____ computer
   c. **How many searches does your grants office provide each year?**
   d. **What percentage of these searches result in proposals submitted?**
   e. **What percentage result in proposals funded?**

4. **Rate how well your office provides the following preproposal contact support services.**
   - Writes and sends letters to get on grantor's mailing list
     _____ does not provide _____ inadequate _____ adequate _____ excellent
   - Assists in getting lists of federal grantees, reviewers, and sample proposals
     _____ does not provide _____ inadequate _____ adequate _____ excellent
   - Assists in getting foundation tax returns
     _____ does not provide _____ inadequate _____ adequate _____ excellent
   - Helps grantseekers determine what to bring and what to wear to visit prospective grantors
     _____ does not provide _____ inadequate _____ adequate _____ excellent

5. a. **Does your grants office provide funds for long-distance phone calls to grantors?**
   _____ yes _____ no
   b. **Does your grants office provide funds for travel to grantors?**
   _____ yes _____ no

Chapter 6

Developing a Proactive Grants System

THE MOST IMPORTANT single aspect of successful grantseeking is initiating contact with grantors early in the proposal-development process. Studies have shown a substantial increase in the success rates of grantees who make preproposal contact with potential grantors. By initiating the grantseeking process early, the proposal developer has the time to contact a grantor well before the deadline and the ability to modify his or her proposal based upon communication with the potential funder.

As the district grants administrator, your challenge is to encourage your grantseekers to contact grantors and, while doing so, to create the impression that your district has a coordinated grants system. If several grantseekers from your school district contact the same grantor to present different grant ideas, it confuses the grantor and makes it appear as if your district has no priorities. Grantors do not feel that they should make decisions that will influence education in a school district without knowing the district's priorities. Because of this, many grantors (both public and private) will review only one proposal from the grantseekers' entire organization.

Your district's grant system needs to take the issue of access to potential grantors into account for three reasons:

1. Preproposal contact means increased success.

2. Uncontrolled access to grantors can result in the submittal of multiple proposals to one funding source and the loss of your district's credibility.

3. An organized system of preproposal contact encourages grantseekers to contact prospective funders, thus freeing up the district office's resources and the district grants staff's time.

In addition, your system should respond proactively and in a timely fashion to grantseekers who are investing their time and effort in developing proposals. They deserve to know what degree of support they will receive from the district grants office and what restrictions will be placed on their contact with grantors. Much of this can be addressed by requiring prospective grantseekers to receive district endorsements in advance. This advance endorsement or "sign-on" by district representatives avoids many problems.

Before getting involved in pursuing a funded proposal, the school district needs to know what types of funders their grantseekers are going to approach and what restrictions or rules the district will be subject to by accepting the funds, including those relative to the following:

- Matching funds or in-kind contributions of space

- Equipment purchase, ownership, maintenance, and inventory

- Release time for personnel—percentage of time and replacement for project workers

- Continuation of the project

A proposal sign-on system allows grantseekers to know where they stand relative to their district's priorities and mission before they invest their time and effort. Projects and proposals that address district priorities should receive more support from the district grants office as well as preference with respect to matching funds, space, and equipment.

Education is the key to instituting a mandatory grants sign-on system that is supported by your administration, teachers, other education professionals, and volunteers. All those involved in your grantseeking process must understand the need for a system that respects your proposal developers' time and effort, maximizes the limited resources of your school district, and maintains your district's credibility with grantors. This system can also alert others to the potential of putting interested groups together in consortia. The advance endorsement or "sign-on" system is extremely helpful to those required to prepare proposals as part of their job and find their time and effort are not fully appreciated.

The first step is to have each of your grantseekers complete a School Grantseekers' Preproposal Endorsement Worksheet (Figure 6.1). Putting a sign-on system in place will allow you to track your grantseekers' progress. Assign a grants office identification and coding number to each preproposal endorsement worksheet and log that number in your database along with the grantseeker's name and school and the steps in proposal development that have been accomplished.

Figure 6.1

SCHOOL GRANTSEEKERS' PREPROPOSAL ENDORSEMENT WORKSHEET

To ensure that you receive maximum benefit from your school and central office's grant-development services, please submit this form to your school principal when you begin to consider seeking grant funds from nondistrict resources.

1. **Grantseeker's Name:** _____

     Phone: _____

2. **Area to be addressed through grants:**

     _____

     _____

3. **How the need to address this area was identified:**

     _____

     _____

     _____

4. **Brief documentation of the need:**

     _____

     _____

     _____

5. **If potential solutions have been developed, please provide a summary of each.**

     _____

     _____

     _____

     _____

6. **Please suggest key personnel to be involved in:**
    *   Development of the proposal _____
    *   Implementing the project if funded (include % of time) _____

7. **List the resources that may be required to implement and maintain the project if the school and district support it.**
    *   School space requirements (sq. footage, special needs) _____
    *   Equipment _____
    *   Supplies, materials_____

8. **Will any matching or in-kind contributions be required of the school or school district?**
     _____ yes   _____ no

     If you have already conducted a search for potential grantors, please attach your list of prospects to this worksheet. By reviewing your list of potential funding sources, we will be able to determine whether any of these grantors are currently being contacted to support other school or district projects. This will minimize the chances of a potential conflict.

     Permission to continue your search for funding will be evaluated. If granted, you will be required to follow the school's grants system to ensure a quality product.

The Tracking Checklist (Figure 6.2) provides your office with a method for each project that is recorded and receives approval:

- District priority
- School/community priority
- Preproposal endorsement worksheet completed
- Preproposal endorsement worksheet returned with status (approved/rejected), signatures, conditions that must be met, and so on
- Search for grants carried out
- Search for linkages carried out
- Proposal being written
- Proposal undergoing review by quality circle
- Submittal process
- Proposal out for signature to _____
- Matching or in-kind contributions needed—amount, type, and funder restrictions
- Special services or assistance required from grants office
- Proposal status—awarded/rejected/pending

By implementing a sign-on system and tracking your grantseekers' proposals through development to submittal, you will be able to prepare a year-end report that includes the following:

- Number of proposal ideas developed
- Number of sign-on sheets returned and the status of each
- Number of proposals under development
- Number of proposals completing a quality review
- Status at year's end (submitted/rejected/awarded/pending)
- Matching funds (pending/awarded)
- Success rate total in dollars

It is difficult if not impossible to recreate this data at the end of the year without some type of sign-on procedure as part of your proactive grants system. In addition, your tracking system will help you see where your grants system is performing well and identify those areas that are not meeting your expectations. For example, if your tracking shows that many grantseekers languish in the proposal-writing stage of development, you can redirect some of the district grants office's resources toward helping them get over this hurdle.

Figure 6.2

TRACKING CHECKLIST

Put a check next to each of the following steps when it has been initiated and when it has been completed and record the date of completion.

Initiated	Completed	Date	
_____	_____	_____	Proposal idea receives priority status by school
_____	_____	_____	Proposal idea receives priority status by school district
_____	_____	_____	Preproposal Endorsement Worksheet completed
_____	_____	_____	Preproposal Endorsement Worksheet returned to proposal initiator with approval conditions/restrictions rejection
_____	_____	_____	Preproposal contact made with prospective grantor by letter, telephone, fax, or face-to-face
_____	_____	_____	Grantor Strategy Worksheet (Figure 6.19) completed and reviewed
_____	_____	_____	Proposal construction completed
_____	_____	_____	Proposal improvement/quality circle exercise completed
_____	_____	_____	Quality circle recommendations for revision made and implemented
_____	_____	_____	Sign-off procedure completed
_____	_____	_____	Matching and in-kind contributions approved and recorded as a district matching commitment
_____	_____	_____	Special services required by grants office provided/completed (list services)

_____

_____

_____

Using Volunteers Effectively

Earlier chapters have encouraged the involvement of parents and other community members in brainstorming problem areas that grant funds could have an impact on and developing solutions to address them. Promoting this positive form of school/community involvement makes the volunteer a vital partner in the grants effort. This is truly what site-based management is all about.

Many theorists believe that positive action is based upon individuals setting their sights on solving problems and improving situations. Dennis Whately, author of *Psychology of Winning,* points out that individuals move in the direction of their dominant thoughts. By identifying solutions and developing positive ideas, your volunteers set in motion a system that moves toward completing the steps necessary to fund these ideas. Part of your role as district grants administrator is to educate and involve your volunteers to the point where they are committed enough to become involved in the most important stage of grantseeking—sharing their excitement and ideas with their friends in corporations, foundations, and government agencies.

The following sample letters and worksheets will help you encourage your school units to build an active volunteer component into their grants system by establishing grants advisory groups. Tailor these materials to your district grants plan.

Grants advisory groups can be set up by school units, departments, subject areas, or community. Individual advisory groups can then send a representative to a larger school district's grants advisory group that sets district priorities and deals with preproposal sign-on, endorsement, commitment of matching funds, and so on.

Worksheet for Planning a Grants Advisory Group

Use this worksheet (Figure 6.3) to help your schools develop a tentative list of the individuals whom they may want to participate in their grants advisory group. They should avoid placing well-intentioned zealots on the group. Although these outspoken individuals may be highly motivated, they can turn off the other group members as well as potential funders because they often lack the listening skills needed to grasp what the

---

Figure 6.3

WORKSHEET FOR PLANNING A GRANTS ADVISORY GROUP

Review the suggested categories of individuals to include and write down names.

Whom to Invite

_____ Parents   _____ Retired teachers

_____ Corporate leaders   _____ Wealthy/influential people

_____ Foundation board members   _____ Others (please add)

_____ College professors/educators

Review the Skills/Resources Needed list below and write the boldface resource description next to the possible committee members you have listed above. Avoid inviting volunteers who are overzealous about children but have no resources or contacts.

Skills/Resources Needed

- **Commitment** to children and education
- **Contacts** with people on foundation/corporate boards
- **Travel** to areas of the state/nation where there are more funders
- Willingness to share **telephone credit card** for grant-related calls
- **Marketing/sales skills**
- **Budgeting** and financial analysis skills
- Access to equipment and materials necessary to produce **audiovisual** aids depicting need
- Other

grantor is looking for. Encourage them instead to look for individuals who will make the grantseeking process less work for your office. Help them assess the skills and resources that each potential member will bring to the group.

Grants Resources Inventory Worksheet

This worksheet (Figure 6.4) lists some of the resource areas that are helpful in grantseeking. The worksheet can be used in several ways. A quick review of the worksheet may trigger the names of potential grants advisory group members. Once they have been identified they can be asked to complete the inventory by noting their own skills and abilities and also listing the names of any other potential members next to the corresponding resource area. For example, if Sylvia Smith is filling out the inventory, she may indicate that she can provide sales skills. She might also indicate that an acquaintance of hers, Michael Doe, might be willing to provide computer programming services.

Figure 6.4

GRANTS RESOURCES INVENTORY WORKSHEET

Please put a check mark next to any resource area in which you can help. Use the section at the end of the worksheet to briefly describe the resources you could provide. If you are willing to contact funding sources, please list the areas of the United States that you visit frequently.

Resource Area

_____ Evaluation of projects
_____ Computer programming
_____ Computer equipment
_____ Printing
_____ Layout and design work
_____ Budget skills, accounting, developing cash flow, auditing
_____ Purchasing assistance
_____ Audiovisual assistance (equipment, videotaping, etc.)
_____ Travel
_____ Long-distance telephone calls
_____ Searching for funding sources
_____ Sales skills
_____ Writing/editing skills
_____ Other equipment/materials
_____ Other

Description of resources:_____

Areas frequently visited: _____

Once the group members have been selected, your school units should not be overly concerned with rules regarding their attendance at group meetings. If the member promises to provide the resources and skills needed, what difference does attendance make? For instance, salespeople who travel a lot may not spend much time in their offices or at home. It may be easy for them to make preproposal contact with a grantor in another part of the state or country but difficult for them to attend meetings.

To offer an example, a very productive sales executive on one of my grants advisory groups never attended a meeting but was instrumental in procuring several grant awards. When he was in a city with a potential grantor, I would e-mail or fax all the pertinent information to him at his hotel. This would include a description of the proposed project and information on the grantor, such as funding history or pattern. He would then set up an appointment with the grantor to discuss the project. After his meeting with the funding source he would e-mail or fax information back to me concerning the appropriate strategy to pursue in the proposal. He was highly successful at getting in to see federal and state grantors as well as foundation and corporate sources. In many cases, he was actually given preferential treatment over the grants and education professionals, who, after all, were *paid* to be there. My advisory group member was donating his time; he was actually being paid to be somewhere else. In reality, the preproposal visit was costing him money. Many grantors will respond favorably to such a committed volunteer.

Your advisory groups need members who are free to travel and who have skills or resources in marketing, budgeting, printing, computer programming, and so on. What could be more ideal than a finished proposal produced by a committee member donating his or her office and secretaries and having the budget checked by their finance department or certified public accountant?

Worksheet for Initiating a Grants Advisory Group

To complete this worksheet (Figure 6.5), discuss your plan to develop grants advisory groups with the faculty and staff in your district and ask them to suggest names of people they would be willing to contact and invite to take part in one of these groups. You may decide to form districtwide groups that focus on district priorities and problems, or you may form groups in each school. Either way, you will be amazed at how many excellent contacts they suggest. Don't be surprised if the spouse of one of your district's longtime volunteers or staff members is the marketing director of a local corporation and that he or she would be happy to donate resources, from graphics to preproposal contact, to your effort.

Figure 6.5

WORKSHEET FOR INITIATING A GRANTS ADVISORY GROUP

Potential Members	Who Will Contact Them	When	Results	Skills/Resources You Expect

Sample Letter to Potential Committee Member

This letter (Figure 6.6) should be tailored to the individual and to the scope of the grants advisory group's work. For example, a small district may have one grants advisory group to assist in all grantseeking activities whereas a large district or one with diverse and critical areas of concern may have several, each focusing on one particular school or problem (such as illiteracy, delinquency, dropout prevention, drugs, alcohol, AIDS education, and so on).

The important point to get across in this letter and in phone conversations with potential group members is that they are not being asked for money. They are being asked to lend their brain power and resources to your grants effort. Grants are provided by foundations, corporations, and government agencies, and any help that advisory group members can give in setting up a meeting or even a telephone conversation with possible funding sources will increase your school's chances of success.

It is important that potential group members know that more than $90 billion will be given away by the federal government in 1999 and approximately $150 billion by private philanthropy and that they are being asked

Figure 6.6

SAMPLE LETTER TO POTENTIAL COMMITTEE MEMBER (INVITATION TO PARTICIPATE)

Note: *You may telephone potential committee members first and then send them this letter, or send them this letter and then telephone them.*

Dear _____:

The children in [name of school/classroom] invite you to become involved in developing and implementing solutions in their education. Your past work in _____ demonstrates your commitment and concern for children, their education, and our community. We are in the process of developing a grants advisory committee, which we would like you to be part of. Your commitment and concern have prompted this invitation to join with a select group of individuals in developing solutions and resources to education-related problems and needs.

I look at the problems associated with educating children as opportunities—to become involved in developing creative solutions to the educational inadequacies that hold our children back from

_____

_____

[Add pertinent statistics. For example, "National reading scores for fourth graders are _____. In our school _____ percent of fourth graders read below this level." Include some outcomes, such as, "Students who lack reading skills _____."]

This letter is your invitation to do something about this problem. [Number] of your fellow citizens are receiving similar invitations to join our informal group. The purposes of the group include:

- Brainstorming suggestions for improving our educational programs for _____ , and
- Capitalizing on the group members' skills and contacts for getting our proposals in front of foundation, corporate, and government funding sources.

Last year corporations and foundations awarded over $20 billion in grant funds. Elementary and middle schools are receiving a growing portion of these funds as private funding sources become more concerned about our children's education. Our knowing whom you know may give us the advantage we need to share in this funding.

Please attend our meeting on [date] at [place] and learn how you can play an important role in our grants development process. A study in *Grants Magazine* indicates that there is up to a 500 percent increase in grants success if the funding source has personal contact with the proposal developer before the proposal is written. A simple phone call to set up an appointment with a prospective funder may elicit a favorable response to our proposal, and *you* could provide this essential contact.

Please set aside the date of _____ to attend our first meeting. I know you will enjoy learning how we can work together to improve our educational system.

Sincerely,

to help get some of that money for your school district. They should be reassured that they will not be involved in asking for a friend's personal donation but only in requesting foundation and corporate funds.

Remember, you and your individual school units establish the requirements for group membership. Individuals might ask how long they must serve. I suggest that you leave it up to them.

Webbing and Linkages

Point out to your district's grants advisory groups the dramatic increase in success that is possible when the prospective grantee makes contact with the potential grantor before the proposal becomes a finished product.

The corporate representatives on your district's grants advisory groups already know the value of linkages who can help them get a foot in the door with a client. The corporate world keeps track of who golfs, plays tennis, and vacations with whom. Being able to tap into this network is worth its weight in gold (that is, grant dollars). Because most corporate grants are funded because of a connection to the community, your district's grantseekers need to gather corporate inside information.

It is estimated that there are only about 3,000 full-time foundation employees working for 41,588 foundations, and only 1,000 foundations have an office, so the most logical way to make preproposal contact with foundations is through one of their 300,000-plus board members. The way to contact them is through a mutual friend or link. The same holds true for corporate executives and government grantors. The key is to educate your grants advisory groups about the importance of sharing their linkages. They must be assured that all information they share will be held in the strictest confidence. When one of your schools has an idea for a project suitable for a grantor that one of your volunteers can communicate with, your office will contact the volunteer to discuss the project and to ask for his or her help in setting up an appointment. The contact may be a simple phone call or a breakfast or lunch meeting to discuss the grantor's current interests and how they relate to your school district's project.

By being actively involved in your district, your volunteers will approach potential funders with attention-grabbers like "We at the _____ school district have developed several solutions to our problem with _____, and we would like to discuss them informally with you." The grants advisory group members' depth of commitment and the detail with which they complete the Foot-in-the-Door Worksheet (Figure 6.7) also depend on their involvement in developing solutions and the degree to which they feel part of the solutions.

___

Figure 6.7

FOOT-IN-THE-DOOR WORKSHEET

Name and Title: _____

Home Address & Phone (Winter & Summer):

_____

_____

Business Address & Phone:

_____

_____

1. **What foundation boards are you currently a member of?**

   _____   _____

   _____   _____

2. **What foundation boards are you a past member of?**

   _____

   _____

3. **What foundation boards do members of your family serve on?**

   Name of Relative   Relationship   Name of Foundation

   _____   _____   _____

   _____   _____   _____

4. **What foundation boards do your friends and associates serve on?**

   Name of Friend/Associate   Name of Foundation

   _____   _____

   _____   _____

5. **What corporations do you have a relationship with?**

   Name of Corporation   Relationship to Corporation

   _____   _____

   _____   _____

6. **What corporate relationships do relatives, friends, and associates have?**

   Relative/Friend/Associate   Corporation   Relationship to Corporation

   _____   _____   _____

   _____   _____   _____

7. **What federal, state, city/county funding agencies do you have contacts in?**

   Name of Agency   Name & Title of Contact
   (Department/Division/Program)

   _____   _____

   _____   _____

   _____   _____

   (continued)

Figure 6.7 (continued)

8. **What contacts do you have with federal, state, and city/county elected officials who could influence education-related appropriations? If the federal official is a senator or representative, indicate what state he or she represents.**

   Name and Title:_____

   Federal/State/City/County? _____

   Which State? _____

   Which City? County?_____

   Name and Title:_____

   Federal/State/City/County? _____

   Which State? _____

   Which City? County?_____

9. **What other clubs, groups, or organizations are you a member of or have a consulting, advisory, or other relationship with?**

   Name of Organization   Nature of Your Relationship

   _____   _____

   _____   _____

Sample Letter—Inventory of Linkages and Resources

The timing of this letter (Figure 6.8) is very important, and the quantity and quality of the linkages derived from it will most likely correspond to the prestige of the grants advisory group member who signs it. For that reason each group's most distinguished member should sign the letter and introduce the concept of linkages at the advisory group meeting. This will increase the likelihood that inventories and worksheets will be completed and returned.

The sample letter (Figure 6.8) and the Foot-in-the-Door Worksheet (Figure 6.7) are self-explanatory. The questions on the worksheet deal with types of funding sources. The volunteers can add any other information they feel would be helpful.

Someone might ask about the appropriateness of giving the Foot-in-the-Door Worksheet to your school district staff. I suggest that you explain the concept to staff at meetings and ask them to voluntarily share their links with the appropriate grants advisory group (school, department, and so on).

My clients who have organized and utilized their linkages have dramatically changed their grantseeking strategies. One organization I work with has decided to concentrate on those foundations and corporations to which they now know they have a linkage. The organization matches

Figure 6.8

SAMPLE LETTER
INVENTORY OF LINKAGES AND RESOURCES

Dear _____:

The problems/opportunities that we have discussed at our grants advisory committee meetings have solutions, but the implementation of the solutions costs money. We will seek this money through grant funds from foundations, corporations, and possibly state and/or federal sources.

Foundations and corporate sources granted over $21 billion in 1997. These funding sources make these awards every year, and every year the funds they distribute will increase. However, these grantors are limited in staff support. In fact, while there are 41,588 foundations, they employ only 3,000 individuals, and fewer than 1,000 have offices. Taking these factors into consideration, it is very important to carefully plan our approach, especially since research indicates a fivefold increase by contacting the grantor before writing the proposal.

That's where you come in. We are not soliciting you for money, nor do we want a list of all your wealthy friends. What we are asking is that you provide us with a list of your friends, associates, and relatives who have a relationship with grantors so that we will know who to call to help us get a foot in the door.

The attached "Foot-in-the-Door Worksheet" is aimed at gathering the information we need. This webbing and linkage information will help us to know when to ask you for your assistance in securing personal or telephone contact with a grantor. Your responses will be kept confidential, and the only person that will have access to this information is [name of individual]. While we are a neighborhood school, we can still reach out to a variety of funding sources, and the linkages you provide us will help us do so.

When our research indicates that we have developed a project that is particularly suited to a funder that you know, we will contact you to discuss the project, the funder, and your desire to assist us. We may just need a foot in the door, or you may want to accompany us on a visit to the potential funding source or even visit them yourself. In any event, we will not contact any of the sources you suggest without your prior approval.

In addition to your suggested sources, it is also very important that you let us know of any grant-related resources that you can provide or help us procure. For example, nothing makes a more powerful statement than a volunteer taking time out from a business trip or a vacation to make contact with a funder. Since the volunteer is not paid to make the visit, he or she has great credibility with the funding source. Remember, the use of resources like your travel itinerary, sales skills, and telephone credit cards for long-distance calls all demonstrate how cost-efficient our grantseeking and proposed solutions can be.

Please review and complete the attached Grants Resources Inventory Worksheet and the Foot-in-the-Door Worksheet before our next meeting on _____ so that we can work together to make a difference. If we do not receive the worksheets before this date, please expect us to call you to arrange to pick them up.

Sincerely,

grantor interests with organizational needs and projects, and by getting their foot in the door they ascertain the level of interest and what changes they need to make in their project to make it more fundable by the grantor.

Your district grants office should look at all the possibilities that your linkages can provide before you seek funds from a grantor with whom you have no contacts.

The District Grants Office's Role in Coordinating Preproposal Contact with Grantors

Preproposal contact is one of the most critical steps to grants success. Why? Contact with grantors in advance of writing a proposal allows grantseekers to do the following:

- Confirm their research

- Learn about changes, additions, and new grantor interests

- Avail themselves of valuable information that will help them prepare their proposals (whether in the form of copies of successful grants, newsletters, or priority statements, this information can be incorporated into the project and proposal)

- Understand the proposal review process and how they can become a reviewer

In short, preproposal contact confirms how your grantseekers can incorporate more of the potential grantor's concerns and perspectives in their proposals.

Preproposal contact is also the area that poses the greatest challenge to grantseekers. Even when they know it will help them, they are reluctant to embrace the practice. Your district grants office can provide the initial support for taking this step with a minimal amount of work. You can play a pivotal role in supplying grantseekers with research on potential grantors and access to the friends of the school system who may help them get a foot in the door. In addition, your proposal sign-on system will ensure that contact is made only with those grantors who have been preapproved.

Review the following worksheets and suggestions and decide which services your district grants office will provide to help your grantseekers with preproposal contact and what aspects of preproposal contact you will encourage your grantseekers to take responsibility for. Just remember that leaving the step of preproposal contact solely up to your grantseekers may adversely affect your district's grant acceptance rate.

I ask many grantseekers why they avoid preproposal contact. Their answers vary, but there is one consistent theme: most people would rather write a proposal and place it in the mail than risk having their ideas rejected in a face-to-face meeting.

Whatever their reasons, you must help your grantseekers put them aside. Point out that preproposal contact is less intimidating if they do their "grants homework" and know enough about the prospective grantor to ask intelligent questions that reflect their knowledge rather than expose their ignorance.

Remember that using your district's linkages will help break the ice and that your volunteers may have much less anxiety about contacting grantors than you or your grantseekers. Ask a volunteer who has sales training for help. She or he may be able to make a cold call on a grantor without any problem.

Whoever contacts the prospective grantor should first review the appropriate grantseekers matrix (Figures 4.5–4.12) to reconfirm the values and interests of the type of funder selected for approach. She or he should then review the research collected on each specific grantor. Naturally, any procedural information gathered on a particular funding source should be followed. In general, however, the following suggestions will be helpful.

How to Contact Government Grantors

Contact government agencies by e-mail, letter, phone, and in person, when possible. The first step is to send the agency a letter or e-mail requesting program information and to be put on the agency's mailing list. When appropriate, use the Sample Letter to a Federal Agency Requesting Information and Guidelines (Figure 6.9). Before doing so, check your federal research to see if the agency has provided an e-mail or website address. It is becoming increasingly common for federal agencies to provide program information and even applications on the Internet.

Next, telephone the agency. The *Catalog of Federal Domestic Assistance* (CFDA) usually gives the program officer's name and the agency's phone number. Keep in mind, however, the possibility that no one in the agency may have ever heard of the individual because she or he transferred to another office quite some time ago.

Introduce yourself to the person who answers the phone and tell him or her that you are calling for information concerning a grant program. Identify the program by the CFDA reference number and name and ask to speak to the program officer or to someone who can answer a few questions.

Figure 6.9

SAMPLE LETTER TO A FEDERAL AGENCY REQUESTING INFORMATION AND GUIDELINES

Date

Name
Title
Address

Dear [Contact Person]:

I am interested in the grant opportunities under [CFDA #], [Program Title]. Please add my name to your mailing list to receive information on this program. I am particularly interested in receiving application forms, program guidelines, and any existing priorities statements.

Please also send any other information that could help me prepare a quality application, such as a list of last year's successful grant recipients and reviewers. I am enclosing a self-addressed envelope for your convenience in sending these lists.

I will be contacting you when it is appropriate to discuss my proposal ideas. Thank you for your assistance.

Sincerely,
Name/Title
Phone Number

It may take one or two referrals to reach the person knowledgeable about the program. Be sure to always ask for the name of the person you are talking to and the phone number and name of the individual you are being transferred to.

Through research, your grantseekers should have collected a considerable amount of information about the potential grantor. This is a good opportunity to validate it. For example, the deadline dates and appropriations in the CFDA can be checked for accuracy.

Tell your new contact what you want! Remember, there are more staff involved in the government grants process than in the foundation or corporate process, and the rules governing freedom of information must be adhered to in tax-supported grantmaking. Staff members are generally willing to provide information.

Your objective is to validate the research that led you to believe that the program was a good match for the project your grantseekers want support for and to discuss their approaches to solving the problem. Ask if you could send the grantor a one-page concept paper and call after it has been reviewed. Also, ask to be put on the grantor's mailing list to receive guidelines, application information, newsletters, and so on.

Review Figure 6.10 and then ask where the agency is in its grants cycle.

Figure 6.10

THE PROACTIVE GRANTSEEKER'S $90 BILLION FEDERAL GRANTS CLOCK

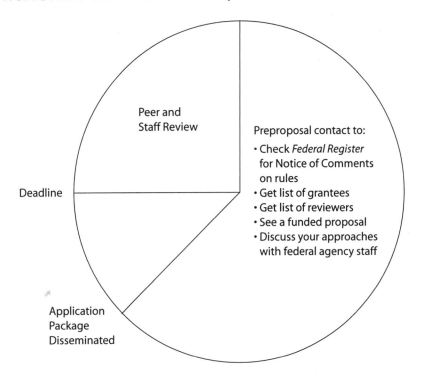

Peer and
Staff Review

Preproposal contact to:

• Check *Federal Register*
  for Notice of Comments
  on rules
• Get list of grantees
• Get list of reviewers
• See a funded proposal
• Discuss your approaches
  with federal agency staff

Deadline

Application
Package
Disseminated

The clock operates Monday through Friday (except federal holidays) 52 weeks per year. The federal government's year begins on October 1 and ends September 30.

Ask if the agency published information about its rules in *The Federal Register*. If so, request the date of publication and page number.

Request a list of last year's grantees. Ask if the list is available on the Internet, or if they will send you a copy. This list of grant winners will help you determine if your applicant school even stands a chance or if it would be better to develop a consortium with other districts, join with your intermediate district, or become part of a college or university's grant. The list of grantees will also tell you who got how much grant money and for what type of projects.

Ask the agency official for information on the agency's peer-review system. Although the *Federal Register* may have information on the points that the reviewers award for each section of a proposal, you need to know who reads the grant application. Knowing the types of reviewers and the reviewers' backgrounds will help your grantseekers decide what writing style to use and how to construct their proposal. In addition, you should ask the program office how someone from your district could become a reviewer.

After the information-gathering phone call is over, the best strategy is for you, one of your grantseekers, or a volunteer to visit the federal agency in Washington. In a two- or three-day visit contact can be made with several possible funders for your schools' different projects.

Some federal programs actually suggest a preproposal meeting. These agencies want potential grantees to submit the best proposals, even if the agencies are unable to fund them. The better the proposals and the greater the number of requests for funds, the more they can prove that their program is needed, should be continued, and should receive increased appropriations.

You could also invite the funding official to visit your school district or applicant school to observe the problem firsthand. The funding official may come if you invite other schools and districts to an informative session on grants presented by the agency.

You may also ask the program officer if he or she plans to attend an education conference or professional meeting being held in your area in the near future. If so, you, one of your coworkers, or one of your grants advisory group members may be able to meet with the official there.

Who should represent the district at such a meeting? If one of your grantseekers cannot attend, send a volunteer or an advocate from your appropriate grants advisory group. Ideally, a district representative (either you or a coworker) and an advocate should go to the meeting together. Two is the magic number when it comes to representation.

Whoever goes, be aware that dress is important. Federal program officers generally dress quite conservatively. However, program officers at the National Endowment for the Humanities usually dress more casually than those in the Department of Education. Generally, the older the bureaucrat, the more conservative the dress.

Dress for Success by John T. Malloy has a section on how to dress for meetings with government bureaucrats. Although many individuals in the world of education are offended by the notion that people are judged by how they are dressed, it is worthwhile to read this book. Malloy's work was originally funded by an education grant. The purpose of the grant was to determine whether classroom leaders' style of dress had an impact on students' learning and retention; research indicated that indeed it did. Very few educators ever read the research findings and fewer still improved their dress habits because of them, but the important point is that your representatives will be judged by what they wear and therefore should dress accordingly.

What should you or other representatives bring to the meeting? Bring materials that help demonstrate the need. These may include photographs and short audiovisual aids (three to five minutes long), such as filmstrips, videotapes, and slide presentations. You can bring a laptop to present computer-generated materials such as a short, full-motion production with sound, but remember that federal offices are often small and may lack sufficient electrical outlets.

In addition, bring information on your community, school district, individual schools, or specific classrooms. But never leave a proposal behind. Federal bureaucrats know that if you bring an already written proposal with you, you are not likely to change it to incorporate any of their suggestions.

Bring a list of questions to ask the program officer. The questions should reflect your knowledge of the Federal Grants Clock and be aimed at validating information you have already collected about the funding source.

Be sure to file copies of all the information gathered on a prospective government funding source and that all contacts and correspondence are recorded on the Record of Face-to-Face Contact, Telephone Contact, and Correspondence that is part of the Federal Research Worksheet (Figure 6.11). In addition, all information collected on agency personnel should be recorded on the Federal Funding Staff History Worksheet (Figure 6.12).

Contacting Foundation Funding Sources

Most foundations do not respond to requests for information. If your research states "no contact except by letter of inquiry, concept paper, or letter proposal," do not send a letter requesting information and guidelines. For those who state that reports or guidelines are available, follow these suggestions.

You may request general information, grant application guidelines, annual reports, and newsletters. The Sample Letter to a Foundation Requesting Information and Guidelines (Figure 6.13) can be used with national general-purpose, special-purpose, community, and family foundations, but not with *all* foundations in these categories. Use the letter to contact only those foundations that state in resource materials such as *The Foundation Directory* that they have application guidelines available.

Note that this is a letter asking for information only. It is not a proposal. If there is no response to it, a telephone call to the foundation is justified.

But, as probably fewer than a thousand foundations actually have offices, telephone contact is very often impossible. In addition, many of the entries in foundation resource directories do not give telephone numbers. Even if a phone number is listed in an entry or on an IRS tax return,

Figure 6.11

FEDERAL RESEARCH WORKSHEET

CFDA No. _____   Deadline Date(s): _____

Program Title: _____   Gov't. Agency: _____

Create a file for the program you are researching and place all the information you gather on this program in the file. Use this Federal Research Worksheet to do the following:

- Keep a record of the information you have gathered
- Maintain a log of all telephone and face-to-face contacts made with the government agency
- Log all correspondence sent to and received from the agency

Agency address: _____   Agency director: _____

Telephone number: _____   Program director: _____

Fax number: _____   Name/title of contact person: _____

Place a check mark (✔) next to the information you have gathered and placed in the file for the foundation.

_____ Program description from CFDA

_____ Letter requesting to be put on mailing list

    _____ sent for _____ received

_____ List of last year's grantees

    _____ sent for _____ received

_____ List of last year's reviewers

    _____ sent for _____ received

_____ Application package—expected availability date

    _____ sent for _____ received

_____ Comments on rules/final rules from *Federal Register*

_____ Notice of rules for evaluation from *Federal Register*

_____ Grant scoring system—point allocation for each section. Source:

_____

_____ Sample funded proposal

_____ Federal Funding Staff History Worksheet

_____ Written summary of each contact made

_____ Grantor Strategy Worksheet

Record of Face-to-Face and Telephone Contact:

Date Contacted	Contacted by	Foundation Contact	Results	Action

Record of All Correspondence Sent and Received:

Date of Correspondence	Purpose of Correspondence	Results/Action

Figure 6.12

FEDERAL FUNDING STAFF HISTORY WORKSHEET

CFDA No. _____

Program Title: _____

Gov't. Agency: _____

1. Name: _____

2. Title: _____
   (Agency Director, Program Director, Program Officer, etc.)

3. Business address: _____

4. Business telephone: _____

5. Birthdate: _____   Birthplace: _____

6. Marital status: _____   Children: _____

7. College/university _____

8. Degree(s): _____

9. Military service: _____

10. Clubs/affiliations: _____

11. Interests/hobbies: _____

12. Board memberships: _____

13. Other philanthropic activities: _____

14. Awards/honors: _____

15. Other: _____

Notes:

do not call the foundation if its description clearly states that there should be no contact except by letter. However, do not despair. Remember that the 40,588 foundations with no offices still have board members that may be contacted through a linkage with a volunteer or staff member.

If you have not gotten a response to your letter, and you are not aware of any instructions prohibiting telephone contact, by all means telephone the foundation and try to arrange a personal visit. If a face-to-face meeting is not possible, use the phone call to ask the same kind of questions you would have asked at a meeting. Ask the foundation official if you can e-mail or fax a one-page summary of your ideas to him. Also ask if you can call him back to discuss the ideas. Arrange a mutually convenient time to call. A conference call involving a linkage person would be ideal.

Figure 6.13

SAMPLE LETTER TO A FOUNDATION REQUESTING INFORMATION AND GUIDELINES

Date

Name
Title
Address

Dear [Contact Person]:

My research on your foundation indicates that you provide application guidelines to prospective grantees. My organization is preparing a proposal in the area of [topic] and I would appreciate receiving these guidelines at your earliest convenience.

I would also appreciate any other information you may have that could help us prepare a quality proposal. Please add us to your mailing list for annual reports, newsletters, priority statements, program statements, and so on.

Since both of our organizations are committed to [subject area] I believe you will find our proposal idea of interest.

Sincerely,
Name/Title
Phone Number

Steps for Contacting Foundation Grantors

If permissible, call the contact person. The dilemma is deciding who should establish a relationship with the funder—a district administrator, grants coordinator, or one of the grantseekers. Because many educators are reluctant to make preproposal contact, you may decide to help your grantseekers get started and then step back.

In any event, the caller may find it helpful to review the needs data first as a reminder that she is calling on behalf of the school district, school, students, field of education, or whatever it is, rather than for any private motive. This may help alleviate nervousness.

The caller should introduce herself and state the purpose of the call. (If a secretary or administrative assistant is reached, ask to talk to the foundation director or to a staff person best able to answer questions.) As with government grantors, one purpose of the call is to validate the information already gathered on the foundation. The caller's questions should reflect knowledge of the foundation's granting pattern and priorities. Another purpose is to ascertain the foundation's interest in the grantseekers' approach to the problem or in increasing educational opportunities for children.

It is important that the caller demonstrate that she is different from other grantseekers and that this foundation has been purposefully selected. For example, the caller may say, "I am contacting the Sebastian Jessica Foundation because it has demonstrated its desire to see expanded parental involvement in elementary and middle schools. My research shows that 40 percent of your funds in recent years were committed to this area."

As with government grantors, the caller should tell the foundation funding source what she wants. For example: "I would appreciate five minutes of your time to ascertain which of the two or three approaches I have developed for the XYZ School would elicit your foundation's support and appeal favorably to your board." Note: You may use the fax approach here to build their interest. For example: "I would be happy to fax a short summary of the proposed solutions to you and to discuss them with you after you have had time to look them over." E-mail with an attached short file is becoming more acceptable. You should inquire about this option.

Ideally, the next step is to meet face-to-face with the funder. You can either go to his location or invite him visit to visit you at the applicant school. By visiting the school, he can observe your district's students and see the needs population or problem firsthand. In either case, the funder will expect to pay his way to visit you, just as he will expect you to pay your way to visit him.

If a visit to the funder is possible, who should go? Whether you visit the foundation or it comes to you, your team should be small—usually no more than two. Select an active and concerned volunteer from your appropriate grants advisory group who is donating his or her time to the proposed project. The other person may be yourself or one of your grantseekers.

The team's style of dress should be similar to that of the foundation official. Again, your grantseekers' research will come in handy here, as well as the book *Dress for Success*. It is important to remember that your goal is to project the appropriate image to the prospective funding source. This is not the time to assert your individuality or state your values. The most important outcome of the visit is that the grantor hear your ideas.

What you bring to the meeting is extremely important. Focus on your objective. What do you expect to accomplish in a person-to-person visit with the potential grantor? You want the following:

- Agreement on the need or problem to be addressed

- To induce the prospective funder to discuss its interest in your grantseekers' solution

- Information on the grants selection process so that your grantseekers can tailor their approach

- To validate your research and in particular to ascertain the appropriateness of the size of the potential grant request

To avoid the common mistake of jumping directly to the money issue, concentrate on bringing material that solidifies agreement on the need or the problem. In many cases, the grantor has difficulty seeing the problem through the eyes of a student or an educator. Use the following techniques to help the funder develop insight into the problem. Your materials should be aimed at educating, rather than convincing, the grantor.

A well-developed presentation on a laptop computer can be very effective, but keep it simple and to the point. Avoid projection systems. Be careful about using technology when requesting a small grant. Your laptop should not cost more than what you are requesting.

A short (three- to five-minute) videotape or slide show, especially one produced by students, can demonstrate the problem very effectively. Whether it is about alcohol abuse or zoology, these tell a compelling story because they enable the funder to *see* the nature of the need. Or a picture book that documents the need may provide the starting point for a discussion of the problem.

Again, the objective of the meeting is to first establish agreement on the need for the project and then to ascertain the funding source's interests and to discuss several approaches or solutions.

Recording Foundation Research and Preproposal Contact

The purpose of preproposal contact is to validate your grantseekers' research on the funding source and to add to that knowledge so that your district can develop a grant-winning strategy. You want your grantseekers to be organized and to take advantage of every possible time-saving technique. Therefore, your district grants office should initiate an electronic or conventional file on every foundation funding source your grantseekers are researching and thinking about approaching. These files should be continually updated and kept together in alphabetical order. Your grantseekers may make copies of these files for their own records, but the original files should be stored in the district grants office. This is a great start toward an organized grants effort.

The Foundation Research Worksheet (Figure 6.14) should be filled out for each foundation that is a possible source of funds. This worksheet will help you keep an up-to-date record of the information and materials gathered. All contact with the potential funding source should be logged on the Record of Face-to-Face Contact, Telephone Contact, and Correspondence portion of that form, even contact that reveals that the grantor has no interest in your project.

Collect as much information as possible on foundation officers, board members, and trustees. This information can help you and your

Figure 6.14

FOUNDATION RESEARCH WORKSHEET

Foundation: _____   **Deadline Date(s):** _____

Create a file for each foundation you are researching and place all the information you gather on this foundation in the file. Use the Foundation Research Worksheet to do the following:

- Keep a record of the information you have gathered
- Maintain a log of all telephone and face-to-face contact with the foundation
- Log all correspondence sent to and received from the foundation

Foundation address: _____   **Name of contact person:** _____

Telephone number: _____   **Title of contact person:** _____

Fax number: _____

Place a check mark (✔) next to the information you have gathered and put in the file for the foundation.

_____ Foundation description from *Foundation Directory* or other source such as DIALOG, SPIN, etc.

_____ Note source: _____

_____ List of grants from IRS Form 990 or *Foundation Grants Index*

_____ Note source: _____

_____ Application information/guidelines

_____ sent for _____ received

_____ Foundation's annual report

_____ sent for _____ received

_____ Foundation's newsletter/other reports

_____ sent for _____ received

_____ Foundation funding staff history

_____ Written summary of each contact made

_____ Grantor Strategy Worksheet

Record of Face-to-Face and Telephone Contact:

Date Contacted	Contacted by	Foundation Contact	Results	Action

Record of All Correspondence Sent and Received:

Date of Correspondence	Purpose of Correspondence	Results/Action

grantseekers figure out strategies to deal with any preferences and biases you may encounter in your contact with a foundation. It will also help you pinpoint links between the foundation, your school district, a volunteer on your grants advisory group, and so on.

Use the Foundation Funding Staff History Worksheet (Figure 6.15) to record the information collected. Keep the worksheet in the appropriate file.

How to Contact Corporate Grantors

Your district grants office should open a file on corporations that may be potential grantors for your schools' projects. Because many corporations are more responsive to an approach through their employees or sales representatives, you may want to line up your linkages before contacting the actual grantor.

The Sample Letter to a Corporation Requesting Information and Guidelines (Figure 6.16) can be sent to those corporations that actually have a grants staff and a preferred proposal format or application form. In general, the larger the corporation, the greater the chance it will have proposal guidelines.

Before you follow up on the letter by telephoning the corporate grantor, review the reasons why you think the company would value your school's project and how the project relates to the company's products or workers. If you do not know who the corporate contact is, ask whoever answers the phone who would best be able to answer your questions about the corporation's grants process. It may be a local plant manager, salesperson, or corporate granting official.

As with foundation and government grant sources, state the reason for your call; for instance, "I am calling to discuss the opportunity of working together on a grant that has mutual benefits to both the XYZ School and the ABC Corporation." Request five minutes of the person's time to answer your questions and suggest that you fax, e-mail, or mail them background information. The purpose of sending background information is to solicit comments so that you can tailor your proposal to the company's needs. Be sure to let the contact know that you are presenting your school's proposal at this point.

Summarize the research that has led you to contact the company. Explain that you are not approaching a hundred corporations but only a select group.

If there is a possibility of a conference call, use any linkages and local employee support that you can. For example, you can demonstrate the voluntary involvement of the corporation's employees in your school district by including one of them in the call.

Figure 6.15

FOUNDATION FUNDING STAFF HISTORY WORKSHEET

Foundation: _____

1. Name of director/board member: _____

2. Title: _____

3. Residence address: _____ Phone: _____

4. Business address: _____ Phone: _____

5. Linkages/contacts (mutual friends/associates who can contact director/board member for you):

   _____
   _____
   _____
   _____

   List any data you have uncovered that might help you do the following:

   - Determine ways to deal with any of contact's preferences and biases
   - Locate other possible linkages between this individual and you/your school's volunteer on your Grants Advisory Group, etc.

6. Birthdate: _____   Birthplace: _____

7. Marital status: _____   Children: _____

8. Employer: _____   Job title: _____

9. College/university: _____   Degree(s): _____

10. Military service: _____

11. Clubs/affiliations: _____

12. Interests/hobbies: _____

13. Other board memberships: _____

14. Other philanthropic activities: _____

15. Awards/honors: _____

16. Other: _____

Notes:

Figure 6.16

SAMPLE LETTER TO A CORPORATION REQUESTING INFORMATION AND GUIDELINES

Date

Name
Title
Address

Dear [Contact Person]:

My research on your company's grant support indicates that we share a concern for children and the importance of positive educational experiences.

[At this stage, mention your linkage if one exists.] [John Smith], your sales representative, suggested I write to request your company's proposal guidelines and requirements for funding a project I believe you will find very interesting.

In an effort to promote the most efficient investment of both our organizations' time, I would appreciate any information relative to your company's funding priorities.

Sincerely,
Name/Title
Phone Number

Corporations may actually spend more time reviewing grants than foundations do. One possible reason is that they have employees and offices, even though employees who act as corporate grants contacts may have several other job responsibilities. This often makes it possible for a grantseeker to meet with the corporate grantor in person.

Because of the growing involvement of corporations in programs such as "Adopt a Classroom," more and more districts are developing historical relationships with the corporations in their area. Naturally, your district grants office should make records outlining the corporation's history with the school district available to the individuals planning to visit the company.

You may even want to invite the corporate person to visit your applicant school to see the problem firsthand and to discuss the corporation's interest in the approaches developed to reduce the problem.

A volunteer might be the best person to meet with a corporate contact. You and your coworkers are being paid by your district to represent it and its schools, but a volunteer is donating time and may even lose income to represent the district. Corporations will be impressed by the quality, commitment, and number of volunteers that your schools can mobilize.

But don't overwhelm the corporate funder with a massive team. Two well-chosen and carefully instructed representatives will be most effective. Again, they should dress similarly to the people they will be meeting and strive to project a serious, businesslike appearance. They should bring along information on the need for the project. As with other funding sources, one of the following might be included:

- A short videotape that documents the need; include facts and, if possible, a testimony or case study for human interest

- A slide-audiotape presentation on the problem or need

- Pictures, charts, statistics, and so on

As corporations have their own management style and vocabulary, it might be a good idea to ask a corporate member of a grants advisory group to help you prepare a short, corporate style presentation to the funding source. This presentation might include colored charts and transparencies.

Recording Corporate Research and Preproposal Contact

Create a file for each of your district's corporate prospects. The corporate files should be kept together in alphabetical order. Again, this will help organize your district's grants effort.

Make sure that contact with each corporate prospect is logged on the Record of Face-to-Face Contact, Telephone Contact, and Correspondence portion of the Corporate Research Worksheet (Figure 6.17). The worksheet will help your office maintain an up-to-date record of the information gathered. It should be updated as additional information and materials are obtained.

Just as it is important to gather personal data on foundation officers, board members, and trustees, it is also important to gather personal data on corporate executives and contributions officers. You can uncover some information on corporate executives by examining various corporate resource materials such as *Standard and Poor's Register of Corporations, Directors and Executives.*

The more information gathered, the better the chances of developing an approach that will appeal to the funding source. In addition, your chances of identifying more linkages to the corporation will increase. However, please note that your grantseekers should not rule out a particular corporation as a funding prospect simply because they are unable to gather personal data on the corporation's funding officials.

The corporate Funding Staff History Worksheet (Figure 6.18) should be used to record the information collected. The worksheet should be stored in the appropriate corporation's file.

Figure 6.17

CORPORATE RESEARCH WORKSHEET

Corporation: _____   **Deadline Date(s):** _____

Create a file for each corporation you are researching and place all the information you gather on this corporation in the file. Use the Corporation Research Worksheet to do the following:

- Keep a record of the information you have gathered
- Maintain a log of all telephone and face-to-face contact with the corporation
- Log all correspondence sent to and received from the corporation

Corporation address: _____   Name of contact person: _____
Telephone number: _____   Title of contact person: _____
Fax number: _____

Place a check mark (✔) next to the information you have gathered and put in the file for the corporation.

_____ Description of corporate giving program from *National Directory of Corporate Giving, Corporate Foundation Profiles,* or other source.
 Note source: _____
_____ Required proposal format, grant application/guidelines
_____ Corporate foundation's 990 IRS tax return
_____ List of corporate officers, sales representatives
 Note source: _____
_____ Corporate product information (the Standard Industrial Classification Code)
_____ Profits/dividends information—financial status of corporation from Dun and Bradstreet's *Million Dollar Directory,* credit rating service, or other source.
 Note source: _____
_____ Corporate funding staff history
_____ Information obtained from Chamber of Commerce (number of employees, payroll, etc.)
_____ Written summary of each contact made
_____ Grantor Strategy Worksheet

Record of Face-to-Face and Telephone Contact:

Date Contacted	Contacted by	Foundation Contact	Results	Action

Record of All Correspondence Sent and Received:

Date of Correspondence	Purpose of Correspondence	Results/Action

Figure 6.18

CORPORATE FUNDING STAFF HISTORY WORKSHEET

Corporation: _____

1. Name of funding executive: _____

2. Title: _____

3. Residence address: _____   Phone: _____

4. Business address: _____   Phone: _____

5. Linkages/contacts (mutual friends/associates who can contact funding executive/corporation for you):

   _____

   _____

   _____

   _____

   List any data you have uncovered that might help you do the following:

   • Determine ways to deal with any of contact's preferences and biases
   • Locate other possible linkages between this individual and you/your school's volunteer on your Grants Advisory Group, etc.

6. Birthdate: _____   Birthplace: _____

7. Marital status: _____   Children: _____

8. College/university: _____   Degree(s): _____

9. Military service: _____

10. Clubs/affiliations: _____

11. Interests/hobbies: _____

12. Other board memberships: _____

13. Other philanthropic activities: _____

14. Awards/honors: _____

15. Other: _____

Notes:

The Grantor Strategy Worksheet

This worksheet (Figure 6.19) should be completed for each funding source your grantseekers are planning to submit a proposal to. It will help you assist your grantseekers in tailoring their proposal to the potential funder's viewpoint.

Every attempt should be made to analyze the funding source's granting history. Even if preproposal contact is not possible, you must at least make sure that the amount your grantseekers are requesting fits the funding source's granting pattern.

Think about who might collaborate with your grantseekers on their proposal and what other groups could submit it so that it might better fit the funder's requirements.

If at all possible, find out who will read and evaluate the proposal. For example, will it be read by staff members? Board members? Program personnel? Outside experts or reviewers? Besides helping your grantseekers write the proposal, this information will be vital to performing a mock review.

The prospective funding sources should be ranked by potential. At this point, your grantseekers should not spend much time writing the proposal. Instead, they should be investing their time analyzing their best prospects for funding.

Although some pieces of vital information will probably be missing, encourage your grantseekers to devise the best strategy they can based on what they know.

Developing a district grants booklet on the concept of preproposal contact has a positive effect on your grants effort. Providing grantseekers with a suggested process for making each type of contact reduces their anxiety and increases their readiness to make the contact. It is unfortunate that many school districts ignore the issue of access to potential grantors. Your grantseekers deserve to understand this process.

Use the worksheets and information in this chapter to help you develop a booklet tailored to your district. The title of the booklet could be "How to Get Approval to Contact Funders and the Preproposal Contact Support Services Provided by the District Grants Office." This would make it clear to your grantseekers that your office has a sign-on system and services that can help them. And even if it doesn't, you could still provide a preproposal contact booklet containing helpful information, worksheets, checklists, and so on.

If your system is more advanced it may be appropriate to include a section in the booklet on the role of the grants advisory committee and a description of your system for recording linkages.

Figure 6.19

GRANTOR STRATEGY WORKSHEET

Potential Grantor: _____   **Priority #:** _____

Deadline: _____

A. Strategy Derived from Granting Pattern

1. $_____ Largest grant to organization most similar to ours

2. $_____ Smallest grant to organization most similar to ours

3. $_____ Average grant size to organizations similar to ours

4. $_____ Average grant size in our area of interest

5. $_____ Our estimated grant request

6. Financial trend in our area of interest over past three years

_____ up   _____ down   _____ stable

7. If yours is a multiyear proposal, how popular have these been with the funding source in the past three years?

_____ Many multiyear proposals funded

_____ Some multiyear proposals funded

_____ Few multiyear proposals funded

_____ No multiyear funding

_____ Not applicable

8. Financial data on funding source: obligation levels for last three years for grants

19_____ $_____   19_____ $_____   20_____ $_____

B. Based on preproposal contact, which solution strategies are the most appropriate for this funding source?

C. Proposal Review System

1. Who evaluates submitted proposals? _____

_____

2. What is the background and training of the evaluators? _____

_____

_____

3. What point system will be followed?_____

_____

_____

4. How much time will be spent reviewing each proposal? _____

_____

D. Use this space to note anything special that will affect proposal outcome.

_____

_____

_____

_____

_____

CHAPTER 6 ASSESSMENT TOOL

Several strategies for developing a proactive grants system are listed on this assessment tool. Put a check mark in front of those that your district already has in place and an "I" in front of those that you need to implement. Rate the effectiveness of those you have in place, using E for exceptional, A for adequate, and NI for needs improvement.

When you have completed your assessment, review the items that you need to implement and those that need improvement and develop a prioritized list of the order in which the items should be addressed. Use a project planner (see Chapter 7) to outline the steps required to make the necessary changes in your system.

Check Mark or I   **Rate: E/A/NI**

_____ Preproposal sign-on system that provides district administrators with advance knowledge of the foundation, corporate, and government programs grantseekers will pursue   _____

_____ Grantors' system for the identification of and compliance with matching and in-kind contribution requirements   _____

_____ System for identifying special space, equipment, and release time needs   _____

_____ System to identify and comply with grantor requirements regarding the inclusion of the program in the district after the completion of the grant-funded project   _____

_____ System to identify and comply with grantor requirements regarding various issues related to the equipment purchased under the grant—special maintenance agreements and so on   _____

A tracking system that provides information on:

_____ Number of ideas developed into proposals   _____

_____ Number of searches provided   _____

_____ Number and identification of individuals who have made preproposal contact   _____

_____ Number and identification of individuals who have employed a proposal review and improvement exercise before submittal   _____

_____ Number of proposals awarded, rejected, and pending   _____

_____ Amount of matching funds committed to awarded grants and required for pending proposals   _____

A program in which volunteers are utilized in the district's grants effort to:

_____ Participate on grants advisory groups   _____

_____ Provide linkages with prospective grantors   _____

_____ Donate resources and skills   _____

_____ Make preproposal contact with prospective grantors   _____

The district grants office's efforts in encouraging and helping grantseekers with preproposal contact with prospective government grantors:

_____ Generates and sends a letter to get on the prospective grantor's mailing list and to request a list of past grantees   _____

_____ Provides assistance in contacting past grantees   _____

CHAPTER 6 ASSESSMENT TOOL (continued)

_____ Generates and sends a letter for the list of reviewers _____

_____ Provides information on how to become a reviewer _____

_____ Helps with telephone calls and personal visits to prospective program officers and
maintains records of all contact _____

_____ Supports travel for preproposal contact _____

_____ Helps procure copies of funded proposals _____

**The district grants office's efforts in encouraging and helping grantseekers with preproposal
contact with prospective foundation and corporate grantors (private grantors):**

_____ Generates and sends a letter to those grantors who have proposal guidelines _____

_____ Provides research and analysis on past granting patterns and history based on IRS 990s _____

_____ Assists in contacting prospective grantors and maintains records of all contact _____

For all grantor types:

_____ District grants office assists in developing a final grantor strategy (completing the
Grantor Strategy Worksheet and so on) _____

Moving from Idea to Project Plan

THIS CHAPTER HELPS grantseekers select the best proposal strategy and create a grant-winning plan that provides for sound project management.

Much of the work of a successful district grants office consists of encouraging and monitoring the pace at which grantseeking occurs. Some zealous grantseekers may view the steps to developing a credible, organized, and ultimately successful proposal as roadblocks inflicted by a system that requires too many forms, worksheets, and approvals. It is usually those with a great idea but a poorly developed plan who create the most problems.

The time to develop an easily administered grant is while it is being constructed, not after the award notice. Sound grants administration principles are grounded in proper planning. An easily administered grant is founded in a proposal that provides an analysis of the tasks that must be carried out to bring about the suggested change and includes the job description of all staff; the requirements for staff; consultants' work descriptions; the cash flow by activity; and an inventory of all supplies, materials, and equipment needed.

In reactive grantseeking, there is a mad rush to finish the proposal by the deadline and no time for preproposal contact with the funder or for review and rewriting. The budget is usually created in the final hour before the proposal is signed and submitted. By then, asking the proposal developer to slow down and create an organized planning document or a spreadsheet that outlines all the activities or methods so cash flow can be projected is out of the question. But should there be a mistake or a legal or credibility problem, the district grants person will be the first to be called before the superintendent.

Your school administrators and district grantseekers must be educated to the increased chances of grants success if they follow a grants plan such as the one suggested in this chapter. The credibility and image of the entire district rest on each proposal submitted to a grantor. Even when grantors must reject your district's proposal, you want them to have read a well-organized document. Some grantseekers mistakenly think they can dazzle them with their brilliance and baffle them with their bull. But grantors usually subscribe to the KISS concept—*Keep It Short and Simple*. They are offended by disorganization because it wastes their valuable time.

A quality proposal is based on an easily understood plan that provides the rationale for the proposed activities and expenditures. Some grantors require that it be described in a budget narrative form. Others prefer to see it visually displayed on a spreadsheet. Even when not required by the grantor, your grant writers should complete a spreadsheet that provides the detail necessary to prepare and negotiate a budget.

Both you and your grantseekers need a project management system that allows you to track each project's progress, locate the equipment purchased under each grant, and maintain your schools' credibility within your district and outside of it. Grantseekers often complain about their inability to control and expend grant funds that are accepted by their school district for proposals they have written. This complaint can be avoided by employing an effective project management system.

Up to this point in your proactive grants system, your grantseekers should have documented a problem and come up with several possible solutions for it. Some will want to send the prospective funder a proposal that outlines several solutions, hoping the funder will select the one it prefers. But you should encourage submitting only proposals with *one* solution—the solution that will appeal most to the grantor.

Your grantseekers' research and preproposal contact should have helped them choose the solution or approach that most likely offers the prospective funder what it wants. If it was possible to procure a copy of a proposal the grantor has funded in the past, this also should have provided them with an idea of what objectives, methods, and format the funder prefers.

Research should at least have uncovered the range of grant awards, including the high, low, and average grant size; geographic preferences; and types of projects preferred. If the proposal requires more funds than a single grantor is likely or able to invest, you will need a project plan that identifies several prospective grantors and the amount of funds needed from each. The plan should also clearly delineate which parts of the project each grantor will fund.

As your grantseekers become more and more involved in developing proposals, you must remind them to view their proposals through the eyes of the funding source and to make every effort to tailor each proposal to each prospective grantor. This reinforces the values-based approach to grantseeking. Remember, the funder may not see the methods, budget, or grant request the same way you and your grantseekers do. In fact, each type of grantor will view these differently. For example, government grantors require longer, well-organized proposals that allow them to easily identify matching or in-kind contributions and may require a written description linking each budget expenditure to a method. In contrast, most corporate and foundation funders prefer a short letter of proposal and a businesslike approach that relies on cost analysis of each step in your plan.

Whatever their type, all grantors require that you have a clearly defined plan. Just as good teachers have well-developed lesson plans, funding sources require grantees to have well-developed plans before they give funds. The Project Planner (Figure 7.1) should help your grantseekers format their grants. (The Project Planner is presented here with permission from the American Council on Education.)

The Project Planner

Think of the Project Planner as a lesson plan or spreadsheet. The proposed plan is developed when the grantseeker (proposal developer) is ready to focus on the solution or approach believed to be the most interesting to the prospective grantor. The plan must show the percentage of time and effort the key staff spends on the project, outline consortium arrangements and the use of consultants, and identify any matching or in-kind contributions the grantseekers' school will provide.

The Project Planner helps your grantseekers develop a clearly defined proposal methodology, plan, and budget. Once completed, it allows them to define and refine several aspects of the project:

1. An adequate staff pattern that describes who is needed to do what tasks when (helping ensure that job descriptions match the tasks that must be accomplished)

2. An easily scanned overview of the prescribed activities and how they relate to costs and the attainment of the objectives

3. A logical framework on which to evaluate the tasks performed by consultants

4. A detailed analysis of the materials, supplies, and equipment related to each objective

Figure 7.1

PROJECT PLANNER

Proposal Developed for: _____   Proposal Year _____

Project Director: _____   Proposed Start Date _____

PROJECT PLANNER

PROJECT TITLE: _____

A. List project objectives or outcomes A. B.

B. List methods to accomplish each objective as A-1, A-2, ... B-1, B-2 ...

	MONTH		TIME	PROJECT PERSONNEL	PERSONNEL COSTS				CONSULTANTS CONTRACT SERVICES				NON-PERSONNEL RESOURCES NEEDED SUPPLIES - EQUIPMENT - MATERIALS				SUB-TOTAL ACTIVITY COST	MILESTONES PROGRESS INDICATORS		
	Begin	End			Salaries & Wages	Fringe Benefits	Total		Time	Cost/Week	Total		Item	Cost/Item	Quantity	Tot cost	Total I,L,P	Item	Date
	C/D		E	F	G	H	I		J	K	L		M	N	O	P	Q	R	S

Total Direct Costs or Costs Requested From Funder

Matching Funds, In-Kind Contributions, or Donated Costs

Total Costs

100%   % of Total

T

5. A defensible budget and cash forecast

6. An efficient way to keep track of in-kind or matching donations

7. A basis for dividing costs among multiple funders

8. A working document that makes it possible to assess the involvement of multiple organizations and the responsibilities of consortium participants and subcontractors

Project Planners appeal most to funding sources that are familiar with and use spreadsheets themselves (corporations, for example). Recently they have become an addition to government proposals. Federal program officers and their grant and contract officers are now trying to pinpoint inflated budget items, and will push grantees to agree to carry out their proposal for less money than originally requested. They are simply trying to negotiate, a process that requires give-and-take. But most grantseekers just take what the federal grantor says it will give. The Project Planner helps your grantseekers to truly negotiate.

Standard federal budget forms use broad budget categories. These make it difficult to demonstrate that a project will be compromised if less money is granted than requested. But a Project Planner shows how a reduction in funds will impede methods or activities and negatively affect the proposal's objectives. This link between cause and effect is crucial to negotiating the final award because the achievement of a proposal's objectives is shown to be directly related to bringing about the degree of change desired by both the grantee and the funder. The Project Planner allows grantseekers to present a clear picture of the relationship between project personnel, consultants, equipment and supplies, and the accomplishment of their school's proposal.

If you and your grantseekers are not familiar with spreadsheets, the Project Planner might seem a bit overwhelming. But there are many ways to complete it, and the only real mistakes one can make are mathematical (incorrect addition, multiplication, and so on).

Look at the Project Planner as a tool that helps your grantseekers identify the costs of carrying out the methods and activities in the proposed plan and how those costs will be divided among all partners in the agreement. They decide how detailed the breakdown of activities should be. The more detailed the breakdown, the easier it is to document the costs assigned to each activity and to defend them in budget negotiations.

The basic purpose of the Project Planner is to provide a clear plan that results in the educational change described in the project objectives. Therefore, we must look at how to develop objectives before we examine the general guidelines for filling out the Project Planner.

Objectives

The district grants office should remind the proposal developers how important it is to develop objectives that demonstrate the type of change the grantor values. Proposed plans should meet or exceed the educational change defined in their objectives. My rule is: no objectives, no need for a plan; no plan, no chance for a grant and no need to bother grantors.

Your district grants office will find that it pays off to provide grantseekers with guidelines for constructing quality objectives that result in quality proposals, which in turn lead to grant awards. Include guidelines for constructing objectives in your district's booklet on how to write a grant-winning proposal.

A well-constructed objective tells the funder what will change and how much if funds are granted. Graduate training may have given you experience in setting affective, cognitive, psychomotor, and behavioral objectives, but many grantseekers do not understand the difference between an objective and a method. Some mistakenly write objectives that focus on the approaches, steps, or methods that will be used to bring about the change. This confuses *what* will be accomplished with *how* it will be accomplished. Objectives deal with what will change; activities and methods tell how it will be brought about.

Objectives should be reviewed to be certain that there is more than one way to achieve each one. If the objective in question suggests that there is only one possible approach, then you are dealing with a solution, not an objective. A well-developed objective focuses on an outcome, implying that more than one strategy could reach it. If your grantseekers are confused about the difference between objectives and methods, ask them why they are performing a particular activity. Their reply may give them a clear sense of what will be measured as they close the gap in the area of need.

An objective provides a measurable way to see how much change should occur by the conclusion of the project. A method tells how it will be accomplished. Objectives say what you want to accomplish, methods say how. Being aware of this distinction can dramatically strengthen a proposal.

Developing objectives may appear tedious, especially when your grantseekers are eager to move on to proposed solutions and proposals. But keep in mind that well-written objectives that focus on measurable change do the following:

- Make the proposal more interesting and compelling to the funder
- Enable grantseekers to measure the changes the proposal suggests
- Increase their school's and the district's reputation as a source of excellent proposals

The Understanding and Creating Measurable Objectives Worksheet (Figure 7.2) may help your grantseekers develop objectives. In addition to suggesting that they review the guidelines for constructing objectives in your district's booklet on how to write grant-winning proposals, you may also suggest that they consider the more detailed guidelines in the *Teacher's Guide to Winning Grants* (see bibliography), but, in general, a well-written objective includes an action verb and statement, measurement indicator, performance standard, deadline, and cost frame.

Action Verb and Statement

The direction of change to be accomplished is based on the information provided on the Needs Worksheet (Figure 3.3) and Goals Worksheet (Figure 3.5). Remember, you and your grantseekers are not suggesting or

---

Figure 7.2

UNDERSTANDING AND CREATING MEASURABLE OBJECTIVES WORKSHEET

Grantors want to be sure that their funding will promote measurable change in the need or gap that the grantseekers' proposal aspires to address.

Review the following sample objective to help learn how to create behavioral objectives that provide measurement indicators:

Train 150 teachers at Jonesboro Elementary School to use the Smith Reading Series.

Now ask yourself what will be measured and what need this objective seeks to address. As you can see, you cannot do so from the information in such an objective. Just because an objective contains a number does not mean it provides a measurement indicator.

Sometimes you can back into a proper objective by asking, "Why?" Why train 150 teachers at Jonesboro Elementary? Maybe Jonesboro students have scored low on standardized reading tests and the school hopes the Smith Reading Series will improve their reading skills.

What should the measurement indicator be? In this example, test scores already exist: a baseline that makes it possible to measure improvement by administering a new test after the Smith Reading Series is implemented.

The objective should thus state how much the scores should improve, over what period of time, and for how much money. Perhaps it should read:

Through use of the Smith Reading Series, increase standardized reading test scores at Jonesboro Elementary School by _____ percent over a twelve-month period, as measured by a post-test, at a cost of $_____.

Training of teachers is not the objective; it's a method or activity prescribed to bring about the objective.

Now put your objective through a similar analysis. What will be measured? Will it demonstrate a reduction in the problem you seek to address? What pretest or baseline data can you use to evaluate your proposal's success?

promising that a goal will be met or a gap entirely eliminated by funding the proposal. You are suggesting that a measurable part of the gap will be closed by means of its prescribed actions, methods, and activities. You are not certain that your proposed approach will be entirely successful, but you believe it will benefit education by at least partially closing the gap and expanding knowledge of what works.

For instance, any project aiming to promote educationally responsible behavior in parents, teachers, and students is unlikely to close the gap entirely. Thus a grant proposal should suggest that the project will lessen, not eradicate, educationally responsible behavior in parents, teachers, and students.

When you ask your grantseekers what will change as a result of a project, some answers will have to do with knowledge and others with values and feelings. In the example just cited, some might specify outcomes in the area of cognition or knowledge, others in the area of attitudes and feelings. Because such issues are complex, suggest that your grantseekers ask for help from the college or university faculty members on their grants advisory group when constructing objectives.

Measurement Indicators

Just as there are many ways to accomplish objectives, there are several ways to measure change. Your grantseekers should begin by asking themselves what students will do differently after experiencing the methods aimed at solving the problem and how the change can be measured. Are there standardized tests or evaluation instruments for this purpose? If not, can a way of measuring the desired change be developed?

In the sample project to increase educationally responsible behavior in parents, teachers, and students, the reduction in the gap between what exists now and what ought to be can be measured in a variety of ways. For instance, we could look for behavior that indicates a developing sense of responsibility: improved grades, decreased absenteeism, higher percentage of students successfully completing their grade, more time spent on homework, more teacher-parent contacts, more parent-child talks about education, and less time spent watching television. We might even develop an Educational Responsibility Scale that contains questions aimed at surveying many of these points.

Performance Standards

A grantor will look at the objectives, note the size of the grant requested, examine the measurement indicators, and compare the amount of the request with the expected amount of change.

For a multiyear project, your grantseekers may want to create objectives stating a one-year goal for change and increase the amount of expected change over subsequent years. For example, in the educationally responsible behavior project, the objective could be to achieve a 25 percent increase in one year and a 40 percent increase by the end of year two.

Deadline

Most government grants are for one year because of the way the federal budget appropriation cycle operates. However, there is a movement in Washington to allow multiyear awards because it is difficult to demonstrate behavioral change in just twelve months. In addition, it often takes a good part of a year just to develop and conduct pretests that provide the baseline data for post-tests.

Thus far in our discussion, the objective of our sample project might be expressed like this:

To increase educationally responsible behavior in parents, students, and teachers in the XYZ Elementary School (action verb and statement) by 25 percent (performance standard) at the end of one year (deadline) and by 40 percent (performance standard) at the end of year two (deadline), as measured by the Educational Responsibility Scale (measurement indicator).

Cost Frame

Your grant developers should include the cost of accomplishing the change in the body of the objective. This will demonstrate that they have total command of their proposal. They know *what* they will measure, *how* they will measure it, *when* it will be accomplished, and *how much* it will cost. This provides a stark reminder of how much it costs to accomplish educational change. The one catch is that your grant developers cannot know the cost until they have completed their project planner. Now that they have a proper objective, they are ready to tackle this task. Caution them to use pencil when completing the project planner so that corrections and changes can be made easily.

Completing a Project Planner

The following general guidelines follow the format of the planner sample shown in Figure 7.1.

Objectives and Methods

In the column labeled A/B, list the project objectives and label each—for example, Objective A, Objective B, Objective C, and so on (if the grantor prefers another format for labeling objectives, use that instead). Under each, list the methods that will be used to accomplish each of the objectives. Think of the methods as the tasks or activities that will be used to meet the need. Label each method under its appropriate objective; for example, A-1, B-1, C-1, and so on.

Month

In column C/D, record the month each activity or task will begin and the month each will end. For example, writing 1/4 signals intent to begin the first month after receiving funding and carry out the activities over four months (sixteen weeks). If the expected start-up month is known, note it here.

Time

In column E, record the number of person hours, weeks, or months needed to accomplish each task listed in column A/B.

Project Personnel

In column F, list the names of key personnel who will spend a measurable or significant amount of time on each task or activity listed and on each objective. (The time has already been recorded in column E.)

Personnel Costs

In the next three columns, list salaries and wages (column G), fringe benefits (column H), and total compensation (column I) for each of the key personnel listed in column F.

Start by coming up with a rough job description by listing the activities each person will be responsible for and the minimum qualifications required. Determine whether each will be full- or part-time by looking at the number of hours, weeks, or months they will be needed. Then call a placement agency to get an estimate of the salary needed to fill the position.

Be sure to include services that will be donated. Put an asterisk next to all donated personnel and remember that these individuals' fringes as well as wages will be donated. Identifying donated personnel is crucial when matching or in-kind contributions are required, and may be advantageous even if not; matching contributions show good faith and make your schools seem a better investment. Indeed, put an asterisk by *anything* donated (such as supplies, equipment, materials) as you complete the remaining columns.

Consultants and Contract Services

In the next three columns, list the time (column J), cost per week (column K), and total cost (column L) of assistance to be provided by consultants and other contractors. These are individuals not in your normal employ who provide services not normally provided by someone in your district. (Note: No fringe benefits are paid to these.)

Nonpersonnel Resources: Supplies, Equipment, Materials

Use the next four columns to list the supplies, equipment, and materials needed to complete each activity and to itemize the associated costs. In column M list the items; in column N list the cost per item; in column O list the quantity of each item; and in column P list the total cost.

Do not underestimate the resources needed to achieve the objectives. Grantseekers should ask themselves and the project's key personnel what is needed to complete each activity. Again, designate donated items with an asterisk.

Subtotal Cost for Activity

Add columns I, L, and P—the totals of personnel costs, consultant and contract services, and nonpersonnel resources—and note the sum in column Q. Your grant developers can do this either for each activity or for each objective. If they do it for objectives, they will have to add the subtotals for all of the activities that fall under the objective.

Milestones and Progress Indicators

In column R, list what you will give the funding source to show them how the project personnel are working toward the objectives (such as a quarterly report). Think of these as milestones or progress indicators.

In column S, record the dates by which the funding source will receive the listed milestones or progress indicators.

Involving Corporate Volunteers

Corporate volunteers can be extremely helpful in preparing the Project Planner. They may have access to computer software that can develop a spreadsheet and a forecast of cash flow for your project. However, as your school's representative to the corporate world, you must be aware of the problems in communication that can occur when you involve corporate people in developing educational programs.

Many corporate staff have been exposed to business seminars on management by objectives, matrix management, total quality management, and the learning organization, to name a few. The management theory vocabulary, and that of the corporate world in general, is much different from that of the field of education. Hence, confusion can result when an educator and a corporate individual work together to develop goals or objectives. For example, in education, goals are long-range desires. They are normally part of a "guiding statement" and are therefore nonmeasurable and usually nonobtainable. In the corporate world, goals are daily steps taken to accomplish objectives—what an educator would call methods or activities. To make matters even more confusing, objectives in the corporate world are long-range and normally part of a guiding statement; in education they are what we want to accomplish and are measurable.

It is easy to imagine how this difference in understanding could extend to a proposal submitted for corporate funding. It would therefore be wise to ask one of your corporate volunteers to review the proposal prior to submission to ensure that the vocabulary is appropriate for a corporate funding source.

Project Planner Examples

One way to complete a project planner is shown in Figure 7.3. In this sample the project director's salary is being requested of the funder, as are the salaries of two graduate students who will assist the director. The services of the project director and the graduate students are being contracted from West State University. Therefore, their time commitments and costs fall in columns J, K, and L on the Project Planner.

The project director will ask West University's Human Subject Institutional Review Board to examine the procedures involved in getting the students, parents, and teachers to agree to write contracts for change. It is anticipated that she will work half-time on the project for twelve weeks during months one through six and full-time for twenty-four weeks during months seven through twelve.

This case shows considerable matching and in-kind contributions, as indicated by the asterisks. For example, the school district is donating the salary and fringe benefits of the project secretary. In addition, a significant portion of matching and in-kind contributions are coming from the Jones Corporation, which is donating the use of its corporate video production facility.

Although these contributions demonstrate frugality, commitment, and hard work, "overmatching" can become an issue. When a proposal has a huge matching component and requires only a small amount of grant funds, a prospective grantor may conclude that the *entire* proposal should be funded through matching and in-kind contributions. Still, most matching components are viewed favorably by grantors.

Grant writers sometimes create a second, more detailed project planner once they receive word that their proposal has been awarded. Figure

Figure 7.3

SAMPLE PROJECT PLANNER

PROJECT PLANNER

A Contract for Educational Cooperation - Parents, Teachers,
PROJECT TITLE: and Students Charting a Course for Involvement

A. List project objectives or outcomes A. B.
B. List methods to accomplish each objective as A-1, A-2, ... B-1, B-2 ...

Proposal Developed for: Project Director: Proposal Start Date   Proposal Year

Activity	Month Begin/End (C/D)	Time (E)	Project Personnel (F)	Salaries & Wages (G)	Fringe Benefits (H)	Total (I)	Time (J)	Cost/Week (K)	Total (L)	Item (M)	Cost/Item (N)	Quantity (O)	Tot cost (P)	Sub-Total Total I,L,P (Q)	Milestones Item (R)	Date (S)
Objective A: Increase educational cooperation of teachers, parents, and students 25% as measured on the Educational Practices Survey in 12 months at a cost of $88,630																
A-1 Develop the Responsible Educational Practices Survey with Advisory Committee	1/2	4	Proj Dir (PD) West Univ.				2	1000	2000	Computer			2500			
Advisory Committee																
a. Write questions and develop a scale of responsibility for parents, teachers, and students			Grad Stud (GS) West Univ.				2	500	1000	Printer			500			
A-2 Administer survey to the target population	2/3	4	2 GS West Univ.				4	500	2000							
a. Develop procedure		4	PD West Univ.				4	1000	4000							
b. Get human subjects approval through West University																
c. Administer survey		4	2 GS West Univ.				4	500	2000	Travel			700			
d. Input survey data		*4	Sec'y West Univ.	800	160	*960	1	1000	1000							
e. Analyze results		1	PD West Univ.				1	1000	1000							
A-3 Develop curriculum	3/6															
a. Review results of pretest given to parents, students, and teachers		1	PD West Univ.				1	1000	1000							
b. Develop a curriculum on responsibility concepts in education for each group (includes workbook and video on each area of curriculum)		5	PD West Univ.				5	1000	5000	Layout & print			1250			
		*8	Sec'y West Univ.	1600	320	*1920				Workbooks	10	200	2000*			
		8	Senior High Video Club - Using Jones							Blank tapes	2	20	40			
			Corp. Video Facility							Video studio	5000	5 hrs	25000*			
- Responsible use of time																
- Homework responsibility																
- Communication skills			PD							Camera edit						
										Character generation						
- Developing contract for change																
A-4 Promote and carry out program	6/12	24	PD West Univ.				24	1000	24000							
a. Use advisory group to announce program		24	Sec'y West Univ.	4800	960	*5760										
b. Public service spots on radio and television																
c. Develop and send home a program																
d. Schedule meetings with parents																
e. Develop a student video										Video camera	1000	6	6000*			
Total Direct Costs or Costs Requested From Funder						0			42000				4990	46990	53%	
Matching Funds, In-Kind Contributions, or Donated Costs						8640			0				33000	41640	47%	
Total Costs						8640			42000				37990	88630	100%	

©David G. Bauer Associates, Inc.
(800) 836-0732

7.4 shows how Activity A-4 from the previous example could be outlined in more detail. Naturally, cost estimates could also be developed for each of these more detailed activities. Keep in mind that some grantors may require such detail.

Using the Project Planner for Budgeting

It is best that you, the district grants administrator, review the Project Planner with the proposal creators to ensure that they have included all the elements necessary to develop a realistic budget and the success of the plan. With this in mind, several key areas need emphasis.

Budget Development and Negotiation

The budget, in whatever form it is requested, should reflect the Project Planner totals for personnel costs (column I), consultants and contract services (column L), and nonpersonnel resources such as supplies, equipment, and materials (column P). By pointing out the importance of subtotaling the costs for each activity in column Q of the Project Planner, you will be ready to help your grantseekers negotiate a grant award. Beginning to discuss the strategy for negotiating the budget while finishing the plan will enable you to set the stage for an accountable and defensible budget.

The negotiation itself, however, should not be based on the budget categories (personnel, consultants, supplies, and so on). Rather, it should be based on the methods or activities that make up the budget totals.

Review with your grantseekers the effect of reducing funds for each activity. What impact would it have on attaining the change indicated in the objective? You may be able to reduce the size of your request by eliminating an activity or two without having much effect on the project; however, if you eliminate too many activities you will probably not be able to accomplish your project as outlined. Instead, it may be preferable to modify the objective and reduce the amount of expected change or the number of students or participants the project will reach.

The district grants office must be involved in negotiating the final award and in altering the objectives and methods to arrive at the final budget. Overzealous grantseekers can become their own worst enemy. In their desire to please the grantor and their excitement over the grant, they want to appease and appear appreciative and congenial. But they may go too far; it might seem as though they would settle for any amount of funding. Without being given reason to think otherwise, the grantor may come to believe that the budget was not realistic to begin with.

Figure 7.4

SAMPLE PROJECT PLANNER

PROJECT PLANNER

PROJECT TITLE: A Contract for Educational Cooperation - Parents, Teachers, and Students Charting a Course for Involvement

Proposal Developed for: _____

Project Director: _____

Proposed Start Date: _____

Proposal Year _____

A. List project objectives or outcomes A. B. B. List methods to accomplish each objective as A-1, A-2, ... B-1, B-2, ...	MONTH TIME		TIME	PROJECT PERSONNEL	PERSONNEL COSTS				CONSULTANTS CONTRACT SERVICES				NON-PERSONNEL RESOURCES NEEDED SUPPLIES - EQUIPMENT - MATERIALS				SUB-TOTAL ACTIVITY COST	MILESTONES PROGRESS INDICATORS		
	Begin	End			Salaries & Wages	Fringe Benefits	Total		Time	Cost/Week	Total		Item	Cost/Item	Quantity	Tot cost	Total I,L,P	Item	Date	
	C/D		E	F	G	H	I		J	K	L		M	N	O	P	Q	R	S	

A-4 Promote and carry out the Responsible Education Partners program

a. Set up a meeting with elementary and junior high teachers to explain the project
   1. Get program on teachers' in-service agenda
   2. Distribute information packet
   3. Have a panel discussion, include representatives from the parents advisory group and the media
   4. Break into small groups to discuss and make recommendations

b. Invite local advertising council to take on program and develop public service announcements

c. Invite parents and students to participate in T.V. Busters as a lead activity
   1. Set up prizes by soliciting local industry to provide focus awards for students who complete a contract to not watch any television for 20 days (except news and educational T.V.)
   2. Send home examples of the responsible use of non-T.V. time
   3. Invite parents to develop a contract for responsible education that includes homework, school contact, and parental involvement

Total Direct Costs or Costs Requested From Funder

Matching Funds, In-Kind Contributions, or Donated Costs

Total Costs

% of Total   100%

©David G. Bauer Associates, Inc.
(800) 836-0732

A well-developed Project Planner and a sound budget counter this. Some grantseekers will try to convince you that a district grants administrator simply cannot understand their high-tech plan. Generally they are merely ill-prepared. When completed accurately, the Project Planner can help you understand the proposal and provide valuable assistance in the negotiation of the final award.

The credibility of the school district depends on the impression the grantor gets when negotiating the final award. Your office must be part of that process in order to administer the funds later.

Matching and In-Kind Contributions

The district grants administrator will be required to document any and all costs that have been designated as matching or in-kind contributions.

Each year more grantors are requiring that school districts demonstrate commitment to their projects through a system of contributions. As funding becomes more limited and competition increases, this practice will become even more common.

How does a school district that needs outside funding to accomplish its projects demonstrate that it has resources to donate to a grant? It might seem paradoxical, but try to look it from the funder's point of view: they want to see commitment!

To help document commitment, your grantseekers should consider the time their advisory group members have volunteered to the project. Can this be considered an in-kind contribution? Ask them to review their Project Planner. Are there any personnel costs or nonpersonnel resources that could be donated instead of requested from the funder? Finally, are there any hidden costs in their schools that could qualify as matching contributions? For example, I once worked on a grant proposal that called for developing an in-service course for teachers as a way of effecting change in the classroom. In seeking to meet the funding source's matching funds requirement, a school administrator revealed that under the teachers' contract the district was required to pay each educator a salary increase after completion of the course. We calculated the average age of the participating teachers and the total number of years that the increase would be paid out to all teachers, multiplied this figure by the salary increase, and were allowed to claim the resulting figure as a match.

I cannot guarantee what a grantor will accept as a matching or in-kind contribution, but be creative. Proposal developers should review their project and look for every possible matching contribution. If they have a grants advisory group, the members may volunteer some of the match by lending the use of facilities and donating equipment, printing, travel, and so on.

Cash Flow

As an administrator, you may or may not be praised for helping to develop the proposal, but you will surely be blamed if problems with cash flow arise. You can avoid trouble with cash flow by doing the following:

- Having a project plan that forecasts your cash requirements properly

- Making your school district aware of the cash forecast by pointing it out in the proposal sign-off process

By analyzing the Project Planner, your proposal developers gain the information necessary to determine their cash flow needs. Column C/D of the planner designates the beginning and the end of each activity, and column Q tells how much money will be required to accomplish each activity. By transferring this information to the Grants Office Time Line (Figure 7.5), your proposal developers will have a fairly accurate estimate of their cash flow needs. Some public and private grantors will accept cash forecasts as an adequate expenditure plan and will provide payment in advance, thus minimizing your district's cash investment.

Grants Office Time Line

The Grants Office Time Line is a visual representation of the proposal's time frame. It also shows an estimate of the cash required to stay on schedule.

From the Project Planner, transfer your activity number to column 1 of the Time Line. Then draw a line from the activity's projected start date to its completion date. For example, if the activity is to begin in the second month of the project and end in the fourth month, draw a line from 2 to 4.

On the far right of the line, write the total cost of the activity from column Q of the Project Planner.

Federal and many state funders require a quarterly cash forecast. In these cases, place the estimated cash forecast in the appropriate quarterly column at the bottom of the Time Line. Estimate the total cash needed for those activities that take place over several quarters or that require advance expenditure, such as equipment purchase.

Your proposal developers will benefit from a booklet on how to create a grant-winning plan. This booklet should include samples of completed project planners tailored to your district along with the federal budget pages that reflect the column totals from the project planners. The booklet should also include instructions on how your district grants office can help grantseekers obtain copies of funded proposals to serve as models.

The subsequent chapters help you move from the Project Planner spreadsheet to the written proposal.

Figure 7.5

GRANTS OFFICE TIME LINE

ACTIVITY NO.	1	2	3	4	5	6	7	8	9	10	11	12	TOTAL COST FOR ACTIVITY
	1st QUARTER			2nd QUARTER			3rd QUARTER			4th QUARTER			TOTAL

QUARTERLY FORECAST OF EXPENDITURES ▲

CHAPTER 7 ASSESSMENT TOOL

Rate how well your district grants office assists your proposal developers in the following areas.

1. **Assistance in developing a work plan and time frames**
   _____ nonexistent
   _____ inadequate
   _____ adequate
   _____ excellent

2. **Assistance in creating measurable objectives**
   _____ nonexistent
   _____ inadequate
   _____ adequate
   _____ excellent

3. **Assistance in developing methods, activities, and time frames**
   _____ nonexistent
   _____ inadequate
   _____ adequate
   _____ excellent

4. **Assistance in developing job descriptions**
   _____ nonexistent
   _____ inadequate
   _____ adequate
   _____ excellent

5. **Assistance in developing quarterly cash flows**
   _____ nonexistent
   _____ inadequate
   _____ adequate
   _____ excellent

6. **Assistance in negotiating final awards**
   _____ nonexistent
   _____ inadequate
   _____ adequate
   _____ excellent

Chapter 8

Creating Winning Corporate and Foundation Proposals

AS YOUR SCHOOL UNITS become more and more interested in pursuing grants from foundations and corporations, the district grants office will be asked more frequently for help in understanding private grantors and constructing foundation and corporate proposals.

These proposals are particularly difficult to construct because private grantors generally do not provide the guidelines, rules, and specificity that government funders do. The district grants office research system should strive to provide grant writers with as much information as possible on preferred proposal formats, but only a few private funders have format guidelines available in print or on a website.

Many reference books and information retrieval systems only state that personal contact with the funding source is prohibited and that grant requests must be made in writing—a letter proposal, letter of inquiry, concept paper, or simply a "letter."

With no more information than that, it is imperative that prospective grantees follow any instructions they *do* receive from the private funding source. For example, restrictions on the length of the letter proposal must be strictly adhered to.

The foundation and corporate grants marketplace is very different from the federal grants arena in other ways as well. As you may recall from Chapter Four, private grantors have few office workers, staff, or paid reviewers and lack well-developed proposal review procedures or predetermined scoring systems for proposal evaluation. Only a very few larger foundation and corporate grantors have a specified proposal format and use experts in the subject area to review proposals. In general, proposals submitted to them are read by board members or trustees, who have a limited amount of time to review the hundreds they receive. Nor are these decision makers usually experts in the fields of interest funded by the organization; few are professional reviewers. But they know what their foundation or corporation is looking for and answer only to their fellow trustees, board members, or stockholders. They prefer short proposals that can be read rapidly. This means your school's proposal must stimulate a prospective funding source's interest right from the beginning and be able to maintain it. The best way for your grantseekers to win the reader's respect is to demonstrate that they have purposefully singled out that particular grantor and have especially tailored their approach to the grantor's needs.

Grantors can sense immediately when one proposal has been "shotgunned" to a list of prospective funders. They know that they were lumped together with others and that their individual values and needs were ignored for the convenience of the grant writer. Considering the forethought and effort you and your grantseekers have invested in the proactive grants process, you definitely do not want your school to be guilty of this.

Remember that you are striving for a 50 percent success rate from your grants system. Foundation or corporate proposals must not, therefore, be direct-mail fund-raising pieces; the return on these is typically less than 1 percent. Foundations and corporations are one of your school's most prestigious groups of potential supporters. You must be sure that the proposal they see reflects your school's best effort rather than the most convenient or easiest solution for the grant writers.

When the funding source has proposal format guidelines, make sure your grantseekers follow them. When no guidelines are available, your grantseekers may use the following proposal format. In addition, you can provide your grantseekers with samples of proposal formats that have produced positive results.

The Letter Proposal

The most common type of proposal to a foundation or corporation takes the form of a letter on your school district's letterhead. If you have a school foundation, consider using its letterhead, especially if the grantor requests your IRS tax exemption status. Most private funders limit the length of letter proposals to two or three pages and do not allow attachments. These are the main components of a letter proposal:

1. An introductory paragraph stating the reason for writing

2. Paragraph explaining why the grantor was selected

3. Needs paragraph

4. Solution paragraph

5. Request-for-funds paragraph

6. Uniqueness paragraph

7. Closing paragraph

8. Signatures

9. Attachments (if allowed)

Have your proposal writers draft a letter proposal for your school's project. Encourage them to include all these components and to use data from their research and Project Planner. Remind them that their letter proposal should be tailored to the grantor's point of view and reflect any information they have on the funding source's preferred format. It is also important to remind your proposal developers that the proposal reader probably will not have a degree in education and therefore might not know or understand as much about the proposed project as they do.

Introduction

Mention in the introduction any linkages or contacts your school may have with the foundation or corporation. These include any of your school's key volunteers who have name recognition with the foundation or corporation or who are on the board of the funding source. Any contacts who have already talked to the foundation or corporation's board members or trustees on behalf of your school district should also be mentioned. But keep the focus on the grantor. Under no circumstances should your letter proposal begin with "We are writing to you because we need . . ." What you need is not the primary concern of grantors; they are concerned about what they value and need. Therefore, place the emphasis on them: "John Smith suggested I contact the Jones Foundation with an exciting project that deals with _____, an area in which our school and your board share a deep concern."

If your school does not have an established linkage or contact with the foundation or corporation, the proposal should start by explaining why your grantseekers selected that particular foundation or corporation to approach or how they knew it would be interested in the educational need addressed in your proposal.

Why the Grantor Was Selected

Your proposal developers should show that they have done their homework by demonstrating their knowledge of the grantor. For foundations, they should invest a few minutes reviewing the organization's IRS 990 PF tax return and analyzing and synthesizing the information. By compiling the statistics on past grants made to the field of education, they might discover an interesting fact or statistic that does not appear in any foundation resource publication. They could also cite a program previously funded by the foundation to demonstrate their familiarity with the foundation's granting pattern and history. For instance, if a foundation's tax return indicates that approximately 25 percent of its grants are related to children, your proposal developers could combine two years of data and say something like this:

> *My research indicates that in a recent two-year period, the Smith Foundation made _____ grants totaling over _____ dollars for projects focusing on children and their ability to successfully compete in our society. Your granting pattern has prompted us to submit to you this proposal for improving our students' competitive edge by enhancing our faculty's ability to involve parents in the education of children attending Neighborville Middle School.*

Corporate grants are more difficult to research than foundation grants because they are not recorded on publicly available records like the 990 IRS PF tax return. Information on corporate grantors will have to be gathered through linkages, preproposal contact, or company workers who have volunteered to assist your school. As competition for corporate grants increases, companies are focusing their support on those nonprofit organizations to which their workers donate their time and money. Corporate volunteer programs and programs such as "Dollars for Donors" try to increase contact with workers and to get them involved in volunteerism. Your grant developers may therefore want to mention volunteerism in the second paragraph: "Harry Higgs, chairperson of our volunteer group and a Jones Corporation employee, has stated that the Jones corporation places a high value on quality education for young people."

Whether you are approaching a foundation or a corporation, this section of your letter proposal should do the following:

- Inform the funder if its employees donate time to your school
- Show that your grantseekers did their homework and are aware of the funding source's giving patterns and priorities
- State your conviction that the grantor is special and has unique needs and interests
- Inspire the grantor to read on because your school has a special request that fits these needs and interests

Although the request for funds usually appears in a later part of the letter (usually along with the budget information), your proposal developers can mention it in this section if they choose. Placing it here avoids the problem of getting a grantor interested in your project only to disappoint them later if it turns out that the amount you request is too much for its grants budget. If your proposal developers decide to put your school's grant request in this section they should compare the amount you are asking for with one of the foundation's or corporation's past grants or with their average grant amount for that area of interest. For example: "It is because of your concern for _____ that we encourage you to consider a grant for $25,000."

The Need for Your Project

The need referred to here is not the proposal developers' need to get the project funded but rather the documented need that your program aims to reduce. However, your proposal developers should not describe your school's project in this section. Unfortunately, overzealous grantseekers have a tendency to jump right into a description of what they want to do. The project and solution should be presented after the funding source understands what the problem is and that it *must* be addressed irrespective of the specific project or grantee. Again, research on the grantor will help your proposal developers tailor the description of the need to them. Your proposal should seek to demonstrate that there is a gap between what exists and what ought to be for your school, community, students, and so on. The more your grantseekers know about the funder's values and perspectives, the better they will be able to document the need. The needs section must do the following:

- Be motivating and compelling so that it captures and maintains the funder's interest

- Demonstrate that your grantseekers have a command of the literature and are aware of the pertinent studies concerning the problem

- Appeal to the perspective and interests of the grantor

Have your proposal developers review their research concerning the granting pattern of the foundation or corporation. Being aware of the types of projects the grantor has funded in the past and where the projects were implemented provides valuable insight and enables your grantseekers to tailor the data presented in the needs section. Federal and state grantors and their paid staff and reviewers expect such material as statistics, literature searches, research references, and quotes, but foundation and corporate readers may be more motivated by the human element, although they too will expect the proposal to reflect a command of the facts. The best avenue to take with a foundation or corporation may be to present a fact-filled story or case study to help them see the problem. The following is an example:

National studies have demonstrated that children watch television an average of _____ hours per day. A survey of the fourth graders at ABC Elementary School showed that their television viewing surpassed the national average by 20 percent. One possible cause of this disparity could be that the children from ABC Elementary School spend more time alone than many children. One fourth-grader surveyed said, "I ride a bus for one hour to get home after school. I'm lonely and tired and my mom doesn't get home until late, so TV is my friend—and a lot better friend than my brother! People who say TV is violent have never lived with my brother."

It is important that your proposal developers determine what type of needs documentation best motivates the prospective grantor. Does the funding source's distribution of past grants demonstrate any specific geographic preferences? What types of grantees have been supported in the past? Can this information help your proposal developers select the right data, studies, or examples to document the need?

When approaching corporate funders, have your proposal developers focus on the corporation's areas of concern and on the locations of company plants or centers of operation. How can the problem addressed in your school's proposal affect the corporation's marketplace and products? You will find that corporations are normally concerned with the education of their future employees, who may well be their employees' children.

Solution

This section of the letter proposal is often difficult to construct because of the limited space available. The previous paragraphs focus on the grantor. If your grantseekers were fortunate enough to make preproposal contact with the funding source to discuss two or three possible solutions to the problem, you can be more confident in choosing one specific approach. But even when your proposal developers have limited insight into which solution the grantor might favor, they still must choose one approach and present it in this paragraph.

Naturally, your grant writers have much more information on the proposed solution than they can fit into a few short paragraphs. The challenge is to decide what information to include and what to exclude. Typically, proposal writers describe the solution in such great detail that they confuse rather than enlighten. This is another area where the administrator can step in. By playing a supportive role, the administrator can help the proposal writers maintain the proper perspective and recognize when they are providing too many details as well as when the proposal's conceptual framework is weak.

The object of this section is to give the prospective grantor a basic understanding of the solution your grant writers have chosen to meet the needs they have outlined. To do this, your proposal developers should try to think like the grantor. Ask them to keep in mind the qualities they would want to see in the solution if they were on the foundation or corporate board.

The Project Planner (see Chapter Seven) can help your grant writers keep the project summary short. If possible, include the Project Planner they have developed as an attachment. If attachments are not allowed, include the Project Planner as page two of a three-page letter proposal. It will clearly demonstrate to the funder the relationship between your project's activities or methods and its success. The Project Planner is also an excellent basis for the budget section or paragraph, particularly when you consider that it can summarize five or more pages of narrative on one spreadsheet! If your grant writers do not want to develop a project planner, remind them that a spreadsheet will be viewed very positively by the businessperson reading the proposal.

Whether or not a project planner is included, the plan or solution must appear interesting, plausible, affordable, and well organized. The objectives should be summarized in such a manner that the funder can envision how funding your school's proposal will shrink the gap between what is and what ought to be.

The letter proposal must focus on one solution—the one that has the greatest chance of matching the values of the prospective grantor. If your grant writers have done their homework, they know what the grantor values and will have described a need that the grantor will agree is important. By this point in the proposal the prospective grantor should believe that it is essential that the gap be closed (indicating commitment) and closed now (indicating urgency) and that to put off funding the proposal will only result in a larger gap later. Readers should feel that they cannot put your school's proposal down until they have read your suggested solution.

The grantor will likely agree that the need your grant writers have described exists, but may disagree with the solution. Even if your grantseekers did their homework, funding sources may have values, feelings, or prejudices that remain hidden. Thus prospective grantors could say any or all of the following:

- That they do not think your solution will work
- That they have already funded a grant that tried the same solution
- That other applicants have better or more interesting solutions

Assuming that by this point the grantor is still interested in the potential benefits of your solution, he or she will move on to the next item in your letter proposal.

Request for Funds

Grantors have limited funds and can finance only a fraction of the proposals they receive. Estimates are that private funders grant only 10 percent of the requests made to them. Ultimately they must judge which proposals produce what benefits for how many in the population or field they are concerned about.

Your school's letter proposal should clearly state the amount of grant funds being requested. If appropriate, have your proposal writers divide the cost of the project by the number of individuals it will serve. This will provide an estimate of the cost per person served. Remember that your school's project will have a "roll-out" or future benefit because each student served will go through life with more skills, better job opportunities, and so on. If your school's proposal deals with parent or teacher training, have your proposal writers roll out the project's benefits to the number of individuals these trained people will come in contact with. When they are describing facilities, have them identify how many students will use the facility over its lifetime. For example: "X number of families will utilize the Middlesex Recreational Facility for Y hours over a ten-year period."

When requesting equipment or technology, divide the cost by individuals served and what the skills they learn are worth over an entire lifetime. Depending on your situation, the cost per person served could be only pennies per hour.

Multiple Funders

If the project requires funding from more than one source, the letter proposal must state the amount requested from each prospective grantor. Thus the request-for-funds section should inform the grantor that your school will be seeking additional grant funds from other corporations or foundations. Your proposal writers should avoid saying, for example, that they *hope* to get funded by the Smith Corporation, the Jones Foundation, and so on. Instead, they should state the exact number of other grantors being approached, the grantors who have agreed to fund the project, the total amount already granted, and the amount outstanding.

For jointly funded projects it is crucial that the grantor know that your proposal is being tailored to each prospective funding source and that your grantseekers have done their homework. Some grantors may be justifiably concerned that their part of the project will be overshadowed by the other grantors or that they will not receive appropriate credit. To ensure that the grantors realize how critical their roles are, a colored highlighter can be used to visually separate each grantor's part of the total project on the Project Planner. By referring to this spreadsheet each grantor will see how integral its contribution is to the success of the whole plan.

Matching Costs and In-Kind Contributions

Required matching costs and in-kind contributions are usually associated with federal grantors, but some foundation and corporate grantors also require that a portion of a project's costs be borne by the grantee. How the district office secures and documents matching or in-kind contributions is particularly important but providing a voluntary match will look good to any funder. Even if a matching or in-kind contribution is not required, you, as an administrator, may still want to include a documented contribution to demonstrate both your and your school district's dedication to the project, because private grantors want to be sure that the organizations they fund are committed to supporting their projects after grant funds are depleted. By demonstrating your school's commitment in advance through a matching or in-kind contribution, you show that you have not applied for the grantor's money without carefully analyzing your own commitment. Matching and in-kind contributions should be designated on your Project Planner with an asterisk. The total should be placed at the bottom of the Project Planner in the column headed "Matching Funds, In-Kind Contributions, or Donated Costs."

What to Do if the Grantor Requests a Budget

Most foundations do not require submission of a formal budget with the letter proposal. Only a few hundred will request that a specific budget format be used.

If your proposal writers have developed a project planner, preparing the budget is a simple task. For a letter proposal budget, they should provide a summary of the major line items on the Project Planner and inform the grantor that more detailed budget information is available upon request.

If no budget format is specified, your proposal developers should present the budget in a paragraph or block form, using a minimum of space and short columns rather than long ones. Here is an example:

We are requesting a grant of $20,000 from the Smith Foundation. To demonstrate our school's support of this important project we will provide $8,000 in matching support. A detailed budget is available upon request.

	Request	Match	Total
Salaries & Wages	$10,000		$10,000
Stipends/Teachers In-Service		7,000	7,000
Consultants/Evaluation	3,000		3,000
Computer Equipment/Software	7,000		7,000
Printing/Materials		1,000	1,000
TOTAL	$20,000	$8,000	$28,000

Uniqueness

Why should your district, school, classroom, or consortium get a grant rather than some other? Because funding sources will debate this issue anyway, why not address the subject first? Couldn't another school successfully initiate the methods and carry out the proposed project? Your proposal writers need a person with a broader perspective to help them develop the answers to these questions. They need you, the administrator, to play the role of cheerleader.

First, their school developed the project idea. Second, your proposal writers documented the school's need. In other words, the opportunity to act is where you are. And third, your project idea was developed with the help of experts in curriculum development, evaluation, and so on. You arranged for their input, gathered them together, and worked with them. In short, your school has already invested many, many hours developing a project that will be a successful model.

But in addition to these strong and valid reasons, you still need to examine more closely why their school deserves the funds necessary to implement the proposed solution. Brainstorm with your proposal writers the qualities that can convince the grantor that their school is indeed the best one to fund. For instance, in addition to superior facilities, you may also have unique individuals whose commitment and expertise make your school the funding source's most logical choice. It is extremely helpful when the administrator or superintendent singles out the commitment of the project director or other key personnel in the body of the proposal. For example, "Jane Doe is slated to direct the project. Ms. Doe has been recognized as an outstanding educator by the State Department of Education and has over twelve years of experience in classroom teaching." The district grants office is the best place to make this kind of input, as it coordinates the sign-off process.

The uniqueness paragraph can also outline the ways that your district's structure will help implement the proposal and, equally important, how the relationship between school and district will work to ensure continuation of the project after the grant ends. With the changes in site-based management, more grantors are becoming aware of the emerging role of the building or community-school principal and will be happy to view the district grants office as the administrative body responsible for ensuring coordination. In addition, grantors are interested in the unique relationship between schools and their districts and in how communities are involved in setting their schools' goals and objectives. The uniqueness paragraph or section provides the opportunity to explain these functions.

Closing Paragraph

In the closing paragraph your proposal writers should reaffirm the school and district's commitment to the project and invite the funder to work with them to achieve the project's goals. They should also reaffirm their willingness to provide the funding source with any additional materials necessary to make the grant decision. The grantor should be invited to visit your school to observe both the need and the unique qualities that your staff and volunteers bring to the project.

A decision needs to be made about whose name and phone number should be included in this paragraph. Most grant writers want to include theirs but may not be available to take calls during the day. And as the superintendent or another district official often signs the proposal, grantors sometimes try to contact them with questions—questions they may not be prepared to answer. To anticipate problems that could arise as a result of grantor contact, place your district grants office phone number in this paragraph, providing that your office's quality control system is good. If need be, your office can arrange a conference call that includes the proposal writer.

Another technique that has proven worthwhile is to keep your district administrator aware of all pending proposals. The district administrator should be aware of who the proposal writer is, his or her phone number, and the total amount requested. In one school I worked at, I taped the list of pending proposals on the pull-out writing wing of the superintendent's desk, along with a reminder to the secretary to forward all calls to my office when the superintendent was unavailable.

The final paragraph might include something like this: "Please contact myself or Jane Doe, the project director, at 555-358-4501 with questions about this proposal."

Signatures

Taking the grantor's point of view into consideration, whose signature from your district will have the strongest impact on the funding decision? The general rule is that the letter proposal should be signed by the highest-ranking individual in the school system—in most cases, the superintendent. Some schools require the signature of an assistant superintendent for instruction, a business officer, or a curriculum specialist. Proposals can be submitted with two signatures, those of the president of the school board and a top-ranking school administrator. It may be appropriate to have two signatures for proposals that require special cooperation, collaboration, or coordination. For example, a consortium proposal between several districts or other nonprofit organizations may have the signatures of all the cooperating parties to demonstrate that the collaboration is real.

Unlike foundation and corporate proposals, a federal application may call for a school board resolution that is documented by the inclusion of a signed copy of the board minutes. Even though private grantors do not require this, they may nevertheless respond favorably to a statement that the school/community and the district have passed a resolution to apply to their foundation or corporation.

Attachments

Most foundations and corporations do not allow or encourage attachments. Attachments may help answer questions that arise during the reading of a proposal, but the problems they create for understaffed foundations and corporations often preclude their inclusion.

What about pictures, videotapes, audiotapes, and slides? It seems that in this age of electronics, these components would be not only allowed but encouraged. During preproposal contact, electronic tools may be highly effective in helping the grantor see the problem. However, it may be inappropriate to include them with the proposal. Remember, not all reviewers have access to playback equipment. The bottom line is to find out what is allowed before submitting the proposal. You can include your school's website address to increase their knowledge about your school, or your e-mail address for questions.

Internal Revenue Service Designation

Most foundation grantors request that you include a copy of your IRS designation as a charitable nonprofit organization. A simple statement that you are a nonprofit is usually not enough. Some foundations have in their bylaws that they do not fund organizations that have not received 501(c)(3) status or equivalent tax identification number.

Most school foundations, many Parent-Teacher Organizations and Associations, and even some school booster clubs have the necessary IRS designation. If you cannot locate one of these groups that will let you use its IRS designation, try the following:

- Consider starting a school foundation.

- Check with other nonprofits in your area whose mission is to benefit children, youth, or education (for example, 4-H, Campfire, Boys and Girls Club).

- Contact your Chamber of Commerce to see if it knows of an education-related 501(c)(3) organization that handles corporate educational contributions.

- Call the United Way and ask if it would be willing to handle the grant money for your school and allow you to use its foundation status.

- Find out if your area has a community foundation that might be willing to handle your grant.

Foundations in some states are joining together to support a common format for applications for grants. New Jersey has moved ahead on this idea, but it is unlikely to catch on rapidly. If your grantseekers follow the guidelines found in the various resource books, make preproposal contact when allowed, and expand their school's informal linkage with funding sources, they can be fairly certain that their proposal's format will be acceptable to their prospective grantor.

Two sample letter proposals, one to a foundation (Figure 8.1) and one to a corporation (Figure 8.2), have been included for your review.

Evaluating the Letter Proposal

The formula for consistent grants success with private grantors has one more element—evaluation. To ensure the integrity of your district grants office and the school district, all proposals should undergo a mock review that mirrors the one that the grantor will perform.

Organizing a Proposal Improvement Group

Invite four or five individuals to form a group that will take part in an activity aimed at improving proposals submitted by the schools in your district. Sometimes called a mock review, this follows the basic concepts of quality circles and total quality management, where employees volunteer to commit their personal time to improving their company's products and services. Encourage the most talented individuals from your district's communities to participate, including parents, students, educators, foundation and corporate board members, and anyone else you would like to involve in your district's proposal-development process. (Including a

Figure 8.1

SAMPLE LETTER PROPOSAL TO A FOUNDATION

Ms. Elaine Finsterwald, Trustee
Smith Foundation
123 Money Place
Clotin, NC 28699

Dear Ms. Finsterwald:

The Smith Foundation is synonymous with the word *children*. Since 1927, your grants have provided creative solutions to the needs of young people in Jonesboro and our state. Your recent annual report highlights your commitment to children's early school years and to family involvement and responsibility in education. The $1.5 million in grants you have awarded over the past three years to strengthen children and their families clearly demonstrates your dedication and concern.

[You could mention previous support to your school district or the number of children who have been touched by any past support. For example, "Your grant to renovate an elementary classroom into the Smith Computer Lab has directly touched the lives of over 5,000 students in four years. Scores on standardized tests have improved 40 percent." If the Smith Foundation has not funded elementary or middle school education directly, show how their support for your school-based project relates to their interest in programs related to the welfare of children, improving family life, parental responsibility and involvement, and so on.]

Previous generations have progressed through our schools with the involvement and encouragement of teachers and parents. Today, classroom leaders lack much of the support they used to get from parents and must compete with television and video games for a child's time and attention.

How much time do children spend watching television versus doing homework? A study of 25,000 middle school children conducted by the Department of Education reported 21.4 hours per week of television versus 5.6 hours of homework. When asked if parents placed limits on television, two-thirds of the parents surveyed said yes, while two-thirds of the children said no. These results suggest that some parents may have a problem setting priorities for their children.

Other results of the study point to the deterioration of parental responsibility and involvement in educational activities. For instance, four out of five parents surveyed reported that they regularly discuss schoolwork with their children, while two out of three children said parents rarely or never discuss schoolwork with them. Apparently the breakdown in communication between parents and children is at crisis proportions.

The need exists to develop and implement programs that encourage parents to become involved in their children's education. This means more than just visiting the school. For example, the Department of Education study also showed that 50 percent of parents had visited their child's school for meetings, but only 33 percent had visited their child's classroom.

What happens when parents take responsibility for working with their children and their children's school?

- Students whose parents discuss schoolwork with them get higher grades.
- Restrictions on television viewing tend to boost grades.

While some adults may think that the way to improve education is to increase funding for schools, taxpayers in Harrison, Arkansas, do not. While national test scores for students in Harrison rank in the

Figure 8.1 (continued)

top 10 percent of the country, Harrison ranks 272d out of Arkansas' 327 school districts in education taxes. The key is parental involvement. Almost 100 parents volunteer for one hour a week at each of the town's elementary schools, and parents and teachers meet each year to establish education goals for the next year.

What can we do in Jonesboro to promote the sharing of responsibility for education among schools, parents, and children? Teachers, parents, and students at the Jonesboro Elementary School have developed a program entitled Responsibility in Education through Academic Partners (REAP). The REAP program is aimed at increasing responsible educational behavior and encouraging parental involvement in the classroom and at home. Teachers will actually work with parents and students to develop tailored, individual contracts to produce increases in all levels of education and the quality of all coursework.

The attached Project Planner outlines each objective and the activities that will foster the changes we desire. From increasing test scores to promoting public and volunteer service, the Jonesboro Elementary School will provide the catalyst through the education and involvement of parents in their children's responsible use of "out-of-school" time. The project is not limited to decreasing television viewing, but "TV Busters" are included in the plan.

We are requesting a grant from the Smith Foundation for $20,000 to initiate this project. Based upon our preliminary work with the teachers and Parent Advisory Committee of Jonesboro Elementary School, we anticipate the involvement of 600 students, 360 parents, and 40 teachers. Your grant funds will represent an investment of $20.00 per person served for the first year of the project. Future funding needs will be significantly less once the materials have been developed under your grant award. Our School District will provide $6,000 of in-kind contributions to support the project.

The Jonesboro Elementary School is fortunate to have Renee Weathers as the project director. Ms. Weathers was named the "Outstanding Teacher of the Year" by the North Carolina State Education Department. She will be assisted by the Parents Advisory Committee, chaired by Sam Price. The Committee is supported by a group of 52 parents, who have already volunteered 200 hours to develop the REAP program and this proposal.

We believe that you REAP what you sow in life, and we invite you to "sow with us" by supporting Responsibility in Education through Academic Partners.

Jonesboro Elementary School's tax exempt status is _____ , and our tax exempt number is _____ . Renee Weathers is available at 200-861-4000 to answer your questions and to provide additional information that will help you arrive at your funding decision.

Sincerely,

Attachment

Figure 8.2

SAMPLE LETTER PROPOSAL TO A CORPORATION

Clyde L. Baker
Contributions Officer
Widget Corporation
4321 Commercial Park
Rocker, NY 14570

Dear Mr. Baker:

John Allen, your marketing manager, advised me to contact you for consideration of a grant from Widget Corporation. John, who has volunteered over 100 hours to our Parents Advisory Committee, has told us of your company's interest in and efforts to promote responsible behavior in your employees and their families. It is with this common interest in mind that Casper Schools request a grant of $20,000 from the Widget Corporation for the Responsibility in Education through Academic Partners Program (REAP).

John Allen has been instrumental in guiding our schools' curriculum group toward understanding the changes technological advances have brought to Widget Corporation and how these changes influence what types of employees and skills your corporation will require in the future.

Technological advances have also brought changes to the family. Everything from health to educational achievement to parent/child communication has been affected by television, videos, and computer games.

We have learned in education that what children devote their time to determines the skills they develop. Unfortunately, our children are devoting an inordinate amount of time to television and computer games. A study of 25,000 middle school children conducted by the Department of Education revealed that the children surveyed spent an average of 5.6 hours per week on homework and 21.4 hours per week watching television. In addition, when asked if parents placed limits on television, two-thirds of the parents surveyed said yes, while two-thirds of the children said no.

We are not suggesting that television viewing is inherently bad. However, the amount of television children watch is one possible indication of the responsibility parents take for their children's "out-of-school" time and ultimately for their education.

A parent's responsible involvement in his or her child's education can also be evaluated by the time spent discussing schoolwork within the family and the type or quality of parental contact with the child's school. The Department of Education's study revealed some disturbing facts in these areas as well.

- Four out of five parents surveyed reported that they regularly discussed schoolwork with their children, while two out of three children said they rarely or never discussed schoolwork with their parents.
- Fifty percent of the parents surveyed reported visiting their child's school for meetings, while only 33 percent had visited their child's classroom.

When you compare what can result from parental involvement and responsibility in education with what can result from a lack of parental involvement and responsibility in education, the problem is clear and the goal evident. Students whose parents discuss schoolwork with them get higher grades, and restrictions on television viewing tend to boost grades.

What can be done? This is the question that brought John Allen and over 100 other parents together to prepare a plan for action. The program they developed is entitled Responsibility in Education through Academic Partners (REAP).

Figure 8.2 (continued)

REAP seeks to involve parents, students, and teachers in generating a monthly educational contract for change. Each signed contract is individually tailored and aimed at developing realistic and responsible educational behavior. Each contract outlines a plan to utilize "out-of-school" time more effectively.

The objectives of the project and the activities aimed at bringing about the desired changes are outlined on the enclosed Project Planner spreadsheet. The activities deal with involving parents and students in setting outcomes for education and presenting alternatives such as "TV Busters," a program initiated by a Minnesota teacher, to help kids break the television habit.

Developing the materials and initiating the program generate the project's major costs. Once established, REAP's volunteers and teachers will keep the program going. What is required now is a grant of $20,000 from Widget Corporation.

The Widget Corporation's support will directly affect the lives and education of 600 students, 360 parents, and 40 educators. Over a four-year period, this one-time grant represents an investment of $5.00 per person served. In fact, since the children that participate in the program will learn what can result from a responsible parental role in education, the benefits will accrue over many, many years.

The Widget Corporation's support will be recognized in the REAP program's informational brochure, and space will be set aside on the brochure's inside cover for a statement from Widget Corporation.

Alice Jones has been selected as the project director. She is eminently qualified and has worked with parents in this region for over twenty-five years. As a sign of commitment, the school district has agreed to provide support services valued at $6,000.

The volunteers have done all they can do. The time is right. Please join with us in sowing the seeds for responsible, parental involvement in education.

Money alone does not ensure a great education. Responsible commitment does. In Harrison, Arkansas, national test scores rank among the top 10 percent in the country, while education taxes rank 272d out of Arkansas' 327 school districts. What's the key? Parental involvement. Approximately 100 parents volunteer one hour per week at each of the town's elementary schools, and parents and teachers work together each year to determine the following year's educational goals.

This project is truly an investment in our community. Alice Jones is ready to provide any additional information you may need to make your funding decision. Please call her at 321-987-0645. Our schools' tax exempt status is _____ and our tax exempt number is _____ .

Sincerely,

---

foundation or corporate board member can provide valuable insight into the private grants review and decision-making process.)

By inviting a variety of individuals to take part *voluntarily,* you are facilitating a positive grants atmosphere that reinforces the commitment that your grant developers have demonstrated. Once volunteers realize how easy it is to develop a quality proposal, they will become valuable resources for your district's grants program and take responsibility for developing their own proposals.

It is much easier (and possibly more enjoyable) to perform a mock review for foundation and corporate proposals than for federal grant applications (see Chapter Ten). One reason is that it is fun to role-play being wealthy foundation or corporate board members. (Only community foundations actively recruit board members that reflect the economic and racial diversity of the geographic area they fund.) Also, it takes less time to read and comment on a letter proposal than a lengthy federal proposal.

Use the sample letter in Figure 8.3 as the basis for your invitation to participate in one of your school's proposal-improvement groups. Basically, you ask individuals to take part in a mock review of a proposal. The volunteers will role-play actual funders and carry out the mock-review process as closely as possible to the real review. They will be relieved to learn that the purpose of the quality-improvement exercise is not to get *their* opinions of the proposal but rather to get their impressions of how the proposal will look to the proposed funder.

In most cases, the group members will spend only five to ten minutes reviewing the proposal. The entire evaluation process will be completed in less than one hour. If the proposal is being submitted to one of the few large foundations that use a longer format and have experts review proposals, you may ask your volunteers to review, comment on, and score the proposal before they meet as a group. Even most large foundations use a format similar to the letter proposal. Whether the foundation allows five

---

Figure 8.3

INVITATION TO PARTICIPATE IN FOUNDATION/CORPORATE PROPOSAL IMPROVEMENT GROUP

Date

Name
Address

Dear _____:

    I would like to take this opportunity to follow up on our conversation to secure your input in assisting our school district in submitting the very best grant proposal possible. We are asking that you review the enclosed proposal from the point of view of a reviewer. The attached materials have been designed to assist you in role-playing the actual manner in which this proposal will be evaluated.

    Please read the information on the reviewers' backgrounds and the scoring system, and limit the time you spend reading the proposal to the time constraints that the real reviewers will observe. The Quality Circle Scoring Worksheet has been provided to help you in recording your scores and comments.

    A meeting of all the mock reviewers comprising our quality circle has been scheduled for [date]. Please bring this worksheet with you to the meeting. The meeting will last less than one hour. Its purpose is to analyze the scores and brainstorm suggestions to improve the proposal.

Sincerely,
Name
Phone Number

pages or ten, the best way to get information on the actual review process is to request it during preproposal contact.

The Proposal Improvement Scoring Worksheet

Complete the first half of this worksheet (Figure 8.4) before your group meeting. Give a copy of the worksheet to each member of the group. The grants administrator or the individual selected to represent your administration should provide the worksheets, set up the meeting, and facilitate the mock-review process.

Figure 8.4

FOUNDATION/CORPORATE PROPOSAL IMPROVEMENT SCORING WORKSHEET

The following information is being provided to help you review the attached foundation/corporate grant application/proposal.

The proposal will be read by:

_____ Funding official   _____ Board members

_____ Funding staff   _____ Other _____

_____ Review committee

Amount of time spent reviewing each proposal:

_____

_____

_____

Socioeconomic background of reviewer(s):

_____

_____

_____

Known biases or viewpoints:

_____

_____

_____

Positive points	**Rank order**
_____	_____
_____	_____

Negative points	**Rank order**
_____	_____
_____	_____

Other comments/suggestions for improvement:

_____

_____

The first half of the worksheet distributed to group members should contain the following information:

- Who reads the proposals
- What is known about their background
- How much time is devoted to reviewing each proposal
- What scoring system or criteria are used for evaluation

Unfortunately, in most cases you will not have much information to record. Remember, private grantors are not required to provide information on their review process. Usually the board members simply read proposals quickly and ask their fellow board members what looks good to them.

How can you help your grantseekers obtain background information on private funding officials? Much valuable information can be found in resource books such as *Who's Who* and *Standard and Poor's Register of Directors and Executives*. There are also regional and even local editions of books that describe wealthy and influential individuals. The printed rosters of many membership groups and service clubs may include valuable background information that will give your grantseekers insight into their members. Provide your group with brief biographies on the funding source's board members, or at least basic information such as ages and educational backgrounds. As your proposals will be based on educational principles, information on the reviewers' backgrounds will help your mock reviewers evaluate the appropriateness of the vocabulary in the proposal.

Also, give the volunteers a description of the funding source and any information you have on the types of proposals they have funded in the past, the number of projects they have funded, and the amount of each grant. If the grantor is a foundation, a copy of its tax return is also helpful. At the start of the meeting, review all the information to be sure the group develops an appropriate impression of the funding source's point of view.

If you are unable to find out the amount of time the grantor is likely to spend reading each proposal, limit the group's time to five minutes.

Instruct your volunteers to read the proposal quickly and to make believe that they have read many such proposals and still have a large stack to review. Ask them to designate any areas that they think would appeal to the grantor with a plus sign and any areas that need improvement with a minus sign.

At the conclusion of the reading time, you can play a very useful role as the group facilitator and recorder, if you believe your volunteers will speak openly in front of you. Or ask a volunteer to record and facilitate.

Instruct the recorder to list the positive points on the worksheet (ask him or her to print instead of write). There is no need for consensus on the ideas listed. The participants may then hold a brief discussion about the positive points, after which they should rank them. Again, the rank should reflect the grantor's perspective, not the mock reviewers'. The mock reviewers should repeat this procedure for the negative areas. The participants should then suggest improvements for any area they think may be viewed negatively by the grantor. If an area of the proposal is unclear, it should be listed as a problem area to be improved.

Do not allow the proposal developers to take part in the mock-review activity. After all, they will not be present to answer questions or offer explanations for the real reviewers. In addition, the proposal developers' presence may prevent the reviewers from offering a frank evaluation of the proposal for fear of hurting the writers' feelings.

The group recorder will provide you with the rankings of positive and negative areas so that you will know how strongly the mock reviewers felt about specific parts of the proposal. This information, plus the group's list of suggestions for improvement, will help the developers rewrite portions of their proposal and put the finishing touches on the final version.

Review the rewritten proposal to be certain that the proposal developers have not overreacted to the criticisms at the expense of the positive areas. Many developers are so sensitive to criticism that, in their zeal to fix the proposal, they place all their energy in the areas to improve; cutting the positive areas to give themselves more space to improve negative ones. The district grants administrator can help avoid this problem by keeping the proposal developers focused on the values and perspective of the funder and by promoting a balance between maintaining the strengths of a proposal while improving the weaknesses.

Submitting the Proposal

Research should have given you the deadlines for proposal submittal. If possible, validate the deadlines through preproposal contact with the grantor. If there are no specific deadlines, try to determine what time of the year your grantseekers' proposal would receive the most favorable review and have the greatest chance of being funded. Many foundations and corporations state that proposals are read periodically, or "as needed." Remind your proposal writers that "as needed" does not mean when *they* need the money or want to start the project. Foundations and corporations do not respond to the constraints of their grantees; they expect the reverse. One corporate foundation typical of many makes its grants decisions in the summer for the next calendar year. So plan ahead!

While you are planning ahead, remind your proposal writers that if there is a deadline, their proposal should be submitted slightly in advance of it. Getting theirs in early eliminates the need for special delivery or express mail service. (But consider using it anyway; it is relatively inexpensive and provides a signed assurance that the proposal was safely delivered.) Also, review the exact wording of the funding source's instructions for submitting proposals. Does the grantor demand that it be *received* by a certain date or *mailed* by then? Many request the former.

As grants administrator, you should initiate an early discussion of deadlines to encourage your proposal writers to aim for an early submittal. This will allow time for a mock review of the proposal, which will increase its chances of being funded. By emphasizing the importance of the mock review and early submittal, you dramatically increase the likelihood that these are carried out. Naturally, it is to everyone's benefit to submit a proposal that reflects your proposal writers' best efforts and is a credit to your district and their school.

A grants office booklet on how to write and evaluate foundation and corporate proposals is an excellent vehicle for promoting awareness and improving the foundation and corporate proposal–development skills of your grantseekers. This booklet should be tailored to your district and could include as examples parts of foundation and corporate proposals that your district has had funded. The booklet should also include instructions for developing proposal-improvement groups at individual school units, unless your grants office plans to carry out all mock reviews and assist in the rewriting of proposals after comments from the mock-review process are discussed with the proposal developers.

CHAPTER 8 ASSESSMENT TOOL

Put a check mark next to the services and educational aids that your district grants office provides to your grantseekers to help them prepare foundation and corporate proposals. For the services and aids provided, indicate how often they are provided (sometimes or always) and whether the quality of the services and aids is poor, good, or excellent.

Put an asterisk (*) next to those services and aids you do not currently provide but would like to in the future.

Assistance in tailoring proposals to the particular values of the potential funding source

_____ sometimes   _____ always   _____ poor   _____ good   _____ excellent

Guidelines on how to construct a letter proposal

_____ sometimes   _____ always   _____ poor   _____ good   _____ excellent

Samples of funded proposals

_____ sometimes   _____ always   _____ poor   _____ good   _____ excellent

Assistance your office provides in the proposal-improvement process:

Instructions on how to organize a proposal-improvement group

_____ sometimes   _____ always   _____ poor   _____ good   _____ excellent

Coordination of the process (e.g., contacts the group participants and sets up the meeting locations, dates, times, refreshments, and so on)

_____ sometimes   _____ always   _____ poor   _____ good   _____ excellent

Provides the proposal improvement group with research on the grantor (e.g., completed proposal improvement scoring worksheets, brief biographies of board members, and so on)

_____ sometimes   _____ always   _____ poor   _____ good   _____ excellent

Provides a trained coordinator to act as the group's facilitator

_____ sometimes   _____ always   _____ poor   _____ good   _____ excellent

Helps proposal developers rewrite proposals utilizing proposal-improvement group recommendations

_____ sometimes   _____ always   _____ poor   _____ good   _____ excellent

Assisting in the Development of Federal Proposals

The operant word in this chapter's title is *assisting.* In some school districts the district grants office staff write all federal proposals. This definitely limits the number that can be handled. However, this number can be dramatically increased by changing the role of the district grants office from writing proposals to assisting others in doing so.

To help your grantseekers prepare federal proposals, consider developing and disseminating a short booklet on the district grants office's role in supporting the construction of federal proposal applications (see Chapter Two). Your office should promote an easy to follow step-by-step district-based system that describes support services, outlines district requirements for support, summarizes roles and responsibilities, and provides time frames for adequate preparation.

Up to this point, your proactive grants system has focused on those aspects of preproposal contact that increase the success rate of federal proposals and provide the tools necessary to create a grant-winning federal application. By the time your grantseekers are ready to actually construct their federal proposal application, they should have already done the following:

- Completed and received proposal sign-on approval

- Made preproposal contact with their prospective federal funding agency

- Completed a Grantor Strategy Worksheet (Figure 6.19)

The Federal Grantseekers' Proposal Checklist (Figure 9.1) lists information, resources, worksheets, and so on that help federal grantseekers develop quality proposals. Your office's files should contain samples of each of the items on the checklist, and you should determine which

---

Figure 9.1

FEDERAL GRANTSEEKERS' PROPOSAL CHECKLIST

Put a checkmark next to those items that you have a copy of:

_____ School Grantseekers' Preproposal Endorsement Worksheet

_____ *Catalogue of Federal Domestic Assistance*—Program description

_____ *Federal Register*—Rules and regulations

_____ *Federal Register*—Announcement of proposal submission deadline

_____ Past grantees for program

_____ List of last year's reviewers or profile of reviewers

_____ Sample funded proposal

_____ Sample of past school district proposal with scores and reviewers' comments

_____ Grantor strategy worksheet

_____ Federal research worksheet

_____ Federal funding staff history

_____ Scoring system to be used in review

---

of these items your office will provide as part of its support services to your grantseekers.

Your grantseekers can gain access to much of the information they need at no cost under the Freedom of Information Act, but you can expedite the process by going to Washington to gather it. In addition to providing your grantseekers with a valuable service, periodic visits to Washington allow you to meet face-to-face with potential funding sources for many of your district's projects.

If you or your grantseekers are unable to get the necessary information otherwise, several education associations and private companies compile many of the items on the Federal Grantseekers' Proposal Checklist and sell the package. Aspen Publishers, Inc., is one (see the bibliography).

It is important that your district grants office be able to recapture data on past federal proposals. To help you do so, keep a grants history of the district's attempts at federal grantseeking. Making reviewers' scores, comments, and other items on the Federal Grantseekers' Proposal Checklist available to your grantseekers will give them a competitive edge and enable them to reflect their knowledge of the grantor in their proposal. The importance of maintaining your district's grants history may seem obvious, but many educational organizations that have been involved in federal grantseeking for decades are not even aware of who in their organization has applied for federal grants or has been a reviewer—information that could prove valuable to current grantseekers.

Your district's success rate in the federal grants marketplace depends on how well your grantseekers do their homework and follow the stringent rules for completing a federal grant application. If the rules state that proposals cannot be more than thirty double-spaced pages, typed in a particular font with no fewer than twelve characters per inch, this means the body of the proposal *cannot* be thirty-one pages, single spaced, or in fine print! Remind your grantseekers to express their creativity through innovative solutions to problems, not through innovative ways to complete an application.

The basic parts of most federal proposals are similar. Differences between agency requirements occur in the preferred ordering of the parts of the proposal, space limitations, the terminology, and the allocation of evaluation points. The basic parts of a federal proposal for an education project are these:

A. Proposal abstract or summary

B. Needs statement

C. Plan of operation for addressing the need

D. Key personnel who will operate the program

E. Budget and cost-effectiveness

F. How the effectiveness of the project will be evaluated

G. Adequacy of resources

H. Assurances

I. Attachments

The Department of Education also requires a special section on meeting the purpose of the authorizing statute (that is, the federal law) that established the granting program.

Federal agencies that fund research in education have one other required component: a section on the project's hypothesis, specific aims, and research design. Because your grantseekers' research will lead them to branches of government other than education, it is crucial to procure as much as possible of the information on the Federal Grantseekers' Proposal Checklist. By doing so, your grantseekers will be able to determine the specific agency's preferred proposal format and scoring system. For example, if your grantseekers' project focuses on math and science, they may look to the National Science Foundation (NSF) as a prospect. NSF's rules on such things as proposal components and length differ from the Department of Education's, but your grants system should provide your grantseeker with the information necessary to submit any proposal in the desired format.

It is most important that the federal proposal be constructed in a manner that the reviewer will understand. The reviewer must be able to read through the proposal rapidly. The salient parts must be evident and well documented so that the reviewer can ascribe a point value to each section. The points assigned to each area and the distribution of any additional points are outlined in each agency's specific proposal guidelines.

Proposal Abstract or Summary

Most proposals require one of these. The abstract may have to fit into a designated space or number of lines. Photoreduction is not allowed. Federal agencies normally state the specific font required so that the proposal can be read without magnification.

There is some disagreement over when in the proposal development process the abstract or summary should be written. Most experts believe it should be written last, as the grant writer reflects on the completed proposal and summarizes each section; others contend that writing the abstract first helps the grantee focus on the ideas the proposal will describe. One must allow for grantseekers' individual differences, but preparing a detailed outline, then writing the proposal, and finally writing an abstract that summarizes the proposal works efficiently for most people.

Whether the abstract is written first or last, make certain that it has the required format and follows all the rules. It should provide a short, concise, and easy-to-read description of the need for the project, the objectives, the solution, and the evaluation. Before writing the abstract, your proposal developers should review the required sections of the proposal and the point system that the reviewers will use to evaluate and rank it. Suggest that they highlight those sections worth the most points and refer to them in the same terms as the federal agency.

To convey as much information as possible in a limited amount of space, some grant writers push the abstract to the margins and cram in as many words as possible. This usually is confusing and difficult to read. The federal response has been to specify font size as well as number of lines. Especially considering that the reviewer may have already read several proposals, a "crammed" abstract could set a negative tone for the entire proposal and lead to a low score.

Use this exercise with your grantseekers to help them prepare to write their abstract. Review the following abstract:

*This project will identify those students at risk for dropping out, will
intervene and provide the motivation and tools necessary to complete
their high school education, and will encourage postsecondary education*

and/or training. Over a three-year period, this project will extend ser-
vices to 450 students including 5 elementary programs that feed into 3
middle schools, which, in turn, feed into 2 high school programs. Activi-
ties in this project will increase coping and daily living skills through
classroom instruction, utilize community volunteers to tutor students
and act as role models, increase awareness and incentive through two
field trips, as well as track school attendance and classroom progress
acting as a mediator between teachers, parents, and students to resolve
problems as they arise.

Now consider whether this abstract does the following:

- Shows that the grantseeker has a command of the need

- Indicates that the project has measurable objectives

- Provides a synopsis of the methods

- Presents the proposal's main points in an interesting manner

The abstract indicates that services will be extended to 450 students, five elementary programs, and three middle schools. It also provides a rough idea of the types of activities prescribed to retain students. And it does this in one sentence of fifty-seven words! However, the abstract does not even hint at the need or give any measurement indicators or criteria for success. Also, based on the abstract, the project appears to be geared to high schools, which raises the issue of why elementary and middle schools will be involved. But before we get too critical, we should note that the project summarized in this abstract was funded for approximately $97,000!

The Needs Statement

This section may also be referred to as the "Search of Relevant Literature" or the "Problem."

The Education Department's General Administrative Regulations (EDGAR) is the system that the Department of Education generally uses to review proposals. EDGAR requires grantseekers to focus on the extent to which their project meets the specific needs recognized in the statute that authorized the program. Therefore, applicants to the Department of Education should be aware of the purposes of the relevant statute and begin their needs section by focusing on how their project will serve those needs or purposes. They must provide a clear description of the needs addressed by the project; how the needs were identified; how the needs will be met; and the benefits to be gained by meeting the needs. One successful grantee demonstrated the extent of the need by including descriptions of the following:

1. *Target Area:* Where the applicant was located and data that identified a significant needs population in the student body

2. *Needs for Services:* What school programs were available, and the void between what is and what should be

3. *How the Needs Will Be Met:* A general description of what was to be done

4. *Benefits to Be Gained:* The anticipated positive outcomes of the project

When developing the needs section, your proposal developers should take into consideration the type of reviewer that will be reading the proposal application and try to determine what the reviewer will find motivating and compelling. The needs section must show that your applicant has a command of the current literature in the field so as to demonstrate his or her credibility. Many excellent proposals lose critical points because the grantee fails to command the respect of the reviewer by overlooking the needs section and placing the emphasis on the project description and plan of operation.

The following "extent of the need" is from a grant funded by the Department of Education for dropout prevention.

The target population to be served by the project has experienced low academic achievement, high public assistance rates, high dropout rates, linguistic and cultural differences, geographic isolation, and inaccessibility to existing career and training information. These conditions have combined to create high unemployment, underemployment, poor self-image, and a resultant low standard of living among these people. Astin's study of college attrition clearly identifies family income as a significant factor which negatively impacts student success in postsecondary education and contributes to high dropout rates. Astin does note, however, that this correlation is influenced by such other "mediation" factors as ability, motivation, financial concerns, and parental education.

. . . The target population occupies a rural mountainous and desert region covering over 8,000 square miles which is larger than the combined area of Delaware, Rhode Island, and Connecticut.

. . . It is pertinent to note that 79.3% of the active job applicants are ethnic minority and that 63.5% had less than a high school diploma.

Facts such as the ones in this excerpt convince the reviewer and the federal staff that the writer is knowledgeable about the subject of the proposal. Statistics in the needs section of a proposal show a command of the situation and make a positive impression, unlike "grant-loser statements" such as:

- Everyone knows the need for . . .
- Current statistics show . . .
- It is a shame our students do not have . . .
- You can't believe the number of times . . .
- Several (many, an increasing number of) students . . .

When reviewers read a needs section containing such weak, banal statements they vent their frustration on the scoring sheet, and the grantseeker loses valuable points. A strong needs statement must cite facts, studies, and references and must reflect the commitment and hard work that went in to gathering them.

Plan of Operation

The federal application may refer to this section as the "Plan of Operation," "Objectives and Methods," or "Project Methodology." The purpose of this section is to describe an organized solution to the need and problem you have identified; it should thus include your proposal's objectives, methods, and activities. Study a funded proposal to see how successful grantees have organized this section.

Review the section in Chapter Seven on constructing behavioral and measurable objectives and then review the following sample objectives from a proposal for an early intervention dropout program. Keep in mind that the proposal was funded for $750,000!

1. *1,500 kindergarten through sixth-grade at-risk students will benefit from the District's effort to institutionalize instructional improvement and variation by comprehensively upgrading all instructional and support services. This will include: attendance monitoring and immediate follow-up on absences; ombudsmen and advocates for students; junior high at-risk student tutoring of early grade at-risk students; extended school day programs; and off-site activities.*

2. *Seventy-five kindergarten through sixth-grade teachers and two paraprofessionals will receive training on topics such as: implementation of effective school postulates, individualizing instruction, thematic instruction, ombudsmen and advocates for students, the city as a resource, training parents, managing at-risk*

student programs, and understanding the needs of ethnic minority (especially Hispanic-American) and low-income students.

3. *Approximately 500 parents of at-risk students will attend 30 to 60 hours of project-sponsored activities focusing on issues such as: basic literacy, parenting, how to help your child with homework, English as a second language, and social issues information about: drugs and alcohol abuse, AIDS, teenage pregnancy, and suicide.*

4. *The results of this program will be publicized and disseminated. Strategies will include: a recruitment video, a video that showcases the progress and achievements of students, a program brochure, TV spot announcements, and presentations at community events.*

Do these objectives describe what will be accomplished or how the project will be done? The latter, but for three-quarters of a million dollars, we should be told what area we can expect to see change in, and how much.

Some of your grantseekers may be misled by objectives that contain numbers. Numbers alone do not mean that an objective is well constructed or even measurable. For example, the aforementioned objectives tell us the number of parents to be trained but not what they will do differently as a result or what impact it will have on students.

The following objective is from another proposal funded by the Department of Education under a different program. It demonstrates the measurable component of an objective much more effectively.

By June 1, 1999, at least 65% of all students enrolled in the academic year program will improve at least 1.5 grade levels in mathematics, language mechanics, language expression, and reading ability as documented by pre-post Comprehensive Tests of Basic Skills scores.

Review Chapter Seven on developing a project planner. The project planner provides an organized approach for developing the proposed plan. Whether or not you or your grantseekers use such a planner, your school's proposal will be evaluated on the thoroughness and clarity of the methods you prescribe to meet the objectives and address the need. Studying a previously funded proposal will provide insight on how successful grantees have organized this section of their proposal.

There are many ways to present the methods or activities. In the following example, the successful grantseeker first presents a main objective, then a subobjective or process objective, and finally the methodologies.

OBJECTIVE 3. UPGRADE BASIC SKILLS

PROCESS OBJECTIVE 3.1: Students will be counseled and tutored during the academic year program to meet their individual academic needs and overcome areas of deficiency.

Methodologies:

a) *Deficiencies of participants will be documented through use of CTBS scores, transcripts, and interviews with teachers, parents, students, and counselors. Through this process, an individual education plan will be prepared based on areas of strengths, but particularly on areas of weakness in which the student needs help. This will be in the form of a contract which the student and counselor will sign to agree to work together to strengthen the academic skills which need improvement.*

b) *The counselor will schedule bi-weekly, after-school tutoring, and counseling sessions to provide academic assistance as well as emotional support.*

Personnel Responsible: Project counselors, tutors, and teachers from each high school.

Resources: Textbooks, testing and teaching materials, media centers of each high school.

Key Personnel

This section provides the reviewer with an indication of your project staff's ability to implement the methods aimed at meeting the objectives and closing the gap between what is and what ought to be.

One dilemma that proposal developers face is that key personnel often have not been hired at the time a proposal is submitted. In that case, the proposal should clearly show that capable staff can be hired or that your school can reallocate individuals who have the necessary skills. Remember, reviewers who otherwise favor a proposal will be put off if they are not convinced that individuals qualified to implement the project are readily available.

Review the following section on key personnel from a funded Department of Education proposal.

Criterion: The quality of the key personnel the applicant plans to use in the project.

Staff will consist of a full-time project director, a full-time assistant project director, four part-time regular school year counselors, four full-time summer counselors, eight college and peer tutors, 12 part-time instructors, and a full-time secretary. Inasmuch as project staff have not been identified at this time, resumes are not included. The partnership would like to affirm that no problems are anticipated in acquiring qualified, experienced, highly competent personnel. At least one week will be scheduled at the beginning of the project for the orientation of staff to the goals, objectives, plan of operation, and so on.

Do you feel confident that this applicant has the expertise necessary to conduct this project? Does the statement that "no problems are anticipated in acquiring qualified . . . personnel" make you feel comfortable? This is like asking someone to bet on an unknown horse simply because you believe it will be a winner. Every grantor wants to know what horses a prospective grantee has in its stable!

In this example, the applicant could have stated that the project director would be reporting to Dr. Smith, who is currently responsible for managing X million dollars or completing Y projects. Note, however, that the prospective grantee did at least follow the key personnel criterion with a detailed description of the major positions mentioned in the body of the proposal.

Keep in mind that many government grantors look at the *appropriate* use of personnel as well as their quality. If you are thinking about minimally involving one outstanding person in many grants, you should be aware that some funders will ask for an outline of the time each staff member will commit to the project and may require that the project director or principal investigator commit a significant percentage of her or his time. In other words, do not have one outstanding and well-known individual spend 2 percent of his or her time on fifty different projects!

Budget and Cost-Effectiveness

Federal program proposal requirements differ, but all require a budget. Your proposal's budget and the items that comprise it may be viewed in relationship to how they affect your students, teachers, or parents. The amount you request may be divided by the number of beneficiaries so that the federal program officer and reviewer can arrive at the cost per person served by the proposal. One of the primary concerns of a reviewer is that the budget request be reasonable and based on the cost of the activities or methods outlined in the proposal. For example, if a project is supposed to provide a model for other schools, it must be affordable enough to be replicated by schools and districts that may not receive grants.

The following sample is from a federally funded proposal. Note that in the actual proposal, references to the cost per student were removed by federal agency staff. This may have been to prevent readers from calculating a formula for what they believed to be the program or agency's "preferred" cost figure.

REASONABLENESS OF BUDGET

Criterion: *Costs are reasonable in relation to the objective of the project.*

Salaries and benefits are based upon institutional schedules and policies. Supplies have been computed on the basis of local vendor prices. Travel and communication costs in such a geographically isolated location may appear to be rather extensive. These have been kept to a minimum with rates on institutional policies.

The overall cost per participant from federal funds amounts to $_____ the first year, decreasing to $_____ the second year and $_____ the third year. The budget is reasonable and cost effective, particularly considering the geographic isolation of the target area.

The federal funding agency may also require a budget narrative, which is an explanation of how the salaries, consultant services, equipment, and materials are related to the completion of each method or activity.

The Department of Education's most common budget information form for nonconstruction projects is ED Form No. 524 (Figure 9.2; instructions, Figure 9.3). If you have completed a project planner (see Chapter Seven), you already have all the information you need to complete ED Form No. 524.

Evaluation

Objectives developed according to the methods suggested in Chapter Seven contain the basic steps for evaluation. Most projects demand some sort of preassessment survey so that baseline data can be gathered. Once the intervention steps or model project has been employed, the original baseline data can be compared with post-test evaluation data to demonstrate change in the target population or reduction of the problem.

Using outside consultants to evaluate the project is preferred by many reviewers in the hope that it may encourage an unbiased, independent evaluation. By discussing the evaluation section with the prospective grantor before submitting the proposal, your grantseekers should be able to determine the funding source's preferences.

The evaluation section of your school's proposal must clearly delineate the following:

- What will be evaluated

- When the pre- and postevaluations will occur

Figure 9.2

ED FORM NO. 524

U.S. DEPARTMENT OF EDUCATION

BUDGET INFORMATION

NON-CONSTRUCTION PROGRAMS

OMB Control No. 1880–0538

Expiration Date: 10/31/99

Applicants requesting funding for only one year should complete the column under "Project Year 1." Applicants requesting funding for multi-year grants should complete all applicable columns. Please read all instructions before completing form.

Name of Institution/Organization

SECTION A - BUDGET SUMMARY
U.S. DEPARTMENT OF EDUCATION FUNDS

Budget Categories	Project Year 1 (a)	Project Year 2 (b)	Project Year 3 (c)	Project Year 4 (d)	Project Year 5 (e)	Total (f)
1. Personnel						
2. Fringe Benefits						
3. Travel						
4. Equipment						
5. Supplies						
6. Contractual						
7. Construction						
8. Other						
9. Total Direct Costs (lines 1-8)						
10. Indirect Costs						
11. Training Stipends						
12. Total Costs (lines 9-11)						

ED FORM NO. 524

(continued)

Figure 9.2 (continued)

Name of Institution/Organization

Applicants requesting funding for only one year should complete the column under "Project Year 1." Applicants requesting funding for multi-year grants should complete all applicable columns. Please read all instructions before completing form.

SECTION B - BUDGET SUMMARY
NON-FEDERAL FUNDS

Budget Categories	Project Year 1 (a)	Project Year 2 (b)	Project Year 3 (c)	Project Year 4 (d)	Project Year 5 (e)	Total (f)
1. Personnel						
2. Fringe Benefits						
3. Travel						
4. Equipment						
5. Supplies						
6. Contractual						
7. Construction						
8. Other						
9. Total Direct Costs (lines 1-8)						
10. Indirect Costs						
11. Training Stipends						
12. Total Costs (lines 9-11)						

SECTION C - OTHER BUDGET INFORMATION (see instructions)

ED FORM NO. 524

Figure 9.3

INSTRUCTIONS FOR ED FORM NO. 524

Public reporting burden for this collection of information is estimated to vary from 13 to 22 hours per response, with an average of 17.5 hours, including the time for reviewing instructions, searching existing data sources, gathering and maintaining the data needed, and completing and reviewing the collection of information. Send comments regarding this burden estimate or any other aspect of this collection of information, including suggestions for reducing this burden, to the U.S. Department of Education, Information Management and Compliance Division, Washington, D.C. 20202–4651; and the Office of Management and Budget, Paper Reduction Project 1875–0102, Washington, D.C. 20503.

General Instructions

This form is used to apply to individual U.S. Department of Education discretionary grant programs. Unless directed otherwise, provide the same budget information for each year of the multi-year funding request. Pay attention to applicable program specific instructions, if attached.

Section A—Budget Summary
U.S. Department of Education Funds

All applicants must complete Section A and provide a breakdown by the applicable budget categories shown in lines 1–11.

Lines 1–11, columns (a)–(e): For each project year for which funding is requested, show the total amount requested for each applicable budget category.

Lines 1–11, column (f): Show the multi-year total for each budget category. If funding is requested for only one project year, leave this column blank.

Line 12, columns (a)–(e): Show the total budget request for each project year for which funding is requested.

Line 12, column (f): Show the total amount requested for all project years. If funding is requested for only one year, leave this space blank.

Section B—Budget Summary
Non-Federal Funds

If you are required to provide or volunteer to provide matching funds or other non-Federal resources to the project, these should be shown for each applicable budget category on lines 1–11 of Section B.

Lines 1–11, columns (a)–(e): For each project year for which matching funds or other contributions are provided, show the total contribution for each applicable budget category.

Lines 1–11, column (f): Show the multi-year total for each budget category. If non-Federal contributions are provided for only one year, leave this column blank.

Line 12, columns (a)–(e): Show the total matching or other contribution for each project year.

Line 12, column (f): Show the total amount to be contributed for all years of the multi-year project. If non-Federal contributions are provided for only one year, leave this space blank.

Section C—Other Budget Information

Pay attention to applicable program specific instructions, if attached.

1. Provide an itemized budget breakdown, by project year, for each budget category listed in Sections A and B.

2. If applicable to this program, enter the type of indirect rate (provisional, predetermined, final or fixed) that will be in effect during the funding period. In addition, enter the estimated amount of the base to which the rate is applied, and the total indirect expense.

3. If applicable to this program, provide the rate and base on which fringe benefits are calculated.

4. Provide other explanations or comments you deem necessary.

- How much change is predicted

- Who will perform the evaluation

- How much the evaluation component will cost

In the example provided on the Sample Project Planner (see Figure 7.3), West University was named as the evaluator; thus the grantee would not be evaluating the effects of its own program. By including a few West University professors in the proposal, the grantee built credibility and demonstrated the efficient use of local resources. Using West University's computer resources and graduate students in the evaluation process also demonstrated the cost-effectiveness of the grantee's proposal.

Adequacy of Resources

Every proposal should include this information whether or not the funding source requests it because it lets the funder know why your school rather than another should receive a grant. You can play a particularly useful role in gathering this information by having the individuals and groups involved in grantseeking brainstorm a list of reasons why your school deserves a grant. The key is to focus on the resources or unique aspects of your school and its personnel that would appeal to the reviewer.

Complete the School Resources Worksheet (Figure 9.4) well in advance of your proposal's due date.

Completing the worksheet can be enjoyable and more worthwhile than it might appear at first glance. First, it encourages grantseekers to focus on the positive aspects of their schools, and by brainstorming the positive, they actually combat the negative. Remember, funding sources are not interested in what is wrong with your school and how bad things are. They want to know what forces are at work to ensure success.

Second, the list of your school's positive attributes will empower your grantseekers as they begin to search for external funds. When a potential grantor asks them why their school should be chosen for a grant, they will be able to cite not one but several reasons.

Update your School Resources Worksheet annually and be sure to list all of your school's positive areas, including staff, advisory committees, and so on. The areas that most influence federal grantors and reviewers include the following:

- *Equipment:* Demonstrate that you have enough standard office equipment (desks, chairs, and so on) to support the additional staff called for in your proposal. If your proposal calls for nonstandard equipment such as modems and VCRs and you are not requesting funds from the grantor to purchase them, make it clear that they

Figure 9.4

SCHOOL RESOURCES WORKSHEET

When considering a grant to our school, the funding source will want to be assured that we have the resources to carry out the proposed project. The prospective funding source will want to know what we are good at. Please take a few minutes to help your school put its best foot forward. Prepare a list of possible answers to the grantor's question of why our school should be awarded a grant.

Resources We Can Offer

Buildings, facilities, space:

_____

_____

Equipment (computers, etc.):

_____

_____

Supplies/materials:

_____

_____

Unique arrangements with other organizations:

_____

_____

Our geographic location:

_____

_____

Student composition/makeup:

_____

_____

Uniqueness of faculty, staff:

_____

_____

Awards, honors, or other recognition we have received:

_____

_____

Other unique, interesting credibility builders:

_____

_____

_____

_____

are being donated by you, the grantee, to the project. Your assurance demonstrates that you have adequate resources.

- *Supplies and Materials:* Any supplies or materials that you will be making available should also be noted. This will strengthen your case.

- *Facilities:* Describe the facilities that will be used to support the project, especially unique or different types such as computer labs, swimming pools, and so on. If another organization will be involved in the project, your proposal should show how facilities will be jointly used or shared to ensure the success of the project.

Assurances

District officials will be required to provide signed assurances that the project will abide by a myriad of federal rules and regulations. Assurances deal with a wide range of issues such as drug-free workplaces and political lobbying. For general information, the *Catalog of Federal Domestic Assistance* (CFDA) outlines required federal assurances.

One area of assurances that many school districts overlook is human subjects review. It is not necessary for your school district to organize an Institutional Review Board (IRB) to examine every federal proposal to assure that the human subjects involved are treated humanely; however, as a grantee you should develop a relationship with your local college or university so that you can arrange to have its IRB review and approve your federal proposals.

Attachments

As we have seen, reactive grantseeking limits the time to write a proposal. Because of this, the applications of reactive grantseekers often have to be submitted without letters of support and agreement from cooperating organizations and community groups. This is a red flag to reviewers. It often diminishes potential grantees' credibility and results in the loss of valuable points. Make sure your grantees take the time to gather letters of support and agreement in advance.

It is a good idea to include their Project Planner as an attachment. Other attachments may include maps, pictures, a layout of the school building, support data for the statement of need, surveys, and questionnaires.

Reviewers find it helpful when a separate table of contents for the attachment section is included in the proposal.

The district grants office may choose to provide assistance in developing the final draft of the proposal. This may mean typing and inputting final drafts into its own computer, or it may mean obtaining the grantseekers' computer disks or output from their work station and transferring it to the district grants offices. The draft copy should be received in your office one to two weeks before the deadline. This will ensure that your office has time to do the following:

- Finalize the budget and quarterly cash requests

- Provide for compliance with the assurances

- Conduct a mock review that mirrors the actual review the proposal will undergo once it is submitted

Consider developing a booklet aimed at helping your grantseekers take a major role in creating federal grant proposals. The booklet should spell out the correct strategies, outline the process, and describe the support services your office can provide to them. Include samples of support materials as well as worksheets that will be completed as a result of carrying out the prescribed process. You can provide your grantseekers with useful examples by including one completed set of worksheets based on an actual federal proposal that your district has submitted for funding.

Providing samples and examples of your district's past efforts in addressing the required components of a federal application will help your grantseekers realize that it can be done. They *can* write winning federal grant proposals!

CHAPTER 9 ASSESSMENT TOOL

1. **Review the Federal Grantseekers' Proposal Checklist (Figure 9.1). Which items do you currently provide for your grantseekers?**

   _____

   _____

2. **Of the items you do not currently provide, which ones do you plan to provide in the future?**

   _____

   _____

3. **Do you travel to Washington to (among other things) pick up copies of successful federal applications for your grantseekers to review?**   _____ yes _____ no

   If no, could you?   _____ yes _____ no

   Will you in the future?   _____ yes _____ no

Chapter 10

Improving the Quality of Federal Grants Applications

The effectiveness of a district grants office should not be measured by the acceptance rate of submitted federal applications or by how much federal grant money is awarded to your district. This is particularly true if the proposals are for federal pass-through dollars that are based on formulas such as the number of students receiving free school lunches, or if the office does not have a significant role in evaluating the quality of federal proposals. Many grants administrators greatly rely on proposal developers to review and edit their proposals. Most school districts do not use quality assurance systems that provide grant writers with valuable feedback to ensure that their proposals represent their best efforts.

Although many districts evaluate the grants administrator's performance by the acceptance rate of submitted proposals, that rate is a function of many variables, some of which cannot be controlled by the administrator, including:

- How much federal money has been appropriated for the program
- The number of projects, sites, or programs to be funded
- How well the school district fits the profile of a priority school
- The quality and background of the district personnel who will work on the project
- The strength of consortia partners
- The in-kind contribution of the district
- The quality and amount of equipment included in the project

The one variable that the grants administrator can have an impact on is proposal quality. Your district grants office can increase the percentage of awarded proposals by teaching grantseekers that one of the best ways to ensure success is to subject their proposals to a mock review or quality circle.

Most grant systems are reactive and operate too close to deadlines to use this quality-enhancement technique. But in a proactive grants system there is enough time for every application to undergo a mock review. Still, selling the concept and breaking away from the last-minute sign-off can be difficult.

However, whether this quality-assurance technique is voluntary or mandated by the district, your grantseekers need this extra help. At this stage of the game, they are tired and frequently just want the proposal out the door. But don't let them jeopardize all their hard work by depriving themselves of the benefit of a quality-assurance exercise. After all, a poorly written and thus rejected proposal can harm their careers. In addition, you, as the district grants administrator, have a great deal at stake because awarded, not rejected, proposals are part of your job. Remember, the experts in government granting programs and the reviewers who read your district's proposals assume that what they review reflects your district's best effort. Plainly speaking, your future depends on how good your district's proposals are.

Because the district grants office is in the position to control the proposal sign-off process, it is logical for it to set up the quality-review process. Your office's involvement gives the process credibility and demonstrates its importance.

Also known as a quality circle, quality assurance program, or mock review, the process requires that several volunteers role-play the actual evaluation or federal review process that the proposal will undergo. The district grants office should be responsible for inviting individuals to participate in the mock review.

The individuals participating in your mock review or quality circle need not be experts in the grants field or in the proposal's subject area. The level of expertise of the quality circle members should resemble that of the reviewers on the federal review committee, but you should also invite several individuals with a "clean" perspective to participate. For example, ask a college student, a secretary, or an accountant. These different perspectives help expose the proposal's weaknesses and strengths. (Some volunteers may also be from your district's grants advisory groups.)

Call, write, or ask them in person to participate in the mock-review process. Let them know that the proposal's chance of success will be greatly improved with their help and that you need and value their fresh perspective. Brief them on the general approach you would like them to take. Explain that though you want a rigorous mock review, it will not take much of their time. You will ask them to spend only as much time reading the proposal as the actual reviewers do. Say that you will send them a package that describes the backgrounds and types of reviewers, the time usually allotted to read the proposal, and the scoring system that the reviewers use. It helps to mention that you want their assistance on only one proposal and that the committee rotates throughout the district. (Indeed, the more mock reviewers you use the more knowledgeable your whole district will become about the grants process.) Make sure that they know they do not have to be experts in the subject but that they should make every attempt to read the proposal from the real reviewers' point of view. The sample letter in Figure 10.1 can be used to invite individuals to participate.

The more your mock-review participants know about the review system used by the federal grantor, the more closely they can simulate the actual review and the greater the benefits. Through preproposal contact, your grantseeker or your office should have developed some insight into how the granting agency selects reviewers, the reviewers' backgrounds, and what type of scoring system they follow. This type of information helps you set the stage for a mock review that closely resembles the official review.

Figure 10.1

SAMPLE LETTER INVITING INDIVIDUAL TO PARTICIPATE IN FEDERAL PROPOSAL QUALITY CIRCLE

Date

Name
Address

Dear _____:

    I would like to take this opportunity to follow up on our conversation to secure your input in helping our school district submit the very best grant proposal possible. We are asking that you review the enclosed proposal from the point of view of a federal reviewer. The attached materials will help you role-play the actual manner in which this proposal will be evaluated.

    Please read the information on the reviewers' backgrounds and the scoring system and limit the time you spend reading the proposal to the time constraints that the real reviewers will observe. A Quality Circle Scoring Worksheet has been provided to assist you in recording your scores and comments.

    A meeting of all the mock reviewers comprising our quality circle has been scheduled for [date]. Please bring this worksheet with you to the meeting. The meeting will last less than one hour. Its purpose is to analyze the scores and brainstorm suggestions to improve the proposal.

Sincerely,
Name
Phone Number

It is best to assume that each federal agency that makes grants follows a different review system. For instance, the National Science Foundation's system is very different from the system used by the National Endowment for the Humanities, and the latter is much different from that of the Department of Education. In some cases different granting programs in the same agency use different review systems. This emphasizes the need for preproposal contact with the funder and early data gathering about the review process.

Either your district grants office or your grantseekers should obtain the following information from the granting agency:

- *Where and How the Review Occurs:* Are the reviewers mailed a package of proposals and asked to review them at home? Do the reviewers meet at one place to review the proposals? If so, for how long? Provide this information to your volunteers and replicate the situation.

- *Average Time Spent Reading Each Proposal:* Most reviewers are very busy people, and the time they spend reading proposals varies greatly.

- *Number of Proposals Each Reviewer Evaluates:* A key element in your role playing is to ask your volunteers to think of your proposal as the last one in a pile. If reviewers each read ten proposals, your school's should be thought of as the tenth.

At the very least, you *must* give the members of your quality circle the point system and time constraints they should abide by. Volunteer mock reviewers often want to do such a good job that they spend more time reviewing the proposal than the real reviewers! Make sure they understand that spending an inordinate amount of time reviewing the proposal is counterproductive.

As mentioned in Chapter Nine, the Education Department generally uses a review system known as EDGAR (Education Department's General Administrative Regulations). However, not every program in the Education Department follows EDGAR. There are variations, and some programs have their own published regulations and a specific set of criteria for evaluating and judging applications for grants. If the program you are interested in does not have a set of published guidelines, it probably follows EDGAR, but always double-check through preproposal contact.

EDGAR's main areas of evaluation are these:

1. The need for the project

2. The significance of the project

3. The quality of the project design

4. The quality of the key personnel

5. The adequacy of resources

6. The quality of the management plan

7. The quality of the project evaluation

To help your volunteers review and evaluate your school's proposal from the proper perspective, provide them with the Department of Education's General Selection Criteria and the optional factors under each criterion (the factors in bold print are mandatory) (Figure 10.2), the Scoring Distribution Worksheet (Figure 10.3), and the Quality Circle Scoring Worksheet (Figure 10.4).

It is important that your district grants office or your grantseekers determine the point values associated with each of the areas on the General Selection Criteria for each grant program they plan to approach. This should be done in preproposal contact with the funding source. Variances in point values from program to program reflect differing emphases and, in some cases, the allowance of grantees with special circumstances to score higher in the review process.

Review with your quality circle the General Selection Criteria Overview and the points assigned to each section. Refer them to the Scoring Distribution Worksheet for help in allocating points. The purpose of the Scoring Distribution Worksheet is to promote consistency in scoring within the range of points allowed for each section. Emphasize the need for a candid evaluation and ask the mock reviewers to avoid inflating a positive score or comment in one section to make up for a low score or comment in another.

Each reviewer should be given a Technical Review Package (Figure 10.5). The worksheets in it are very similar to those used by federal reviewers, which makes the mock review resemble the real review as much as possible. In addition, getting acquainted with these worksheets gives the mock reviewers experience that will prove valuable if they are ever selected to review grant applications and proposals for a federal program.

The district grants office can reproduce the worksheets in the Technical Review Package. Providing them to your mock reviewers in the form of a package will keep the committee focused on each section of the proposal and on the important areas each section contains.

The major difference between the worksheets your reviewers will be using and those used by actual reviewers is in the request for suggestions for improvement. As the mock reviewers identify the weaknesses in the proposal, ask them to list any suggestions that would reduce or eliminate the weaknesses. Stress that the proposal developers still have time to incorporate new ideas into the proposal. Sometimes mock reviewers are

---

Figure 10.2

DEPARTMENT OF EDUCATION: GENERAL SELECTION CRITERIA

Need for Project

- Severity of problem
- Need for services to be provided
- Extent to which project addresses needs of students at risk of educational failure
- Extent to which project addresses needs of disadvantaged individuals
- Extent to which project identifies and addresses nature and magnitude of gaps and weaknesses in services, infrastructure, or opportunities
- Extent to which project prepares personnel for fields with shortages

Significance

- National significance
- Significance of problem or issue to be addressed
- Potential of project to increase knowledge or understanding of educational problems, issues, or effective strategies
- Potential of project to increase knowledge or understanding of rehabilitation problems, issues, or effective strategies
- Likelihood that project will result in system change or improvement
- Potential of project to contribute to development and advancement of theory, knowledge, and practice in field of study
- Potential for generalizing from findings or results
- Likelihood of project to yield findings that may be used by other appropriate agencies and organizations
- Likelihood of project to build local capacity to provide, improve, or expand services that address the needs of the target population
- Extent to which project involves development or demonstration of promising new strategies that build on or are alternatives to existing strategies
- Effective use of product resulting from the project (i.e., information, materials, processes, techniques, etc.)
- Dissemination of results in a manner that will allow others to use the information or strategies
- Potential replicability of the project or strategies
- Magnitude of the results or outcomes, especially improvements in teaching and student achievement
- Magnitude of the results or outcomes, especially improvements in employment, independent living services, or both, as appropriate
- Importance or magnitude of the results or outcomes likely to be attained by the proposed project

Quality of the Project Design

- Extent to which goals, objectives and outcomes are clearly specified and measurable
- Extent to which design is appropriate to, and will successfully address, the needs of the target population or other identified needs
- Extent to which there is a conceptual framework underlying the proposed research or demonstration activities and the quality of that framework

(continued)

Figure 10.2 (continued)

- Extent to which proposed activities constitute a coherent, sustained program of research and development in the field, including, as appropriate, a substantial addition to an ongoing line of inquiry
- Extent to which the proposed activities constitute a coherent, sustained program of training in the field
- Extent to which the proposed project is based upon a specific research design, and the quality and appropriateness of that design, including the scientific rigor of the studies involved
- Extent to which the proposed research design includes a thorough, high-quality review of the relevant literature, a high-quality plan for research activities, and the use of appropriate theoretical and methodological tools, including those of a variety of disciplines, if appropriate
- Extent to which the design of the proposed project includes a thorough high-quality review of the relevant literature, a high-quality plan for project implementation, and the use of appropriate methodological tools to ensure successful achievement of project objectives
- Quality of the proposed demonstration design and procedures for documenting project activities and results
- Extent to which the design for implementing and evaluating the proposed project will result in information to guide possible replication of project activities or strategies, including information about the effectiveness of the approach or strategies employed by the project
- Extent to which the proposed development efforts include adequate quality controls and, as appropriate, repeated testing of products
- Extent to which the proposed project is designed to build capacity and yield results that will extend beyond the period of Federal financial assistance
- Extent to which the design of the proposed project reflects up-to-date knowledge from research and effective practice
- Extent to which the proposed project represents an exceptional approach for meeting statutory purposes and requirements
- Extent to which the proposed project represents an exceptional approach to the priority or priorities established for the competition
- Extent to which the proposed project will be coordinated with similar or related efforts, and with other appropriate community, state, and Federal resources
- Extent to which proposed project will establish linkages with other appropriate agencies and organizations providing services to the target population
- Extent to which the proposed project is part of a comprehensive effort to improve teaching and learning and support rigorous academic standards for students
- Extent to which the proposed project encourages parental involvement
- Extent to which proposed project encourages consumer involvement
- Extent to which performance feedback and continuous involvement are integral to the design of the proposed project
- Quality of the methodology to be employed in the proposed project
- Extent to which fellowship recipients or other project participants are to be selected on the basis of academic excellence

Quality of Project Services

- **Quality and sufficiency of strategies for ensuring equal access and treatment for eligible project participants who are members of groups that have traditionally been underrepresented based on race, color, national origin, gender, age, or disability** (mandatory factor)

Figure 10.2 (continued)

- Extent to which services to be provided by the proposed project are appropriate to the needs of the intended recipients or beneficiaries
- Extent to which entities that are to be served by the proposed technical assistance project demonstrate support for the project
- Extent to which the services to be provided by the proposed project reflect up-to-date knowledge from research and effective practice
- Likely impact of services to be provided by the proposed project on the intended recipients
- Extent to which training or professional development services to be provided by the proposed project are of sufficient quality, intensity, and duration to lead to improvements in practice among the recipients of those services
- Extent to which the training or professional development services to be provided by the proposed project are likely to alleviate the personnel shortages that have been identified or are the focus of the proposed project
- Likelihood that the services to be provided by the proposed project will lead to improvements in the achievement of students as measured against rigorous academic standards
- Likelihood that the services to be provided by the proposed project will lead to improvements in the skills necessary to gain employment or build capacity for independent living
- Extent to which the services to be provided by the proposed project involve the collaboration of appropriate partners for maximizing the effectiveness of project services
- Extent to which the technical assistance services to be provided by the proposed project involve the use of efficient strategies, including the use of technology, as appropriate, and the leveraging of nonproject resources
- Extent to which the services to be provided by the proposed project are focused on those with the greatest needs
- Quality of the plans for providing an opportunity for participation in the proposed project of students enrolled in private schools

Quality of Project Personnel

- **Extent to which applicant encourages applications for employment from persons who are members of groups that have traditionally been underrepresented based on race, color, national origin, gender, age, or disability** (mandatory factor)
- Qualifications, including relevant training and experience, of the project director or principal investigator
- Qualification, including relevant training and experience, of key project personnel
- Qualifications, including relevant training and experience, of project consultants or subcontractors

Adequacy of Resources

- Adequacy of support, including facilities, equipment, supplies, and other resources, from the applicant organization or the lead applicant organization
- Relevance and demonstrated commitment of each partner in the proposed project to the implementation and success of the project
- Extent to which the budget is adequate to support the proposed project
- Extent to which the costs are reasonable in relation to the objectives, design, and potential significance of the proposed project
- Extent to which the costs are reasonable in relation to the number of persons to be served and to the anticipated results and benefits

(continued)

Figure 10.2 (continued)

- Potential for continued support of the project after Federal funding ends, including, as appropriate, the demonstrated commitment of appropriate entities to such support
- Potential for the incorporation of project purposes, activities, or benefits into the ongoing program of the agency or organization at the end of Federal funding

Quality of the Management Plan

- Adequacy of the management plan to achieve the objectives of the proposed project on time and within budget, including clearly defined responsibilities, time lines, and milestones for accomplishing project tasks
- Adequacy of procedures for ensuring feedback and continuous improvement in the operation of the proposed project
- Adequacy of mechanisms for ensuring high-quality products and services from the proposed project
- Extent to which time commitments of the project director and principal investigator and other key project personnel are appropriate and adequate to meet the objectives of the proposed project
- How the applicant will ensure that a diversity of perspectives are brought to bear in the operation of the proposed project, including those of parents, teachers, the business community, a variety of disciplinary and professional fields, recipients or beneficiaries of services, or others, as appropriate

Quality of the Project Evaluation

- Extent to which the methods of evaluation are thorough, feasible, and appropriate to the goals, objectives, and outcomes of the proposed project
- Extent to which the methods of evaluation are appropriate to the context within which the project operates
- Extent to which the methods of evaluation provide for examining the effectiveness of project implementation strategies
- Extent to which the methods of evaluation include the use of objective performance measures that are clearly related to the intended outcomes of the project and will produce quantitative and qualitative data to the extent possible
- Extent to which the methods of evaluation will provide timely guidance for quality assurance
- Extent to which the methods of evaluation will provide performance feedback and permit periodic assessment of progress toward achieving intended outcomes
- Extent to which the evaluation will provide guidance about effective strategies suitable for replication or testing in other settings

reluctant to criticize or make suggestions lest the proposal writers take offense. If this is a problem, keep them anonymous. Have your office type their handwritten comments and suggestions before they are given to the proposal developers.

Your volunteers can review the proposal at home, school, or work, or they may prefer to meet to combine their scores and discuss the proposal's positive and negative points. The arrangement you decide on should be

---

Figure 10.3

SCORING DISTRIBUTION WORKSHEET

The numerical scores you assign to an application's response to the selection criteria must be consistent with the comments you write. Comments and scores should reflect the same overall assessment. You should never attempt to mitigate a negative comment with a positive score, or vice versa.

Comments indicate whether the application's response to the selection criteria is poor, adequate, or good; scores indicate *how* poor, adequate, or good. If 10 points are possible, 0–2 points is poor, 5–7 points is adequate, and 8–9 points is superior. Four points means the response is merely weak, whereas 8 indicates it is above average. Whatever amount of total points is possible, use the midpoint of the scale as adequate and choose your scores accordingly. Do not hesitate to use the full range of points. It is perfectly acceptable to assign a score of 10 or 0, for example. Your guiding rule should be consistency in rating.

Always go back and check your scores to make sure that you have written them correctly and used the appropriate point scale. You should also double-check the scores on the summary page of the Technical Review Form to make sure that they match the scores listed under each selection criterion and that the final total has been computed without error.

You may want to use the following table as a guide when assigning points:

Total	Poor	Weak	Adequate	Superior	Outstanding
25	0–8	9–12	13–19	20–23	24–25
20	0–6	7–9	10–15	16–18	19–20
15	0–4	5–7	8–11	12–13	14–15
10	0–2	3–4	5–7	8–9	10
5	0–1	2	3	4	5

---

based on how the federal reviewers perform the review and your volunteers' time constraints. Note that performing the mock review in a group enables the administrator to play a key role as group facilitator. This in itself will reinforce the value placed on the review. It is best if the proposal writers are not at this meeting so that the group members will be as candid as possible.

Ask the volunteers to read the proposal and to evaluate and score each section before moving to the next. Have them put a plus sign beside those areas they think the reviewer will consider positive and a minus sign beside those areas they think will be viewed negatively. Stress that identifying both the positive and negative aspects of each section helps the proposal developers understand the mock reviewers' scores and enables them to improve the negative areas without changing or eliminating the positive aspects.

Send or give your volunteer reviewers the Quality Circle Information Worksheet (Figure 10.6) and any additional information you and your grantseekers have gathered that might help them role-play. For example,

Figure 10.4

QUALITY CIRCLE SCORING WORKSHEET

The following information is being provided to assist you in reviewing the attached federal grant application/proposal.

The Setting—The proposals are read at:

_____ The reviewer's location

_____ The federal agency's location

_____ Another site selected by the federal agency

The Time Factor

Number of proposals the reviewer evaluates: _____

Amount of time the reviewer spends evaluating each proposal: _____

Areas to be Scored	Points/Area	Comments/Suggestions

Total Points _____

What is the background and training of the evaluators? _____

_____

_____

What point system will be followed? _____

_____

_____

How much time will be spent reviewing each proposal?_____

_____

_____

Use this space to note anything "special" that will affect proposal outcome. _____

_____

_____

_____

_____

_____

_____

Figure 10.5

TECHNICAL REVIEW PACKAGE

Technical Review Form

School Application No. _____

CFDA No. _____

Federal Program: _____

Applicant Organization: _____

Selection Criteria	Maximum Points	Assigned Points
Need for project	_____	_____
Plan of operation	_____	_____
Quality of key personnel	_____	_____
Budget cost-effectiveness	_____	_____
Evaluation plan	_____	_____
Adequacy of resources	_____	_____
Significance of project	_____	_____
Total Points	_____	_____

SUMMARY COMMENTS

Strengths: _____

_____

Weaknesses and Suggestions for Improvement: _____

_____

Extent of the Need for the Project

Maximum Points _____   Awarded _____

1. What needs does the applicant identify?
2. How did the applicant identify those needs; that is, what specific documentation or evidence does the application offer to support the applicant's assessment of need?
3. Does the applicant identify too many or too few needs for the proposed time frame and resources of the project?
4. Are the outlined needs well defined so that the project can be focused on them, or are they generic?

Strengths: _____

_____

Weaknesses and Suggestions for Improvement: _____

_____

Plan of Operation

Maximum Points _____   Awarded _____

1. How well is the project designed?
    *   Are project objectives consistent with stated needs?
    *   Are project activities consistent with project objectives?
    *   Are project objectives measurable?
2. How will the applicant use its resources and personnel to achieve each objective?

(continued)

Figure 10.5 (continued)

3. Has the applicant developed an effective management plan that will ensure proper and efficient administration of the project?
4. Do project milestones represent a logical progression of times and tasks?
5. Does the applicant propose a realistic time schedule for accomplishing objectives?
6. Will the proposed activities accomplish the project's objectives successfully?
7. Are the educational approaches planned based on sound research that indicates they will be successful for the population to be served?
8. Does the project have clearly developed plans for providing equal access to eligible participants who are members of traditionally underrepresented groups (racial or ethnic minorities, women, handicapped persons, elderly persons)?

Strengths: _____

_____

Weaknesses and Suggestions for Improvement: _____

_____

Quality of Key Personnel

Maximum Points _____   Awarded _____

1. Do the job descriptions adequately reflect skills needed to make the project work?
2. Are the duties of personnel clearly defined?
3. What relevant qualifications do the proposed personnel possess, especially the project director? (Focus on their experience and training in fields related to the objectives of the project, though other information may be considered.)
4. Will proposed personnel need to be trained for the project?
5. How much time will the proposed personnel actually devote to the project?
6. To what extent does the applicant encourage employment applications from members of traditionally underrepresented groups (ethnic or racial minorities, women, handicapped persons, elderly persons)?

Strengths: _____

_____

Weaknesses and Suggestions for Improvement: _____

_____

Budget and Cost-Effectiveness

Maximum Points _____   Awarded _____

1. Is the budget adequate to support the project's proposed activities?
2. Are overall project costs reasonable in relation to project objectives?
3. How much of the project's total cost is devoted to administrative costs?
4. Are budget items sufficiently justified?
5. Is the budget padded?

Strengths: _____

_____

Weaknesses and Suggestions for Improvement: _____

_____

Figure 10.5 (continued)

Evaluation Plan

Maximum Points _____   Awarded _____

1. Are the proposed methods of evaluation appropriate to the project?
2. Is the proposed evaluation objective?
3. Will the proposed evaluation methods measure the effectiveness of project activities in meeting project objectives?
4. Will the evaluation plan produce valid and reliable data concerning the accomplishment of project objectives?
5. Does the evaluation plan measure the project's effect on the project audience?

Strengths: _____

_____

Weaknesses and Suggestions for Improvement: _____

_____

Adequacy of Resources

Maximum Points _____   Awarded _____

1. Are the proposed facilities adequate for project purposes?
2. Will the proposed equipment be adequate for project purposes?
3. Does the applicant have access to special sources of experience or expertise?

Strengths: _____

_____

Weaknesses and Suggestions for Improvement: _____

_____

Significance of Project

Maximum Points _____   Awarded _____

1. Does the applicant demonstrate the significance of the problem or issue to be addressed?
2. Is the project likely to have national significance, increase knowledge or understanding, result in change or improvement, yield findings that can be replicated, and so on?
3. Is the magnitude of the results or outcomes outlined?

Strengths: _____

_____

Weaknesses and Suggestions for Improvement: _____

_____

information on last year's grantees may be useful, especially if the grantee mix is likely to remain the same.

Review with the developers the scores they received from the mock reviewers on each section of their proposal. Pay particular attention to the positive points. Focus on how to improve areas that were unclear and did not read well. They will probably be able to explain away most problems to you, but remind them that they will not get that chance in the real review. By coordinating the mock-review process but not participating in the actual proposal critique, you are in a perfect position to summarize the volunteers' scores and comments and to review them with the grantseekers in a nonthreatening manner. The results should identify the areas of the proposal that need to be improved and those that should remain the same.

When rewriting and retyping is required, make sure you volunteer any support services your office can provide. Remember that your grant writers are tired. Think of them as racehorses in the home stretch. They

---

Figure 10.6

QUALITY CIRCLE INFORMATION WORKSHEET

The following information is being provided to assist you in reviewing the attached federal grant application/proposal.

The Setting—The proposals are read at:

_____ The reviewer's location

_____ The federal agency's location

_____ Another site selected by the federal agency

The Time Factor

Number of proposals the reviewer evaluates: _____

Amount of time the reviewer spends evaluating each proposal: _____

Background of Reviewers

Age range: _____

Educational background: _____

_____

Known viewpoints or biases:_____

_____

List of last year's reviewers available? _____ yes _____ no

(If yes, please attach) _____

Other Information

Applications/proposals received by the agency last year: # _____

Grants awarded by the agency last year: # _____

Dollar range for proposals from schools such as ours: $ _____

need a little prodding to make the finish line, but don't whip them! This is exactly the time for a true leader to display his or her skills at getting the volunteers and staff to invest the extra effort that translates into grants success. For example, making your office's secretary available for editing goes a long way in ensuring that the mock reviewers' suggestions are incorporated into an improved proposal. Once all the necessary revisions have been made, the proposal is finally ready for submittal.

Submittal

Most grants offices handle the final submittal of federal applications. They coordinate signatures and usually provide copying services so that federal requirements are met for the following:

- Sign-off—original signatures of appropriate school officials
- Inclusion of school board resolutions endorsing the project
- Endorsement of matching funds or in-kind contributions
- Number of copies of proposal
- Binding instructions
- Application transmittal—mail postmark or delivery date
- Federal assurances and compliance
- Notification of state or other governmental agencies or coordinating bodies

The Federal Submittal Checklist (Figure 10.7) lists many of the areas that must be addressed at submittal. If your district grants office is not responsible for these areas, designate those individuals who will be held accountable.

School District Sign-Off Procedure

The final sign-off is considerably easier if your system has a sign-on or proposal endorsement sheet that lists the areas of concern identified by administrators before the grantseekers receive district endorsement to contact federal grantors. This form contains the comments, conditions, restrictions, and signatures of those individuals who would be affected by the proposed grant. Now it is appropriate to include these same individuals on your district sign-off form. Technically, and legally, the federal proposal can be submitted after receiving the district's authorizing signature, but if your sign-on form requests endorsement by other district officials, curriculum groups, or advisory groups, seek their sign-off and endorsement before the proposal is submitted. Naturally, your grants office should also be included in the sign-off process.

Figure 10.7

FEDERAL SUBMITTAL CHECKLIST

Duplicate each area of the completed application that needs to be double-checked and initialed by the party responsible for ensuring that the area has been completed according to the federal grantor's regulations.

Initialed   **Area**

Proposal Submission Instructions

_____   Logging center address: _____

_____

_____

_____   Sent by: _____ U.S. Postal Service

_____ Return receipt requested

_____   _____ Other mail service

_____   _____ Return receipt requested

_____   Number of copies sent _____

_____   Required cover sheet completed

_____   Signature of district officials

Page no. _____   Signature _____

Page no. _____   Signature _____

_____   **Proposal Parts** (For each part, note restrictions on page length and actual number of pages)

	Allowed # of Pages	Actual # of Pages
Abstract	_____	_____
Authorizing statute	_____	_____
Need	_____	_____
Objectives	_____	_____
Methods	_____	_____
Budget	_____	_____
Letters of endorsement	_____	_____

Restrictions of Type Font, Number of Lines, Margins, Charts, and Graphs

Assurances Required

_____   Drug-free workplace

_____   Employee assurances

_____   Human subjects' approval

_____   Debt and debarment certification

_____   Certification regarding lobbying

_____   Certification for contracts, loans, cooperative agreements

It is helpful to include a copy of each individual's sign-on sheet to help them remember their original concerns. For example, if bus transportation is included in your grantseekers' proposal, the individual responsible for district transportation should have the opportunity to review the commitments that the proposed grant could require.

Matching fund requirements or in-kind contributions that will support the project should be outlined on the sign-off form. This ensures that administrators are aware of their financial responsibility.

Include information on any formula that requires increasing district financial support in future years of the grant. Some school administrators see only the first year and 100 percent federal support and fail to recognize or plan for year two or three that will require a 25 or 50 percent match.

It is important that the district individuals who are asked to sign off understand that the purpose of the process is to keep them informed of the concerns they expressed at the time of sign-on or endorsement. The sign-off forms should have specific instructions about how long individuals have to review the proposal and how it will be passed to each individual for signature. A brightly colored cover sheet that outlines the instructions is recommended. The District Sign-Off Worksheet in Figure 10.8 will help you develop a form tailored to your district's needs.

Authorized Signatures

The federal form most often encountered by educators seeking government grants is the Standard Form (SF)-424 (Figure 10.9; instructions for its use are in Figure 10.10). It is the facesheet or the first page for applications submitted for federal assistance and is usually supplied in every federal application package.

In many grant application packages, the name of the federal agency and the CFDA number will already be on the SF-424. It is important to your sign-off system that the individual who is your district's authorized representative place his or her signature on your district's sign-off form and in the appropriate place on SF-424 (or other places that may require a signature). One technique to ensure the appropriate signatures is to use a system of colored plastic paper clips or colored Post-Its. Place a colored clip or tab next to the names of those individuals who must sign the district sign-off sheet and instruct them to locate the same colored clip or tab in the proposal and to sign there as well.

Line 18.4 of the SF-424 calls for the signature of the district's authorized representative. It is a good practice to have the school board pass a resolution designating the district's authorized signature and place it on file.

Figure 10.8

DISTRICT SIGN-OFF WORKSHEET

District ID # _____

Project title _____

_____

Proposal developer(s) _____

_____

Funding source _____

Program _____

Matching and in-kind contributions included in proposal _____

_____

School district policy requires that the attached proposal receive your review and endorsement. Please sign this form, indicating your approval of this project and your support for any special provisions or requirements (see partial list below). The page numbers appearing next to your name refer to the pages in the proposal that you are required to sign. Please do not sign any page unless indicated.

IMPORTANT: DO NOT PLACE THE SIGNED PROPOSAL IN DISTRICT MAIL OR TRANSMITTAL. THE PROPOSAL MUST BE MOVED TO THE NEXT SIGNATURE BY [TIME] VIA [COURIER]. PLEASE CALL _____ WHEN SIGNED.

(A copy of the comments and concerns you raised when you signed the original proposal sign-on sheet has been attached to help you determine if and how these issues have been addressed.)

Special Considerations Relative to this Proposal

_____ Space and/or equipment requirements

_____ Transportation

_____ Released time

_____ Continuation and future support

_____ _____

_____ _____

_____ _____

Signature Required   **Proposal Page Number(s)**

_____   _____

_____   _____

_____   _____

_____   _____

_____   _____

_____   _____

Figure 10.9

APPLICATION FOR FEDERAL ASSISTANCE SF-424

APPLICATION FOR FEDERAL ASSISTANCE		OMB Approval No. 0348-0043
	2. DATE SUBMITTED	Applicant Identifier

1. TYPE OF SUBMISSION:		**3. DATE RECEIVED BY STATE**	State Application Identifier
Application ☐ Construction ☐ Non-Construction	Preapplication ☐ Construction ☐ Non-Construction	**4. DATE RECEIVED BY FEDERAL AGENCY**	Federal Identifier

5. APPLICANT INFORMATION

Legal Name:	Organizational Unit:
Address *(give city, county, State, and zip code)*:	Name and telephone number of person to be contacted on matters involving this application *(give area code)*

6. EMPLOYER IDENTIFICATION NUMBER *(EIN)*: ☐☐ – ☐☐☐☐☐☐☐	**7. TYPE OF APPLICANT:** *(enter appropriate letter in box)* ☐
8. TYPE OF APPLICATION: ☐ New ☐ Continuation ☐ Revision If Revision, enter appropriate letter(s) in box(es) ☐ ☐ A. Increase Award B. Decrease Award C. Increase Duration D. Decrease Duration Other*(specify)*:	A. State H. Independent School Dist. B. County I. State Controlled Institution of Higher Learning C. Municipal J. Private University D. Township K. Indian Tribe E. Interstate L. Individual F. Intermunicipal M. Profit Organization G. Special District N. Other (Specify) _____
	9. NAME OF FEDERAL AGENCY:

10. CATALOG OF FEDERAL DOMESTIC ASSISTANCE NUMBER: ☐☐ – ☐☐☐ TITLE:	**11. DESCRIPTIVE TITLE OF APPLICANT'S PROJECT:**

12. AREAS AFFECTED BY PROJECT *(Cities, Counties, States, etc.)*:	

13. PROPOSED PROJECT		**14. CONGRESSIONAL DISTRICTS OF:**	
Start Date	Ending Date	a. Applicant	b. Project

15. ESTIMATED FUNDING:		**16. IS APPLICATION SUBJECT TO REVIEW BY STATE EXECUTIVE ORDER 12372 PROCESS?**
a. Federal	$ .00	a. YES. THIS PREAPPLICATION/APPLICATION WAS MADE AVAILABLE TO THE STATE EXECUTIVE ORDER 12372 PROCESS FOR REVIEW ON:
b. Applicant	$ .00	
c. State	$ .00	DATE _____
d. Local	$ .00	
e. Other	$ .00	b. No. ☐ PROGRAM IS NOT COVERED BY E. O. 12372 ☐ OR PROGRAM HAS NOT BEEN SELECTED BY STATE FOR REVIEW
f. Program Income	$ .00	**17. IS THE APPLICANT DELINQUENT ON ANY FEDERAL DEBT?**
g. TOTAL	$ .00	☐ Yes If "Yes," attach an explanation. ☐ No

18. TO THE BEST OF MY KNOWLEDGE AND BELIEF, ALL DATA IN THIS APPLICATION/PREAPPLICATION ARE TRUE AND CORRECT, THE DOCUMENT HAS BEEN DULY AUTHORIZED BY THE GOVERNING BODY OF THE APPLICANT AND THE APPLICANT WILL COMPLY WITH THE ATTACHED ASSURANCES IF THE ASSISTANCE IS AWARDED.

a. Type Name of Authorized Representative	b. Title	c. Telephone Number
d. Signature of Authorized Representative		e. Date Signed

Previous Edition Usable
Authorized for Local Reproduction

Standard Form 424 (Rev. 7-97)
Prescribed by OMB Circular A-102

Figure 10.10

INSTRUCTIONS FOR THE SF-424

> Public reporting burden for this collection of information is estimated to average 45 minutes per response, including time for reviewing instructions, searching existing data sources, gathering and maintaining the data needed, and completing and reviewing the collection of information. Send comments regarding the burden estimate or any other aspect of this collection of information, including suggestions for reducing this burden, to the Office of Management and Budget, Paperwork Reduction Project (0348-0043), Washington, DC 20503.
>
> **PLEASE DO NOT RETURN YOUR COMPLETED FORM TO THE OFFICE OF MANAGEMENT AND BUDGET. SEND IT TO THE ADDRESS PROVIDED BY THE SPONSORING AGENCY.**

This is a standard form used by applicants as a required facesheet for preapplications and applications submitted for Federal assistance. It will be used by Federal agencies to obtain applicant certification that States which have established a review and comment procedure in response to Executive Order 12372 and have selected the program to be included in their process, have been given an opportunity to review the applicant's submission.

Item: Entry:

1. Self-explanatory.

2. Date application submitted to Federal agency (or State if applicable) and applicant's control number (if applicable).

3. State use only (if applicable).

4. If this application is to continue or revise an existing award, enter present Federal identifier number. If for a new project, leave blank.

5. Legal name of applicant, name of primary organizational unit which will undertake the assistance activity, complete address of the applicant, and name and telephone number of the person to contact on matters related to this application.

6. Enter Employer Identification Number (EIN) as assigned by the Internal Revenue Service.

7. Enter the appropriate letter in the space provided.

8. Check appropriate box and enter appropriate letter(s) in the space(s) provided:

    -- "New" means a new assistance award.

    -- "Continuation" means an extension for an additional funding/budget period for a project with a projected completion date.

    -- "Revision" means any change in the Federal Government's financial obligation or contingent liability from an existing obligation.

9. Name of Federal agency from which assistance is being requested with this application.

10. Use the Catalog of Federal Domestic Assistance number and title of the program under which assistance is requested.

11. Enter a brief descriptive title of the project. If more than one program is involved, you should append an explanation on a separate sheet. If appropriate (e.g., construction or real property projects), attach a map showing project location. For preapplications, use a separate sheet to provide a summary description of this project.

Item: Entry:

12. List only the largest political entities affected (e.g., State, counties, cities).

13. Self-explanatory.

14. List the applicant's Congressional District and any District(s) affected by the program or project.

15. Amount requested or to be contributed during the first funding/budget period by each contributor. Value of in-kind contributions should be included on appropriate lines as applicable. If the action will result in a dollar change to an existing award, indicate _only_ the amount of the change. For decreases, enclose the amounts in parentheses. If both basic and supplemental amounts are included, show breakdown on an attached sheet. For multiple program funding, use totals and show breakdown using same categories as item 15.

16. Applicants should contact the State Single Point of Contact (SPOC) for Federal Executive Order 12372 to determine whether the application is subject to the State intergovernmental review process.

17. This question applies to the applicant organization, not the person who signs as the authorized representative. Categories of debt include delinquent audit disallowances, loans and taxes.

18. To be signed by the authorized representative of the applicant. A copy of the governing body's authorization for you to sign this application as official representative must be on file in the applicant's office. (Certain Federal agencies may require that this authorization be submitted as part of the application.)

SF-424 (Rev. 7-97) Back

Copies

It is critically important to follow the guidelines exactly and to double-check the font, page size, number of pages allowed, and number of copies and originals required.

Binding

The district grants office should be responsible for binding the application to ensure that the federal agency guidelines are followed precisely. Generally, spiral-bound proposals are not accepted but pressure binders and staples are. Be sure clips and staples are in the correct location (that is, the upper left or right corner).

Assurances

Chapter Eleven outlines the federal regulations, assurances, and guidelines needed to administer federal grant funds. At this point in the submittal process you must indicate on your SF-424 that your district has complied with the Review by State Executive Order 12373. Certain federal programs require that you notify state government officials of your application for federal funds. Not all require this, and even programs that have been reviewed by the state and not recommended for funding have been awarded. The purpose of the state review process is to ensure that the state knows about the project and that it is not in conflict with a state plan or program.

The application package will inform you of this requirement, and the list of State Single Points of Contact (Figure 10.11) will provide you with a name of a person to call in your state's office. But because that individual may no longer be there, telephone the office to check on the information for your state.

Application Transmittal

The district grants office is usually responsible for ensuring that all the federal requirements for transmittal are carried out. The application transmittal information differs from one federal agency to another. (More and more federal programs are making their applications available and accepting proposals over the Internet. For example, the National Science Foundation uses an electronic submittal system known as Fast Lane.) Check with the program officer or contact person to confirm the preferred method of transmittal.

Department of Education grant application packages and forms are available on the Internet at http://ocfo.ed.gov/. The agency's nonelectronic transmittal instructions are shown in Figure 10.12.

Figure 10.11

STATE SINGLE POINT OF CONTACT LISTING MAINTAINED BY OMB

In accordance with Executive Order #12372, "Intergovernmental Review of Federal Programs," Section 4, "the Office of Management and Budget (OMB) shall maintain a list of official State entities designated by the States to review and coordinate proposed Federal financial assistance and direct Federal development." This attached listing is the OFFICIAL OMB LISTING. This listing is also published in the Catalog of Federal Domestic Assistance biannually. Please direct all questions and correspondence about intergovernmental review to: Daisey Millen, Telephone: (809) 774-0750, FAX: (809) 776-0069.

ARIZONA

Joni Saad
Arizona State Clearinghouse
3800 N. Central Avenue
Fourteenth Floor
Phoenix, Arizona 85012
Telephone: (602) 280-1315
FAX: (602) 280-8144
e-mail: jonis@ep.state.az.us

ARKANSAS

Mr. Tracy L. Copeland
Manager, State Clearinghouse
Office of Intergovernmental Services
Department of Finance and Administration
1515 W. 7th St., Room 412
Little Rock, Arkansas 72203
Telephone: (501) 682-1074
FAX: (501) 682-5206

CALIFORNIA

Grants Coordinator
Office of Planning and Research/State
Clearinghouse
1400 Tenth Street, Room 121
Sacramento, California 95814
Telephone: (916) 323-7480
FAX: (916) 323-3018

DELAWARE

Francine Booth
State Single Point of Contact
Executive Department, Office of the Budget
540 S. duPont Hi., Suite 5
Dover, Delaware 19901
Telephone: (302) 739-3326
FAX: (302) 739-5661

DISTRICT OF COLUMBIA

Charles Nichols
State Single Point of Contact
Office of Grants Management and
Development
717 14th Street, N.W. - Suite 1200
Washington, D.C. 20005
Telephone: (202) 727-6537
FAX: (202) 727-1617
e-mail: charlesnic@yahoo.com or cnichols-ogmd@dcgov.org

FLORIDA

Cherie L. Trainor
Coordinator
Florida State Clearinghouse
Department of Community Affairs
2555 Shumard Oak Boulevard
Tallahassee, Florida 32399-2100
Telephone: (850) 922-5438 or (850) 414-5495
FAX: (850) 414-0479
e-mail: cherie.trainor@dca.state.fl.us

GEORGIA

Debra S. Stephens
Coordinator
Georgia State Clearinghouse
270 Washington Street, S.W. - 8th Floor
Atlanta, Georgia 30334
Telephone: (404) 656-3855
FAX: (404) 656-7901
e-mail: ssda@mail.opb.state.ga.us

ILLINOIS

Virginia Bova
State Single Point of Contact
Illinois Department of Commerce and Community Affairs
James R. Thompson Center
100 West Randolph, Suite 3-400
Chicago, Illinois 60601
Telephone: (312) 814-6028
FAX: (312) 814-1800

INDIANA

Frances Williams
State Budget Agency
212 State House
Indianapolis, Indiana 46204-2796
Telephone: (317) 232-5619
FAX: (317) 233-3323

IOWA

Steven R. McCann
Division for Community Assistance
Iowa Department of Economic Development
200 East Grand Avenue
Des Moines, Iowa 50309
Telephone: (515) 242-4719
FAX: (515) 242-4809

KENTUCKY

Kevin J. Goldsmith, Director
John-Mark Hack, Deputy Director
Sandra Brewer, Executive Secretary
Intergovernmental Affairs
Office of the Governor
700 Capitol Avenue
Frankfort, Kentucky 40601
Telephone: (502) 564-2611
FAX: (502) 564-2849

MAINE

Joyce Benson
State Planning Office
184 State Street
38 State House Station
Augusta, Maine 04333
Telephone: (207) 287-3261
FAX: (207) 287-6489

MARYLAND

Linda C. Janey, JD
Manager, Clearinghouse and Plan Review Unit
Maryland Office of Planning
301 W. Preston Street - Room 1104
Baltimore, Maryland 21201-2305
Telephone: (410) 767-4491
FAX: (410) 767-4480
e-mail: Linda@mail.op.state.md.us

MICHIGAN

Richard Pfaff
Southeast Michigan Council of Governments
660 Plaza Drive - Suite 1900
Detroit, Michigan 48226
Telephone: (313) 961-4266
FAX: (313) 961-4869

MISSISSIPPI

Cathy Mallette
Clearinghouse Officer
Department of Finance and Administration
455 North Lamar Street
Jackson, Mississippi 39202-3087
Telephone: (601) 359-6762
FAX: (601) 359-6764

Figure 10.11 (continued)

MISSOURI

Lois Pohl/Carol Meyer
Federal Assistance Clearinghouse
Office of Administration
P.O. Box 809
Room 915, Jefferson Building
Jefferson City, Missouri 65102
Telephone: (573) 751-4834
FAX: (573) 522-4395

NEVADA

Heather Elliott
Department of Administration
State Clearinghouse
Capitol Complex
Carson City, Nevada 89710
Telephone: (702) 687-6367
FAX: (702) 687-3983

NEW HAMPSHIRE

Jeffrey H. Taylor
Director, N.H. Office of State Planning
Attn: Intergovernmental Review Process
Mike Blake
Office of State Planning
2 1/2 Beacon Street
Concord, New Hampshire 03301
Telephone: (603) 271-2155
FAX: (603) 271-1728

NEW MEXICO

Nick Mandell
Local Government Division
Room 201, Bataan Memorial Building
Santa Fe, New Mexico 87503
Telephone: (505) 827-4991
FAX: (505) 827-4948

NEW YORK

New York State Clearinghouse
Division of the Budget
State Capitol
Marsha Roth
Albany, New York 12224
Telephone: (518) 474-1605
FAX: (518) 486-5617

NORTH CAROLINA

Chrys Baggett, Director
North Carolina State Clearinghouse
Office of the Secretary of Administration
116 West Jones Street - Suite 5106
Raleigh, North Carolina 27603-8003
Telephone: (919) 733-7232
FAX: (919) 733-9571

NORTH DAKOTA

Jim Boyd
North Dakota Single Point of Contact
Office of Intergovernmental Assistance

600 East Boulevard Avenue
Department 105
Bismarck, North Dakota 58505-0170
Telephone: (701) 328-2094
FAX: (701) 328-2308

RHODE ISLAND

Kevin Nelson
Review Coordinator
Department of Administration
Division of Planning
One Capitol Hill, 4th Floor
Providence, Rhode Island 02908-5870
Telephone: (401) 222-2656
FAX: (401) 222-2083

SOUTH CAROLINA

Omegia Burgess
State Single Point of Contact
Budget and Control Board
Office of State Budget
1122 Ladies Street - 12th Floor
Columbia, South Carolina 29201
Telephone: (803) 734-0494
FAX: (803) 734-0645

TEXAS

Tom Adams
Single Point of Contact, State of Texas
Governor's Office of Budget and Planning
Director, Intergovernmental Coordination
P.O. Box 12428
Austin, Texas 78711-2428
Telephone: (512) 463-1771
FAX: (512) 936-2681
e-mail: tadams@governor.state.tx.us

UTAH

Carolyn Wright
Utah State Clearinghouse
Office of Planning and Budget
Room 116 State Capitol
Salt Lake City, Utah 84114
Telephone: (801) 538-1535
FAX: (801) 538-1547

WEST VIRGINIA

Judith Dryer
Chief Program Manager
West Virginia Development Office
Building #6, Room 645, State Capitol
Charleston, West Virginia 25305
Telephone: (304) 558-0350
FAX: (304) 558-0362

WISCONSIN

Jeff Smith
Section Chief
State/Federal Relations
Wisconsin Department of Administration
101 East Wilson Street - 6th Floor

P.O. Box 7868
Madison, Wisconsin 53707
Telephone: (608) 266-0267
FAX: (608) 267-6931

WYOMING

Matthew Jones
State Single Point of Contact
Office of the Governor
200 West 24th Street
State Capital, Room 124
Cheyenne, Wyoming 82002
FAX: (307) 632-3909

TERRITORIES

GUAM

Mr. Giovanni T. Sgambelluri
Director
Bureau of Budget and Management Research
Office of the Governor
P.O. Box 2950
Agana, Guam 96910
Telephone: 011-671-472-2285
FAX: 011-671-472-2825

PUERTO RICO

Norma Burgos/Jose E. Caro
Chairwoman/Director
Puerto Rico Planning Board
Federal Proposals Review Office
Minillas Government Center
P.O. Box 41119
San Juan, Puerto Rico 00940-1119
Telephone: (809) 727-4444 or (809) 723-6190
FAX: (809) 724-3270 or (809) 724-3103

NORTHERN MARIANA ISLANDS

Mr. Alvaro A. Santos, Executive Officer
Office of Management and Budget
Office of the Governor
Saipan, MP 96950
Telephone: (670) 664-2256
FAX: (670) 664-2272
Please direct all questions and correspondence
about intergovernmental review to:
Ms. Jacoba T. Seman,
Federal Programs Coordinator
Telephone: (670) 664-2289
FAX: (670) 664-2272

VIRGIN ISLANDS

Nellon Bowry
Director, Office of Management and Budget
#41 Norregade Emancipation Garden Station
Second Floor
Saint Thomas, Virgin Islands 00802
Please direct all questions and correspondence
about intergovernmental review to:
Daisey Millen
Telephone: (809) 774-0750
FAX: (809) 776-0069

Figure 10.12

APPLICATION TRANSMITTAL INSTRUCTIONS

An application for an award must be mailed or hand-delivered by the closing date.

Applications Sent by Mail

An application sent by mail must be addressed to the U.S. Department of Education, Coordination and Control Branch, Attention: CFDA #84._____ (Be sure to include the correct numeric and alpha description—e.g., 84.320A), 400 Maryland Avenue, S.W., Washington, D.C. 20202-4725.

An application must show proof of mailing consisting of one of the following:

(1)   A legibly dated U.S. Postal Service Postmark.

(2)   A legible mail receipt with the date of mailing stamped by the U.S. Postal Service.

(3)   A dated shipping label, invoice, or receipt from a commercial carrier.

(4)   Any other proof of mailing acceptable to the U.S. Secretary of Education.

If an application is sent through the U.S. Postal Service, the Secretary does not accept either of the following as proof of mailing:

(1)   A private metered postmark, or

(2)   A mail receipt that is not dated by the U.S. Postal Service.

An applicant should note that the U.S. Postal Service does not uniformly provide a dated postmark. Before relying on this method, an applicant should check with its local post office.

An applicant is encouraged to use registered or at least first-class mail. Each late applicant will be notified that its application will not be considered.

Applications Delivered by Hand/Courier Service

An application that is hand-delivered must be taken to the U.S. Department of Education, Coordination and Control Branch, Room 3633, General Services Administration National Capital Region, 7th and D Streets, S.W., Washington, D.C. 20202-4725.

The Coordination and Control branch will accept deliveries between 8:00 a.m. and 4:30 p.m. (Washington, D.C. Time) daily, except Saturdays, Sundays, and Federal holidays.

Individuals delivering applications must use the D Street Entrance. Proper identification is necessary to enter the building.

In order for an application sent through a Courier Service to be considered timely, the Courier Service must be in receipt of the application on or before the closing date.

Proof of receipt by any federal agency is a must. Always request written notification of receipt. Some federal programs have a return postcard that verifies your proposal has been logged in at the federal agency or the log-in center. Many programs require that the applicant complete and sign a checklist included in the proposal application. The district grants office's address, not that of one of the grant writers, should appear as the return address.

Your efforts could benefit from a grants booklet that describes the importance of using the proposal-improvement/mock-review process before submittal (see Chapter Two). A booklet that outlines the support services your office provides and describes your role in sign-off and application transmittal not only helps move proposals through your system more smoothly but provides a way to focus on issues that could be overlooked, such as matching and in-kind requirements.

CHAPTER 10 ASSESSMENT TOOL

Proposal Improvement Process

1. **Who ensures that each proposal leaving your district represents the highest quality possible?**

   _____ No one

   _____ The proposal developer/grantseekers

   _____ The district grants office

   _____ Other district office

   _____ Other (specify) _____

2. **Does your district currently use a quality circle or proposal improvement group to perform mock reviews of proposals before they are submitted to prospective funding sources:**

   _____ yes   _____ no

   If yes, is the mock review process: _____ mandatory   _____ voluntary

Put a check mark next to the services your grants office currently provides and an asterisk (*) next to those it does not provide now but will in the future.

   _____ Invites individuals to participate in the mock review

   _____ Provides mock-review participants with a packet of materials containing a description of the backgrounds and types of reviewers, the time usually allotted to read the proposal, and the scoring system that the reviewers will use

   _____ Provides worksheets designed specifically to help participants review and evaluate proposals—e.g., General Selection Criteria, Scoring Distribution Worksheet, Quality Circle Worksheet, Technical Review Worksheet, Quality Circle Information Worksheet, and so on

   _____ Reviews the scores received from the mock reviewers, with the proposal developers focusing on the proposal's positive and negative points

   _____ Provides support services when proposal rewriting and retyping are required

Sign-Off System

1. **Who in your district handles the final submittal of federal applications?**

   _____ District grants office

   _____ Other district office

   _____ Other (specify) _____

   (continued)

CHAPTER 10 ASSESSMENT TOOL (continued)

Put a check mark next to the services your district grants office currently provides and an asterisk (*) next to those it does not provide now but will in the future.

_____ Coordinates signatures

_____ Provides individuals who must sign off on the proposal with a copy of their sign-on sheet to help them remember their original concerns so that they can determine whether action was taken to eliminate or reduce problems foreseen at that time

_____ Provides individuals asked to sign off with a sign-off sheet that identifies any and all commitments (resulting from accepting and carrying out the federal grant (e.g., matching and in-kind requirements, formulas for future financial commitments, special requirements for space, personnel, equipment, and so on)

_____ Tracks the sign-off process and institutes a system for moving the sign-off sheet from one individual to the next in a timely fashion

_____ Ensures that the federal regulations, assurances, and compliances to administer the federal grant funds are understood and can be met

_____ Makes sure that all application guidelines have been followed (e.g., number of copies necessary, binding requirements, and so on)

_____ Carries out all federal requirements for transmittal

Chapter 11

Administering Federal and Private Grant Funds

THE PREVIOUS CHAPTERS outline the broader responsibilities and challenges that the district grants office must deal with to help their schools attract more grant funding. But many such offices are not yet involved in preproposal contact, developing linkages, or other techniques for increasing grants success. Administrators from these offices perhaps view themselves as fiscal agents, accountants, or bookkeepers responsible for administering grant funds. Although the fiscal functions of a grants office are critical to a district's eligibility for grants, the office should have other responsibilities as well.

It should be the gatekeeper between the district's grantseekers and potential grantors, because even one error in communication between the two can result in the immediate rejection of a proposal.

The proposal writer, in some ways, is like a child waiting all year for his birthday. He wants to know what he'll get, and he wants to know now! So before your proposal writers call to see what they might be getting later, it is imperative that you give them explicit instructions about contacting grantors when a proposal is still in play.

Federal Grantor Contact After Proposal Submission

Once your school's proposal has been logged by a federal grantor, it is considered to be in submission. During this time it will be assigned to a review panel and spend several months in the review process.

To put it bluntly, a federal agency will consider contact by you or your grantseekers during this time as an attempt to unfairly influence the review and outcome. So contact with the funder should be made only on the rare occasion when further information should have an impact on its decision, as when one of the following is the case:

- A new advance in education allows you to drastically cut the grant amount requested (because of new equipment, software, assessment tools, or the like)

- Another grantor has agreed to partially fund the project, so you need less money

- You need to pull your school's proposal from submission because another funding source has decided to fund it totally

Short of these or other dramatic reasons, instruct your grantseekers to avoid contact with the grantor while their proposal is being reviewed.

There is a healthy sense of paranoia in Washington concerning the peer-review process; in fact, congressional involvement in the grants award process has been investigated several times by federal watchdog agencies. Grant awards are supposed to be determined by peer review that is based solely on published selection criteria and therefore removed from political intervention. To avoid any problems, just remember that contact by elected officials on your behalf or by your grantseekers while their proposal is in submission could be viewed as an attempt to influence or subvert the review process, which could result in the disqualification of your proposal.

Foundation or Corporate Grantor Contact After Proposal Submission

Contact with federal bureaucrats may be a legal issue during this period; with corporate and foundation grantors it may be an ethical issue. Considering how few grant-related employees most private grantors have, contacting them may also be difficult. The situations in which contact with foundation and corporate grantors are allowed should basically be the same as with federal grantors. Significant changes in the requested amount should be forwarded in writing to the grantor with a brief but thorough explanation of what has occurred and how it will modify your proposal. Significant changes in a proposal should be relatively rare.

Any contact aimed at influencing the proposal outcome should be through the linkage your district has to the grantor's staff or board members. It's okay to tell your contacts or links that you submitted a proposal; indeed, your grants office should forward a copy of the submitted proposal to them with a note of thanks for the help. They may then mention the submitted proposal to other board members as they golf or dine, or speak on your behalf when the proposal comes up for review. The choice of if, when, and how to act is up to them—but they must know of your submittal first.

Dealing with Rejection or Acceptance

Dealing with proposal outcomes is a good topic for one or more booklets (see Chapter Two), the information in which could also be placed on your website. These booklets should outline the steps proposal developers must take when their proposal is rejected or awarded by public or private grantors. Don't overload and frustrate your grantseekers by giving them federal guidelines and a myriad of assurances that must be complied with before their grants are awarded. They will respond much more favorably to a short, well-written booklet that summarizes the information they need. Build your grants system from the point of view of the grantee and the grantor. Ask how much the grantee needs to know about grant rules and regulations and how much assistance your office can provide. What would you require and feel comfortable with if it were your money and you were the grantor?

Trying to develop an inclusive grants document, some districts have developed a manual with hundreds of pages of forms, rules, and detailed procedures. This is too much.

Rejected grantseekers need encouragement. A short booklet on what to do when a proposal is rejected should deal with the rejection in an educational and problem-solving manner. In addition, coordinating your grantseekers' response to rejection can enhance your district's image with the grantor and increase your chances for future funding.

A similar document on what to do when a proposal is awarded will enhance your office's working relationship with your grantseekers and with the grantor. The booklet should clearly define everyone's role: grantee, grantor, and grant administrator. All want to get good projects under way, but getting off on the right foot is best for everyone.

Basically, two district grants administration systems must be dealt with, private and public.

Private Grantors

Private grantors do not require as many forms or operate under as many rules as their government counterparts. But they do expect that the funds they grant will be handled in a businesslike manner.

Rejected Proposals

What is the district grants office's role when the private grantor rejects the proposal? Disgruntled grantseekers want to put the disappointment behind them and generally forget to send or e-mail a thank you letter. Therefore, your office should take a lead role in helping unsuccessful grantseekers continue the process by suggesting that they do so. It will have little or no bearing on the rejected proposal, but may have significant impact on the outcome of resubmittal or new submittal. Review the Sample thank you Letter if Rejected by a Foundation or Corporation (Figure 11.1). The purpose of this note or letter is to thank the funding source for investing time in reviewing your proposal and to advise them of your intentions to reapply. The letter could also ask why the proposal was rejected. Most private grantors won't respond, but by asking you demonstrate that your district wants to learn all it can from the rejection.

Awarded Proposals

Your district grants office's role in the proper administration of a grant award begins with the recognition of the award and continues through to completion of the project and the submittal of evaluation and closeout forms. All contact with the grantor should flow through that office. A thank you should be sent as soon as the amount of the award is established and agreed upon by both the grantor and the district. The thank

---

Figure 11.1

SAMPLE THANK YOU LETTER IF REJECTED BY A FOUNDATION OR CORPORATION

Date

Name
Title
Address

Dear _____:

On behalf of our students, staff, and volunteers I would like to thank you for the time and effort you spent reviewing our school's proposal entitled _____. We realize that your [foundation/corporation] cannot fund all of the proposals sent to you and that it is difficult for you to provide applicants with comments and suggestions. However, there are a limited number of funding sources who are as committed to _____ as you are. Therefore, we would like to know what our prospects for success are if we resubmit the proposal with changes. In addition, we would like to know if you know of any other funding sources who are specifically interested in projects that benefit _____.

Please contact _____ of my staff at _____ to briefly discuss these matters or fax us your comments and ideas at _____. Once again, thank you for your time and cooperation.

Sincerely,
Name/Title
Phone Number

you letter should be signed by your highest-ranking district administrator or another person deemed most credible by the grantor. It could be the school board president, the principal, a volunteer, a linkage, or even a corporate employee who is a volunteer in your district. The letter could be jointly signed by an administrator and a volunteer.

The thank you letter should request information on the transfer of funds to the district, special payment procedures or schedules, and any preferences of the grantor concerning public relations or news releases (see Figure 11.2).

Figure 11.2

SAMPLE THANK YOU LETTER IF AWARDED BY A FOUNDATION OR CORPORATION

Date

Name
Title
Address

Dear _____:

I would like to extend a thank you on behalf of our school's staff members and volunteers who worked on the proposal your [foundation/corporation] has decided to fund. Your support will help improve education in our community and demonstrates your commitment to tomorrow's future.

Our school district would benefit from knowing what your [foundation/corporation] specifically liked about our proposal and what areas you felt were weak. We look forward to your critique and comments.

_____ of our staff will be in charge of administering the project you are funding. _____ has ____ years of experience in the grants field and you may contact her/him directly. She/he can be reached at [phone number] and/or [fax number]. You will find that our school district's grants administration system is very efficient. Be assured that we follow Certified Public Accountant Guidelines.

[If your notification of acceptance did not outline the procedure for the transfer of funds of any reporting procedures the funding source may have, request that information here.]

[If your award notice states that you must submit your school's 501(c)3 IRS number, place it here. If you do not have the necessary 501(c)3 status, request that the grantor make the funds payable to another nonprofit youth-related group in your community that will subcontract the project and disseminate the funds to your district.]

I encourage you to visit our school and observe the project firsthand. Please advise me of when you may be interested in making an on-site visit so that I can coordinate our schedules.

I would also like to know if you have any special preferences concerning public relations or news releases.

Once again, thank you for your support.

Sincerely,
Name/Title
Phone Number

Acceptance of funds by a school district can pose problems for some foundations. Many stipulate that their awards can be received only by nonprofits that have a 501(c)(3) tax-exempt status or equivalent from the IRS. Foundations prefer this so that fiscal responsibility rests with the recipient of the award.

Your district is a nonprofit but may not have 501(c)(3) status. If your district does not have a school foundation or other 501(c)(3)-designated group, you may need to request that your award be given to a 501(c)(3) that will process the grant on your district's behalf. For example, you could use your local community foundation or a 501(c)(3)-designated education or youth group in your area to act on your behalf in accepting and disseminating the funds.

Ultimately you should set up your own school foundation. David G. Bauer Associates can provide your district with information on setting up a school foundation and a list of consultants who specialize in this field (see information at end of book).

Most foundations, corporations, and fraternal and social groups expect that your grants administration system will follow the American Institute of Certified Public Accountants (AICPA) guidelines on record keeping. For more information contact AICPA, 1211 Avenue of the Americas, New York, NY 10036-8775, (212) 596-6200. Its website is http://www.aicpa.org/

When it comes to budget changes and closeout, it is difficult to receive written approval for budget reallocation from all but the largest of foundations and corporations. Ninety percent of private grantors meet only one or two times per year and are focused on reading and acting on new proposals. If you wait for permission to reallocate funds between budget categories, you may never receive a notice of approval or it will arrive after the grant is completed. Because foundations make grants from a trust or fund and must, by IRS rules, grant at least 5 percent of the value of their assets each year, you will create problems if your school district returns unused funds from the previous year. One approach is to notify the grantor that your office will be transferring funds from one budget category to another in thirty days unless you receive notification to the contrary.

Private grantors expect you to follow your district's normal business procedures for contracting, bidding, purchase, maintenance, and inventory of equipment. Your district grants office should have an inventory control system that identifies the source of funds, the location, and the maintenance records of all equipment purchased on a grant.

Public Grantors

Federal and state funding requirements are not nearly as exasperating as some make them out to be. The guidelines and regulations are quite clear and reasonable when you consider that the rules are meant to safeguard tax dollars. The federal bureaucrats that you made preproposal contact with are generally very helpful and when approached correctly will assist your efforts to operate an effective and responsible grants administration system.

Rejected Proposals

What can the district grants office do when a federal or state proposal is rejected? Help grantseekers learn as much as possible from the experience. Toward this end, send a thank you letter requesting information on the scores and comments of the reviewers. This will help your grantseekers learn what they did that was correct and what could have been better. As the district grants administrator, you are in a good position to discuss the comments and scores with the federal or state program official because you are not ego-involved in the proposal and can accept and use the information provided to help your grantseekers improve the proposal for resubmission. You position your school district in a positive manner by thanking the official for her or his time during preproposal contact, for any materials provided, and for the effort of the staff involved in the evaluation process.

Even if the federal or state agency sends the reviewers' comments without your requesting them, a thank you letter is still in order. You can tailor the sample letter in Figure 11.3 to your system. (Although this letter is for federal funding sources, note that it can be adapted to state funding sources as well.)

Awarded Proposals

As previously mentioned, it is good policy to inform your grantseekers that contact with the grantor after their proposal has been submitted can seriously jeopardize the proposal's outcome. Based on your grantseekers' research and preproposal contact, you may have an idea of when the proposal outcome will be announced. If so, you can contact your congressperson's office to alert him or her to a possible upcoming announcement of a federal grant award to your district. Be certain your congressperson knows you do not want or expect him or her to contact or pressure the agency concerning your proposal. Your purpose is to alert him or her regarding the expected decision and to coordinate the

---

Figure 11.3

SAMPLE THANK YOU LETTER IF REJECTED BY A FEDERAL FUNDING SOURCE

Date

Name
Title
Address

Dear _____:

    Thank you for the time and effort you and your reviewers spent evaluating our school's proposal, [title]. We realize that you are able to fund only a small portion of the proposals submitted to your program and are resolved to make our rejection a positive learning experience.

    We would find it most beneficial if you could send us your reviewers' comments and scores and any suggestions you may have for improving our proposal. I have enclosed a self-addressed label for your convenience. [If the federal grantor has already sent you the reviewers' comments, thank them for their effort.]

    Our district staff and volunteers who have worked on this project are interested in reapplying for funds. We will be contacting you to discuss whether you would look favorable on resubmission of our proposal with changes and if you might be interested in one of the other two strategies we have developed.

    We would appreciate any information that would help us get ready for the next submission, including information on how to become a reviewer so that we might learn about and become more familiar with the review process.

    Thank you again for your past consideration.

Sincerely,
Name/Title
Phone Number

---

announcement of funding. This is a valuable opportunity to use the grants mechanism to alert the public to your district's efforts to obtain resources from outside the district.

Ask your congressperson to contact your district grants office if and when he or she is informed of your award. All federal applications require identification of the applicant's congressional district. When a proposal is selected for funding, the system is designed to notify the congressperson's office—often before notifying the grantee. You may even read about your award in the newspaper before you receive official notice. If your congressperson informs you of the award, suggest that the congressional office and your district superintendent's office develop a joint public relations release to the media.

Whether or not your district grants office takes this opportunity to work with your congressperson, your office should lead the way in submitting a thank you letter to the grantor. The letter should include requests for reviewers' comments (your grantseekers want to learn what they did correctly and what they could have done better), procedures for instituting a grant payment plan, forms that will be necessary for periodic reports, and a completed address label to use in returning the requested information.

Your thank you letter should also acknowledge the grantor's work in reviewing the proposal and contain an invitation to visit the district. Tailor the sample letter in Figure 11.4 to your system. (Although this sample letter is for federal funding sources, note that it can be adapted to state funding sources as well.)

Figure 11.4

SAMPLE THANK YOU LETTER IF AWARDED BY A FEDERAL FUNDING SOURCE

Date

Name
Title
Address

Dear _____:

I would like to extend a thank you on behalf of our school district's staff members and volunteers who worked on the proposal being funded by your program. The support provided through your program will greatly benefit our students and improve education in our community. We look forward to carrying out this proposal with a dedication and standard of quality that will be a positive reflection on your program/department.

In order for the individuals who developed this proposal to get as much as possible out of the experience, we would appreciate the reviewers' comments and your critique of the proposal. I have enclosed a self-addressed label for your convenience.

You will find that our school district's grants administration systems is very efficient. _____ of our staff will be in charge of administering the project your program is funding. He/she has _____ years of experience in the federal grants field and can be reached at [phone number]. Her/his fax number is _____.

Please advise us of any problems common to the administration of a grant such as ours and how to avoid them. Please also send us any necessary completion forms and information on your program's record-keeping requirements.

I encourage you to visit our school and observe the project firsthand. Please advise me of when you may be interested in making an on-site visit so that I can coordinate our schedules.

Once again, thank you. We appreciate the time and effort you, your staff, and your reviewers spent evaluating our proposal.

Sincerely,
Name/Title
Phone Number

The requirements you now face about record keeping, budget changes, cash requests, equipment, and inventory control are all covered in the Office of Management and Budget's circular A-110. This circular is entitled "Uniform Administrative Requirements for Grants and Agreements with Institutions of Higher Education, Hospitals, and Other Nonprofit Organizations." The twenty-six-page circular, with its updates, budget forms, and cash request instructions, is your guide to federal rules regarding your district's grant. Available from the U.S. Government Printing Office—Superintendent of Documents, or on the Internet at http://www.doleta.gov/regs/omb/index.htm, the circular covers pre-award requirements, postaward requirements, after-the-award requirements, and contract provisions in an appendix.

The following is a summary of the information contained in the circular. Refer to the most current circular for specific information on each of the sections within each of the subparts:

- *Subpart A—General:* Purpose, definitions, effect on other issuances, deviations, subawards

- *Subpart B—Pre-Award Requirements:* Purpose, pre-award policies, forms for applying for federal assistance, debarment and suspension, special award conditions, metric system of measurement, Resource Conservation and Recovery Act, certifications and representations

- *Subpart C—Postaward Requirements:*

   Financial and Program Management—purpose of financial and program management, standards for financial management systems, payment, cost sharing or matching, program income, revision of budget and program plans, nonfederal audits, allowable costs, period of availability of funds, conditional exceptions

   Property Standards—purpose of property standards, insurance coverage, real property, federally owned and exempt property, equipment, supplies and other expendable property, intangible property, property trust relationship

   Procurement Standards—purpose of procurement standards, recipient responsibilities, codes of conduct, competition, procurement procedures, cost and price analysis, procurement records, contract administration, contract provisions

   Report and Records—purpose of report and records,　monitoring and reporting program performance, financial reporting, retention and access requirements for records

Termination and Enforcement—purpose of termination and enforcement, termination, enforcement

- *Subpart D—After-the-Award Requirements:* Purpose, closeout procedures, subsequent adjustments and continuing responsibilities, collection of amounts due

- *Appendix A—Contract Provisions*

When you consider that most of your district's requirements are equal to those called for under the government circulars, federal grant funds should not instill fear and trepidation in your district.

Most grants administrators' problems occur when their business office is involved in controlling purchase orders and bidding contracts. The business office may follow federal guidelines, but their purchase orders may not be seen by your grants office, and even though the correct procedure is followed the project director of the grant may purchase items not called for in the proposal. The business officers' responsibility is to make sure that there are funds available under the budget category and to bid out the purchase, not to look at the proposal's objectives and methods and question the project director relative to changes in purchase.

Similar problems occur when the grants office is not involved directly in personnel transactions. Even when the district personnel office follows federal guidelines for hiring, without a direct link to the grants office and to the functions that the proposed grant employee will perform, some project directors may abuse the system and hire inappropriate grant personnel.

In an effort to lower the payroll for central administration, some districts reduce the number of grants administration staff. The need may be real, but the district's ability to attract outside resources is directly related to the quality of its grants administration system. Therefore, districts that reduce the staff and the administrative functions performed by their grants office risk not only their credibility but also their access to future funds.

In addition, an inefficient grants administration system can mean the loss of funds intended to reimburse the grantee for costs of carrying out projects that are difficult to charge directly to the grant. These indirect costs include those needed to provide classrooms, office space, security, restrooms, payroll, personnel support, and so on. Although these reimbursable costs clearly play a critical role in supporting a district, they can be overlooked or undercharged if a district does not have a diligent, knowledgeable grants administration staff.

For example, many school districts are aware of their indirect cost rate for restricted federal programs (the restricted cost rate) but unaware of their rate for unrestricted federal programs (the unrestricted cost rate).

Districts that find themselves in this predicament often apply their restricted rate to all federal grant programs, even programs that allow them to use the unrestricted rate. In one school district I worked with, the grants administration staff was unaware of the district's unrestricted rate, so it applied the 2 percent restricted rate to all federal grants. With a little work, I was able to negotiate an unrestricted rate of 26 percent, which resulted in $25,000 more in reimbursed indirect costs from just one grant!

As you can see, the decentralized grants program exposes the school district to oversights as well as to legal and ethical problems. Even the most well-intentioned and ethical project director needs a system of checks and balances, which the grants office can provide.

CHAPTER 11 ASSESSMENT TOOL

Put a check mark next to those services and resources currently provided by your district grants office and an asterisk (*) next to those you do not provide now but would like to provide in the future. Rate the services and resources currently provided.

_____ Monitors contact with grantors between the time that a proposal is submitted and the time the decision is announced

     _____ inadequate   _____ adequate   _____ excellent

_____ Helps proposal developers handle a rejection, learn from the experience, and take the necessary steps to set the stage for resubmission

     _____ inadequate   _____ adequate   _____ excellent

_____ Helps proposal developers handle an award, thank the grantor, request necessary information, and avoid common pitfalls

     _____ inadequate   _____ adequate   _____ excellent

_____ Maintains an equipment inventory control system that identifies the source of funds, the location, and a maintenance record of all equipment purchased on a grant

     _____ inadequate   _____ adequate   _____ excellent

_____ Policy and procedures for procurement

     _____ inadequate   _____ adequate   _____ excellent

_____ Policy and procedures for personnel

     _____ inadequate   _____ adequate   _____ excellent

Put a check mark next to those items your grants office has access to. Record the location of the item and, when appropriate, the date of its publication. Put an asterisk (*) next to those items you do not currently have access to but would like to have access to in the future.

For Administering Private Funds

_____ Institute of Certified Public Accountants five volume guide

    Location: _____

    Date of publication: _____

_____ Generally Accepted Accounting Principles

    Location: _____

    Date of publication: _____

_____ 501(c)(3) Tax Exempt Status or an organization that will act on your behalf in accepting and disseminating private funds

For Administering Public Funds

_____ Office of Management and Budget's circular number A-110 and its updates and attachments, budget forms, and cash request instructions

    Location: _____

    Date of publication: _____

Chapter 12

Getting More People Involved in the Grants Process

However your superiors evaluate you as district grants administrator, your position will not be needed if your staff and volunteers do not attract grants. With this in mind, it is difficult to understand why many grant administrators manage grant funds procured from someone else's efforts day after day without ever examining the following:

- Why proposal developers volunteer their time to prepare grant proposals

- What they get out of the process

- How a grants office can encourage more individuals to become involved in grantseeking

- Why some staff and volunteers are reluctant to become involved in grantseeking

- How this noninvolvement could be reversed or diminished

- The policies, procedures, and support services a grants office can use to increase the number of awarded grants

It is remarkable that a force as potent as the multibillion-dollar grants marketplace has produced so little research on why project directors involve themselves in grantseeking. In higher education the reasons for involvement are thought to be related to job advancement, tenure, and the publish-or-perish atmosphere that exists in the world of academic research. However, many very successful college and university grantseekers continue to invest their time in the process of grantseeking even after they are tenured and have earned a rank that cannot be rescinded.

Grantseekers continue to develop proposals even if they have to do it in their spare time. Few receive release time or extra pay for writing proposals: making extra money after the grant is awarded is not a motivator because most grantors provide repayment to the grantee's organization for the time grantseekers need to be released from their regular duties in order to carry out the project. It is possible to derive some income from a funded proposal for work performed over the summer, but even this is not a strong motivator. Federal grant rules restrict the salaries of individuals working on a grant to their regular pay scale and will not pay for time invested in writing the proposal because this is considered a cost incurred before the award date.

So what does motivate individuals to involve themselves in the stressful and often disappointing process of grantseeking? According to scholars Sharol Jacobson and Mary O'Brien's 1992 study in *Image: Journal of Nursing Scholarship* (24:1, 45-49), probably the following:

- Personal and social rewards

- Feelings of accomplishment, increased self-esteem, and social gain

- Material and career rewards, including travel, extra space, equipment, support staff, and increased professional recognition, as exemplified by invitations to become a peer reviewer or speaker at professional meetings

- Impact on the grantee's organization, including public relations opportunities and increased credibility for the grantee's department and school

Review these satisfiers. What does your district grants office do to foster your grantseekers' sense of accomplishment, recognition, and self-esteem? Identify your existing strategies on the Grantseekers' Satisfiers Worksheet (Figure 12.1).

Many of the techniques listed on the worksheet can be relatively inexpensive to initiate or expand by using a little creativity. For example, one grants office administrator I worked with funded his grants-recognition program in a rather interesting way. During a discussion with a corporate volunteer on his grants advisory committee, he asked about the techniques the volunteer's corporation employed to encourage workers to strive for superior performance. He was pleasantly surprised to discover that the corporation placed great emphasis on the acknowledgment of superior performance on the job. In fact, the list of recognition techniques and rewards used by the corporation was rather extensive and included airline travel, vacations, plaques, honorary dinners, and the use of corporate public relations personnel to write and distribute press releases. Ultimately, the discussion culminated in a grant from the corporation to fund the grant administrator's recognition program!

Figure 12.1

GRANTSEEKERS' SATISFIERS WORKSHEET

Review the following list of techniques that can be used to promote a positive grants atmosphere. Put a check mark next to those that are currently part of your grants system and evaluate each for its effectiveness. Put an asterisk next to those that you would like to incorporate into your district's system.

Recognition

_____ Publish the list of proposal initiators in district or school newsletter when projects receive official endorsement and sign-on
_____ very effective   _____ effective   _____ not effective

_____ Official announcement of intent to apply (announcement made at _____)
_____ very effective   _____ effective   _____ not effective

_____ Publication of notice of award (published in _____)
_____ very effective   _____ effective   _____ not effective

_____ Provide PR release to local newspapers (newspapers_____)
_____ very effective   _____ effective   _____ not effective

_____ Official announcement of award _____
(announcement made at _____)
_____ very effective   _____ effective   _____ not effective

_____ Invitation to present grant findings at:
_____ school/community committee meetings
_____ school board meetings
_____ teacher in-service workshops
_____ regional/national meetings
_____ other _____
_____ very effective   _____ effective   _____ not effective

_____ Recognition at special awards/dinner presentation
_____ very effective   _____ effective   _____ not effective

_____ Presentation of plaques, pins, and so on
_____ very effective   _____ effective   _____ not effective

_____ Promotion of grantseeking as evidenced by increased support in
• Space
_____ very effective   _____ effective   _____ not effective
• Equipment
_____ very effective   _____ effective   _____ not effective
• Released time
_____ very effective   _____ effective   _____ not effective
• Secretarial assistance
_____ very effective   _____ effective   _____ not effective
• Travel budget to visit grantors
_____ very effective   _____ effective   _____ not effective
• Long-distance telephone budget
_____ very effective   _____ effective   _____ not effective

The grants administrator didn't have to sell the corporation on the idea of a recognition program. Corporations are already aware of the benefits of satisfying an individual's need for achievement and recognition. Survey your corporate advisory committee members to collect information on the recognition programs that hotels, restaurants, health care facilities, stores, and manufacturers in your community use. But remember, corporate recognition programs reward work well done on the job. Your recognition program will reward work that occurs in addition to regular job duties as well as the amount of funding your grantseekers can generate for their schools and the district.

What about the stressful aspects of grantseeking? According to one study, managing the budget tops the list of stress-inducing factors. One respondent wrote:

> *I was totally shocked by how my project and I were treated by the school's financial manager. People are always proposing ways in which my funds can be used for some other purpose in the school. Every requisition I send is questioned. I feel like I'm regarded either as a potential embezzler or at best as a financial incompetent and that my project is some sort of goose laying golden eggs.*

This grantee provides a pretty clear indication of why some successful grantseekers may not be excited about creating their next proposal!

Fortunately, you can identify and remedy problems such as this by requesting that your grant recipients evaluate your grants office's services on an annual basis. Other stressful experiences may not be under your office's control and therefore may not be as easy for you to deal with such as:

- The incompatibility of the grantee's accounting system and the grantor's budget categories and allowable expenditures
- Compliance with the grantor's financial reporting requirements
- Problems hiring and supervising project personnel
- Frustration over the bid process and obtaining equipment
- Fatigue and emotional distress
- Inadequate administrative support

The Evaluating Your Grants Office Worksheet (Figure 12.2) will help you identify the areas in your grants system that are causing frustration.

Some grants administration staffs take an adversarial position when dealing with grantees. This is unfortunate because their role should be that of a service provider. The district grants office should provide

---

Figure 12.2

EVALUATING YOUR GRANTS OFFICE WORKSHEET

Rate how good your grants office is at providing assistance in the following areas:

1. **Development of proposal ideas**
    _____ exceptional   _____ satisfactory   _____ needs improvement

2. **Organization and development of a grants strategy**
    _____ exceptional   _____ satisfactory   _____ needs improvement

3. **Searching for potential grantors**
    _____ exceptional   _____ satisfactory   _____ needs improvement

4. **Procuring lists of grantees and reviewers and sample proposals**
    _____ exceptional   _____ satisfactory   _____ needs improvement

5. **Making preproposal contact**
    _____ exceptional   _____ satisfactory   _____ needs improvement

6. **Developing proposal budgets**
    _____ exceptional   _____ satisfactory   _____ needs improvement

7. **Organizing quality circles and mock reviews**
    _____ exceptional   _____ satisfactory   _____ needs improvement

8. **Proposal sign-off and submittal**
    _____ exceptional   _____ satisfactory   _____ needs improvement

9. **Developing follow-up with grantors including procuring reviewer comments when available**
    _____ exceptional   _____ satisfactory   _____ needs improvement

10. **Adminstration of projects including:**
    *   Hiring personnel
        _____ exceptional   _____ satisfactory   _____ needs improvement
    *   Purchasing equipment
        _____ exceptional   _____ satisfactory   _____ needs improvement
    *   Procuring supplies
        _____ exceptional   _____ satisfactory   _____ needs improvement
    *   Submitting reports
        _____ exceptional   _____ satisfactory   _____ needs improvement

11. **Overall cooperation of the grants office**
    _____ exceptional   _____ satisfactory   _____ needs improvement

---

services aimed at helping its customers, your grantseekers, have a satisfying experience so that they keep developing proposals. The grants office's motto should be "us *for* them" rather than "us *versus* them."

Your office can demonstrate its willingness to reach out to grantseekers by developing and disseminating a booklet that examines and addresses the stressful aspects of successful grantseeking. You may even organize a learning session for grantees that outlines how to deal with common areas of stress. No matter how you decide to handle this delicate issue, any and all of your efforts should be aimed at improving your school district's grants administration system.

CHAPTER 12 ASSESSMENT TOOL

1. **Does your district currently recognize proposal development efforts in any special ways?**

   _____ yes   _____ no

   If yes, how? _____

   _____

   _____

   _____

2. **Does your district currently recognize successful grantseekers in any special ways?**

   _____ yes   _____ no

   If yes, how? _____

   _____

   _____

   _____

3. **Rate how good your district grants administration system is at:**

   - Providing timely and accurate account balances to grant recipients

     _____ poor   _____ good   _____ excellent

   - Supporting changes in budget categories

     _____ poor   _____ good   _____ excellent

   - Encouraging the appropriate hiring and supervising of project personnel

     _____ poor   _____ good   _____ excellent

   - Helping in the bid process and the purchasing of equipment

     _____ poor   _____ good   _____ excellent

   - Assisting in compliance with grantor requirements

     _____ poor   _____ good   _____ excellent

Chapter 13

Supporting Planning and Resource Development

IN ADDITION to supporting a proactive grants system with a focus on locating grants for education programs and projects, your district grants office can provide valuable assistance in districtwide long-range and strategic planning. As most plans require new or expanded funding in addition to the reallocation of current district resources, who would be more valuable than the district grants administrator as a member of the strategic planning team?

Planning

The grants administrator who heads a reactive grants system is seldom asked to participate in such a proactive activity as planning for the future. Failure to involve the grants administrator in the district's planning function results in using district funds for programs, buildings, and equipment that could and should have been procured through grants. By supporting new and creative programs with district funds, the grants office is often left with the responsibility of locating support for programs and projects that are extremely difficult to fund through the grants mechanism.

In these instances, the grants office's order of involvement in the planning process should be changed from last to first. By having an early and active role in the planning function, the grants administrator can help the district develop strategies that capitalize on the opportunities provided by the grants marketplace.

For example, it would be much better for a district to expend a small amount of money on a needs-assessment project to help create a credible grant-winning federal proposal than to expend a small amount of money on a large problem that results in little or no change. This is the kind of insight the district grants administrator can provide to the strategic planning team. But to do so, the administrator must keep up with changes in grantor priorities and demonstrate leadership in changing the system. In addition, the grants office must be viewed as a potent and dynamic force in funding educational advancement.

Influencing Legislation

To have an impact on the current crisis in education, more grant programs need to be created and more funds must be appropriated at both the state and national levels. Realizing this, it may be difficult for your grants office to stay away from influencing legislation. You must, however, because you have probably signed assurances that federal grant funds will not be utilized to lobby for more grant funds and because your nonprofit status makes it illegal for you to lobby. But your grants office can take an active role in making sure that the educational organizations your district belongs to continue to educate state and federal elected officials to make enlightened decisions related to education. In addition, it can provide your school board and superintendent with the leadership and direction needed to help them make your students' needs known in your state capital and in Washington.

The district grants office is the logical place to keep information on elected officials that may be needed to help others make their opinions and support known. This information should include linkages, committee assignments, addresses, phone numbers, and so on.

It is important that you make elected officials understand that they should work to create grant funds that all schools can apply for. You do not want them to encourage a grant to your district that is not based on competition and peer review. Specifically, you do not want an elected official to place a clause or restriction on a noneducation bill that mandates an education grant to your district if it is passed. This is referred to as earmarking federal legislation, and it is not held in high esteem in the grants marketplace.

Earmarking has been on the increase in recent years, but it should be avoided just as lobbying should be. Earmarking public funds (state or federal) brings discredit to the grants system and can result in a negative reaction from other districts. In addition, federal bureaucrats do not like to handle earmarked grant funds because the proposal (which is not even written at the time the bill is passed) is not required to compete with other proposals. Peer review has no effect, and thus a political grants decision, not a professional decision by experts in the field, will be made.

This type of irresponsible behavior subverts the purpose of peer-reviewed competitive grantseeking and reduces the grants process to a contest of political strength. Many institutions of higher education have developed a written policy that requires the return or refusal of any grant funds made available through earmarking. Only time will tell how elementary and secondary educational institutions will fare. Ethics are easy to support until resources shrink and needs become critical.

Your district grants office should censure earmarking for ethical reasons and also because there would be no need for your office if earmarking was the grantseeking method of choice. There would only be a need for an office of political influence.

A booklet aimed at educating district leaders may help you expand your office's traditional role. This document could take the form of a position paper or even a proposal to position the grants office as a vital component of your district's planning and resource-development process.

CHAPTER 13 ASSESSMENT TOOL

Does your district have a strategic planning team?

_____ yes _____ no _____ not sure

If yes, do you serve on it? _____ yes _____ no

If you do not serve on it, have you ever requested to do so? _____ yes _____ no

Put a check mark next to the activities your grants office currently does to position itself as a valuable partner in your district's planning and resource-development process. Rate your effort at these activities.

_____ Keeps current on grantor priorities and informs district administration of future funding and grant opportunities

_____ poor _____ good _____ excellent

_____ Takes an active role in ensuring that the organizations your district belongs to educate state and federal elected officials to make enlightened decisions related to education

_____ poor _____ good _____ excellent

_____Provides your school board and superintendent with the direction needed to help them make your students' needs known in your state capital and in Washington

_____ poor _____ good _____ excellent

Chapter 14

Evaluating and Improving Your District's Grants Effort

EACH CHAPTER in this book encourages you to evaluate your district's grants system and to consider ways it can be improved. Some administrators may think it unwise to invest in their grants systems when they are being asked to make drastic cuts in so many other areas. But investing in grantseeking by expanding the scope and role of your district grants office provides a great payoff—an increase in funding. Encouraging staff and volunteers to invest their spare time in the worthwhile effort of grantseeking is critical not only to positioning your grants office for the future, but to developing the resources needed to address the problems in your school district and improve education.

Review each chapter and reevaluate your grants system's areas of weakness. Place the action steps or techniques you would like to implement to deal with these weaknesses on a project planner. Your project planner should ultimately outline how you will move your grants office into the future and provide the basis for your grants plan.

The Grants Plan Sample Project Planner (Figure 14.1) lists activities that could be used to increase a district's ability to gain access to the grants marketplace. However, the sample is not intended to be replicated. Your grants office should develop an individualized grants plan tailored to your district.

Use the same approach you would use to prepare a proposal to develop your Grants Plan. By doing so, you will find it easier to capture your administration's interest and commitment.

As with a proposal, you must first outline the need. To demonstrate your district's need for an improved grants system, you must present a clear picture of what exists now. This will help accentuate the problems that need to be remedied or addressed and set the stage for the activities or methods you will prescribe to solve or alleviate these problems.

Figure 14.1

GRANTS PLAN SAMPLE PROJECT PLANNER

PROJECT PLANNER

PROJECT TITLE: Grants Plan – Sample Project Planner

Proposal Developed for: _____

Project Director: _____ Proposed Start Date _____ Proposal Year _____

A. List project objectives or outcomes A. B.
B. List methods to accomplish each objective as A-1, A-2, ... B-1, B-2, ...

| | MONTH Begin End C/D | TIME E | PROJECT PERSONNEL F | PERSONNEL COSTS Salaries & Wages G | Fringe Benefits H | Total I | CONSULTANTS CONTRACT SERVICES Time J | Cost/Week K | Total L | NON-PERSONNEL RESOURCES NEEDED SUPPLIES – EQUIPMENT – MATERIALS Item M | Cost/Item N | Quantity O | Tot cost P | SUB-TOTAL ACTIVITY COST Total I,L,P Q | MILESTONES PROGRESS INDICATORS Item R | Date S % of Total |

A. Program Objective – Increase the number of proposals submitted by the school district by 50% in one year.

A-1 Method – Initiate a community grants advisory committee in six schools.

a. Develop list of potential members
b. Invite to meeting (phone and mail)
c. Involve group in reviewing school's needs, problems, and opportunities
d. Brainstorm solutions
e. Divide group by problem area
f. Develop a linkage survey of contacts with grantors and resources that they will share

A-2 Method – Create a proposal development package for district/community.

a. Develop a proposal sign-on/idea endorsement procedure
b. Tailor worksheets for idea generation and key search word development
c. Print and disseminate package

A-3 Method – Set up a grants library.

a. Purchase state foundation book
b. Purchase Foundation Grants Index
c. Purchase Foundation Directory

Total Direct Costs or Costs Requested From Funder
Matching Funds, In-Kind Contributions, or Donated Costs
Total Costs

100%

©David G. Bauer Associates, Inc.
(800) 836-0732

Figure 14.1 (continued)

PROJECT PLANNER

PROJECT TITLE: Grants Plan - Sample Project Planner

Proposal Developed for: _____

Project Director: _____

Proposed Start Date _____

Proposal Year _____

A. List project objectives or outcomes A. B. B. List methods to accomplish each objective as A-1, A-2, ... B-1, B-2 ...	MONTH Begin C/D	MONTH End	TIME E	PROJECT PERSONNEL F	PERSONNEL COSTS Salaries & Wages G	PERSONNEL COSTS Fringe Benefits H	PERSONNEL COSTS Total I	CONSULTANTS CONTRACT SERVICES Time J	CONSULTANTS CONTRACT SERVICES Cost/Week K	CONSULTANTS CONTRACT SERVICES Total L	NON-PERSONNEL RESOURCES NEEDED SUPPLIES - EQUIPMENT - MATERIALS Item M	Cost/Item N	Quantity O	Tot cost P	SUB-TOTAL ACTIVITY COST Total I,L,P Q	MILESTONES PROGRESS INDICATORS Item R	Date S
A-4 Method - Set up a computer-based grants searching system.																	
a. Select database for federal grants searching																	
b. Set up federal searching system																	
c. Select database for foundation/corporate grants searching																	
d. Set up foundation/corporate searching system																	
A-5 Method - Provide searches to grantseekers																	
B. Program objective - Increase quality of proposals and acceptance rate.																	
B-1 Method - Develop a proposal writer's guide.																	
a. Write guide and tailor worksheets																	
b. Print and disseminate guide																	
c. Provide information on how grantseekers can obtain help getting lists of grantees, reviewers, etc.																	
d. Provide information on how to make preproposal contact and how to get assistance in this area																	
B-2 Method - Develop a quality circle/mock review of proposals.																	
a. Assist in getting list of review/evaluation criteria																	
b. Complete descriptions of reviewers for role playing																	
c. Ask potential grantseekers to take part in mock review																	

Total Direct Costs or Costs Requested From Funder
Matching Funds, In-Kind Contributions, or Donated Costs
Total Costs

100%   % of Total

©David G. Bauer Associates, Inc.
(800) 836-0732

What Exists Now

Consider the following questions:

- How many proposals does your office handle per year? What is its success rate?

- How much money do you apply for, and how much are you awarded?

- How does your office deal with the new challenges and pressures posed by decentralized grantseeking?

- How does it handle the risks inherent in having all the schools in your district looking for grants at the same time? (Use case studies or examples of damage to your district's image, or quote a grantor concerning the confusion caused by the submittal of multiple proposals from the same school district.)

- How knowledgeable are your schools' staffs about the grants marketplace, and what is the attitude toward grantseeking? (If necessary, survey your schools to gather this valuable baseline data.)

- What are your district grants office's constraints in terms of resources (staff time, current workload, grants administration requirements, and so on)?

One technique to document your office's current workload is to develop a grants office yearly planner. Purchase an erasable plastic-coated perpetual calendar and plot your district's major proposal deadlines, blocking out the preparation time needed for each proposal. This visual aid will help illustrate how your current resources are expended relative to the major proposals that your office handles.

The yearly planner can also be used to help you develop your personnel's vacation schedules and accurately estimate heavy work periods. Because the district's major proposals will have deadlines that are either published months in advance or fall at approximately the same time each year, you can anticipate when your office's sixty-hour work weeks will occur and show your staff how they happen at just about the same time each year!

What Could Be

The next section of your plan should state the goals and objectives of your future grants office. Before you can get your district excited about the methods you want to use to improve the grants system, you must show the powers that be what could happen if your office can improve its access to the grants marketplace.

Use any wish lists you have obtained from school units to show how the education system could be improved in your district if your grants office were able to match your people's ideas and solutions with potential funding sources.

Quote several well-chosen statistics that document your grants potential:

- The number of foundations in your state that fund projects in education and other related areas

- The number of grants awarded by these foundations annually and their dollar value

- The number of corporations you could approach with an improved system

Also, explain how the expansion and improvement of your grants system could result in more federal and state grant funds and how an expanded grants effort could help community groups prepare proposals or work with your school on consortium grants.

The Solution

As you now know, the only real way to close the gap between what is and what could be is to develop a proactive grants system. This will probably require a total shift in the way your district grantseekers currently view the grants process. It is your office's responsibility to educate them on the necessity for preproposal contact and proposal-improvement groups and to support them in a system that uses these techniques to increase grant success.

Your Grants Plan should be designed to influence your district to support the changes necessary and to provide more funds to pay for them. However, if your district supports the changes but cannot provide the financial backing, you have one other option. You can get a grant to support the necessary changes!

By the time you have finished developing your plan you will have clearly documented the return on your investment in an improved grants system. Surely there must be corporations or foundations in your area that are interested in investing in a plan aimed at improving education and moving your schools into the future.

You could interest a larger number of potential funders in your plan by redefining it and changing its focus from improving your district's grants system to developing a community grants system to support youth and education throughout your community. At first glance it may look as though the approach could mean a lot more work for your office. However, your community-based organizations would still be responsible for writing their own proposals. Your office would simply provide them with searches for potential funders. In reality, the community grants system approach may not be that much more work for your office, and it would allow for consortia approaches that could dramatically increase your fundability by making many more grant opportunities available to you.

A Sample Proposal to Fund Your Grants Office (Figure 14.2) is provided to help you develop your own proposal.

Figure 14.2

SAMPLE PROPOSAL TO FUND YOUR GRANTS OFFICE

By surveying each of the schools in our district we identified our educational system's [or community's] most critical needs and developed a prioritized list of projects and programs to address these needs. For example, the math and science scores of our district's sixth-grade students have fallen _____ percent below those of our neighboring school district and _____ percent below our state norms. Because of this we have decided that one of our top priorities is to develop and implement a program to help parents, teachers, and community members become responsible partners in enhancing our district's math and science curriculum.

Unfortunately, this program and some of the other solutions to our district's [community's] most pressing problems cannot be funded through our district's current resources. The money is just not there. But we can utilize the grants marketplace to implement solutions to improve our educational system [community].

Instead of approaching our taxpayers to fund the programs needed in our district through increases in the school budget, we should improve our district's ability to access the billions in grants awarded annually by corporations, foundations, and the federal government.

Corporations grant approximately $_____ billion each year to educational institutions. Our best corporate grant opportunities lie with the largest employers in our community, who are concerned about the ability of our schools to serve their future employment needs. When approached they will realize that they could benefit by helping to ensure that our young people have a superior education.

Foundations provided competitive grant opportunities totaling over $_____ last year. Approximately _____ percent of these funds were granted to education. Our state alone has _____ foundations with assets totaling $_____, and our district should be able to tap into some of these resources.

The federal government supports the largest grant programs to education. Last year our district grants office was directly involved in preparing _____ federal proposals that resulted in $_____. Some of these government funds were provided to our schools based on a formula that involved the need and the number of students in a particular group, and some were a result of the competitive grants process.

Our district's overall proposal success rate (foundation, corporate, and federal) is currently _____ percent. However, when you look at competitive proposals only, our rate drops to _____ percent.

Figure 14.2 (continued)

One explanation for this may be found in a survey we conducted of our district personnel a few months ago. The survey results revealed that in general, district personnel are not very knowledgeable of the grants marketplace and do not know much about grantseeking.

We believe that we could augment our district resources significantly by developing a dynamic grants office and investing in a system that teaches our district personnel and our hundreds of volunteers how to effectively use the grants marketplace.

The attached project planner outlines the steps necessary to develop a dynamic grants office in our district and details the cash expenditures and the rationale for each expense. It also provides the basis for the necessary job descriptions.

We would like the _____ Foundation/Corporation to join with us in working toward our goals to:

1. Increase the number of proposals developed to meet our school district's mission and improve the quality of these proposals.

2. Increase the acceptance rate of submitted proposals and consortium efforts.

3. Promote involvement of community organizations in developing solutions to school/community problems.

4. Promote community efforts at locating and attracting grant-funding opportunities for youth and education.

The following objectives have been developed to move our schools toward these goals.

- Increase the number of proposals submitted by our schools by _____ percent in one year.
- Increase the number of grants awarded to our schools by _____ percent in one year.
- Increase the number of school-community consortium proposals by _____ percent in one year.
- Increase grant funding for priority projects and bring in $_____ in outside resources.

We need your help to achieve these objectives. Specifically, we are requesting a grant of $_____ from [company/foundation] to help us fund our Grants Office. As I am sure you will agree, this project addresses [corporations/foundation's] concern for quality education and the young people in our community in a unique and innovative fashion. Further, the amount of our request is commensurate with your granting history.

[Corporation's/Foundation's] grant would amount to $_____ per student served by our district. However, it has the potential to generate $_____ per student served in dividends by year three of the project. When compared to the funds we expect to realize as a result of our improved grants system, this project is clearly an excellent investment.

If you have any questions or wish to discuss this proposal further, please contact my office or [name], our grants administrator, at [phone number].

Bibliography

Federal Government Grant Resources

Catalog of Federal Domestic Assistance (CFDA)
CFDA is the government's most complete listing of federal domestic assistance programs, with details on eligibility, application procedures, and deadlines, including the location of state plans. It is published at the beginning of each fiscal year, with supplementary updates during the year. Indexes are by agency program, function, popular name, applicant eligibility, and subject. It comes in looseleaf form, punched for a three-ring binder. **Price:** $72 a year. **Order from:** Superintendent of Documents, P.O. Box 271954, Pittsburgh, PA 15250-7954, (202) 512-1800, www.gsa.gov/fdac/default.htm

Commerce Business Daily
This government contracts publication, published five times a week, announces every government Request for Proposal (RFP) that exceeds $25,000, as well as upcoming sales of government surplus. **Price:** $274 to $324 a year depending on postage. **Order from:** Superintendent of Documents, P.O. Box 271954, Pittsburgh, PA 15250-7954, (202) 512-1800, cbdnet.access.gpo.gov

Congressional Record
This covers the day-to-day proceedings of the Senate and House of Representatives. **Price:** $295 a year. **Order from:** Superintendent of Documents, P.O. Box 271954, Pittsburgh, PA 15250-7954, (202) 512-1800, www.access.gpo.gov/su_docs/aces/aces150.html

Federal Register
Published five times a week (Monday through Friday), this supplies up-to-date information on federal assistance and supplements the *Catalog of*

Federal Domestic Assistance (CFDA). It includes public regulations and legal notices issued by all federal agencies and presidential proclamations. Of particular importance are the proposed rules, final rules, and program deadlines. An index is published monthly. **Price:** $607 a year with indexes, $555 a year without. **Order from:** Superintendent of Documents, P.O. Box 271954, Pittsburgh, PA 15250-7954, (202) 512-1800, www.nara.gov/fedreg/

National Science Foundation (NSF) E-Bulletin
Provides news about NSF programs, deadline dates, publications, and meetings, as well as sources for more information. Available electronically. Readers without Internet access can send requests for a print-on-demand monthly edition to paperbulletin@nsf.gov. **Price:** free. **For information contact:** National Science Foundation, 4201 Wilson Boulevard, Arlington, VA 22230, (703) 306-1234, www. nsf.gov/home/ebulletin

NIH Guide for Grants and Contracts
Published weekly. **Price:** free. Electronic access now available. **For information contact:** National Institutes of Health, Institutional Affairs Office, Building 1 Room 328, Bethesda, MD 20892, (301) 496-5366, www.nih.gov/grants/guide

U.S. Government Manual
This paperback gives the names of key personnel, addresses, and telephone numbers for all agencies, departments, and so on, that constitute the federal bureaucracy. **Price:** $41 a year. **Order from:** Superintendent of Documents, P.O. Box 371954, Pittsburgh, PA 15250-7954, (202) 512-1800, www.access.gpo.gov/nara/nara001.html

Academic Research Information System, Inc. (ARIS)
ARIS provides timely information about grant and contract opportunities, including concise descriptions of guidelines and eligibility requirements, upcoming deadline dates, identification of program resource persons, and new program policies for both government and nongovernment funding sources. Reports are available in printed and electronic versions. **Price:** depends on version and whether the subscription is institutional or individual. For Biomedical Sciences Report, Social and Natural Science Report, or Humanities Report, order or call for pricing information from Academic Research Information System Inc., The Redstone Building, 2940 16th Street Suite 314, San Francisco, CA 94103, (415) 558-8133, www.arisnet.com

Education Daily
Price: $598 for 250 issues. **Order from:** Aspen Publishers Inc., 7201 McKinney Circle, Frederick, MD 21704, (800) 638-8437.

Education Grants Alert
Price: $329 for fifty issues. **Order from:** Aspen Publishers Inc., 7201 McKinney Circle, Frederick, MD 21704, (800) 638-8437.

Federal Directory
This includes names, addresses, and phone numbers of federal government agencies and key personnel. **Price:** $300 a year. **Order from:** Carroll Publishing, 1058 Thomas Jefferson Street NW, Washington, DC 20007, (202) 333-8620.

Federal Grants and Contracts Weekly
This contains information on the latest Requests for Proposals (RFPs), contracting opportunities, and upcoming grants. Each issue includes details on RFPs, closing dates for grant programs, procurement-related news, and newly issued regulations. **Price:** $349 for 50 issues. **Order from:** Aspen Publishers Inc., 7201 McKinney Circle, Frederick, MD 21704, (800) 638-8437.

Federal Yellow Book
This directory of federal departments and agencies is updated quarterly. **Price:** $290. **Order from:** Leadership Directories Inc., 104 Fifth Avenue, 3rd Floor, New York, NY 10011, (212) 627-4140.

Health Grants and Contracts Weekly
Price: $379 for 50 issues. **Order from:** Aspen Publishers Inc., 7201 McKinney Circle, Frederick, MD 21704, (800) 638-8437.

Washington Information Directory, 1999/2000
This directory is divided into three categories: agencies of the executive branch, Congress; and private or "non-governmental" organizations. Each entry includes the name, address, telephone number, and director of the organization along with a short description of its work. **Price:** $110. **Order from:** Congressional Quarterly Books, 1414 22nd Street NW, Washington, DC 20037, (800) 638-1710.

Foundation Grant Resources

Many of the following research aids can be found through the Foundation Center Cooperating Collections Network. If you wish to purchase any of them, contact The Foundation Center, 79 Fifth Avenue, Dept. FJ, New York, NY 10003-3076, (800) 424-9836, or, in New York State, (212) 807-3690, fax (212) 808-3677, http://www.fdncenter.org

AIDS Funding: A Guide to Giving by Foundations and Charitable Organizations, 5th edition
Over six hundred grantmakers who have stated or demonstrated a committment to AIDS-related services and research are identified here. **Price:** $75. **Order from:** The Foundation Center, 79 Fifth Avenue, Dept. FJ, New York, NY 10003-3076, (800) 424-9836, or, in New York State, (212) 807-3690, fax (212)808-3677, http://www.fdncenter.org

Corporate Foundation Profiles, 10th edition
This book contains detailed analyses of 195 of the largest corporate foundations in America. An appendix lists financial data on hundreds of smaller grantmakers. **Price:** $155. **Order from:** The Foundation Center, 79 Fifth Avenue, Dept. FJ, New York, NY 10003-3076, (800) 424-9836, or in New York State, (212) 807-3690, fax (212) 808-3677, http://www.fdncenter.org

Directory of Operation Grants, 4th edition
Profiles on more than eight hundred foundations receptive to proposals for operating grants. **Price:** $59.50. **Order from:** Research Grant Guides, P.O. Box 1214, Loxahatchee, FL 33470, (561) 795-6129, fax (561) 795-7794. No credit card or telephone orders accepted.

Foundation and Corporate Grants Alert
Price: $297 for fifty issues. **Order from:** Aspen Publishers Inc., 7201 McKinney Circle, Frederick, MD 21704, (800) 638-8437.

The Foundation Directory, 1999 edition
The most important single reference work on grantmakers in the United States, this includes information on foundations having assets of more than $2 million or annual grants exceeding $200,000. Each entry includes a description of donor interests and its address, telephone number, current financial data, contact person, and IRS identification number. Six types of index are included: donors, officers, and trustees; geography; types of support; subject; foundations new to edition index; and foundation name index. The index to donors, officers, and trustees is very valuable in developing links to decision makers. **Price:** $215 hardcover, $185 softcover. **Order from:** The Foundation Center; see above.

The Foundation Directory Part 2, March 1999
This provides information on over 4,900 midsize foundations with grant programs that award between twenty-five and one hundred thousand dollars. Published biennially. **Price:** $185 for *Part 2*; $485 for hardcover *Directory, Supplement,* and *Part 2*; $455 for softcover *Directory, Supplement,* and *Part 2*. **Order from:** The Foundation Center; see above.

The Foundation Directory Supplement, September 1999
This updates the *Directory* so that users will have the latest addresses, contacts, policy statements, application guidelines, and financial data. **Price:** $125 for *Supplement*; $320 hardcover for *Directory* and *Supplement*; $290 for softcover *Directory* and *Supplement*. **Order from:** The Foundation Center; see above.

Foundation Giving Watch
News and the "how-tos" of foundation giving are provided in this monthly newsletter, along with a listing of recent grants. **Price:** $149 for twelve issues. **Order from:** Gale Group, P.O. Box 9187, Farmington Hills, MI 48333-9187, (800) 877-8238.

The Foundation Grants Index, 1999 edition
This is a cumulative listing of over 86,000 grants of $10,000 or more made by over a thousand major foundations. A recipient name index, a subject index, a type of support/geographic index, a recipient category index, and an index to grants by foundation are included. **Price:** $165. **Order from:** The Foundation Center; see above.

Foundation Grants to Individuals, 11th edition
This directory provides a comprehensive listing of over 3,800 independent and corporate foundations that provide financial assistance to individuals. **Price:** $65. **Order from:** The Foundation Center (see above).

Foundation News
Each bimonthly issue covers the activities of private, company-sponsored, and community foundations, direct corporate giving, and government agencies and their programs, and includes the kinds of grants being awarded, overall trends, legal matters, regulatory actions, and other areas of common concern. **Price:** $48 annually or $88 for two years. **Order from:** Council on Foundations, P.O. Box 96043, Washington, DC 20077-7188, (202) 466-6512.

The Foundation 1,000, 1998/1999 edition
The 1,000 largest U.S. foundations are profiled by foundation name, subject field, type of support, and geographic location. An index allows you to target grantmakers by the names of officers, staff, and trustees. **Price:** $295. **Order from:** The Foundation Center (see above).

Foundations of the 1990s, May 1998
This publication describes more than 9,000 independent, community, and corporate foundations that have incorporated as grantmaking institutions in the United States after 1990. **Price:** $150. **Order from:** The Foundation Center (see above).

Foundation Reporter

This annual directory of the largest private charitable foundations in the United States supplies descriptions and statistical analyses. **Price:** $415. **Order from:** Gale Group, P.O. Box 9187, Farmington Hills, MI 48333-9187, (800) 877-8238.

Grant Guides

Thirty-five *Grant Guides* are available in a variety of areas such as children and youth, alcohol and drug abuse, mental health, addictions and crisis services, minorities, the homeless, public health and diseases, and social services. Each provides descriptions of hundreds of foundation grants of $10,000 or more recently awarded in its subject area. Sources of funding are indexed by type of organization, subject focus, and geographic funding area. Of the thirty-five guides, eight are in the field of education, including elementary and secondary education, higher education, libraries and information services, literacy, reading and adult/continuing education, scholarships, student aid and loans, science and technology programs, and social and political programs. **Price:** $75 each. **Order from:** The Foundation Center (see above).

Guide to Funding for International and Foreign Programs, 4th edition (May 1998)

This includes over eight hundred funding sources that award grants to international nonprofit institutions and projects, as well as over six thousand grant descriptions. **Price:** $115. **Order from:** The Foundation Center (see above).

Guide to U.S. Foundations, Their Trustees, Officers, and Donors (April 1998, 2 vols.)

Includes information on over 40,000 U.S. private, corporate, and community foundations and an index to the individuals who establish, manage, and oversee them. **Price:** $215. **Order from:** The Foundation Center (see above).

National Guide to Funding for Elementary and Secondary Education, 4th edition (May 1997).

Over 2,400 sources of funding for elementary and secondary education and over 6,300 grant descriptions listing organizations that have successfully approached these funding sources are included in this guide. **Price:** $140. **Order from:** The Foundation Center (see above).

National Guide to Funding for the Environment and Animal Welfare, 4th edition (June 1998)

Includes over two thousand sources of funding for environment- and animal welfare–related nonprofit institutions and projects, as well as over

4,800 grant descriptions. **Price:** $95. **Order from:** The Foundation Center (see above).

National Guide to Funding in Arts and Culture, 5th edition (May 1998)
This guide includes over 5,200 sources of funding for arts- and culture-related nonprofit organizations and projects, as well as over 12,700 grant descriptions. **Price:** $145. **Order from:** The Foundation Center (see above).

National Guide to Funding in Health, 5th edition (April 1997)
This guide includes over 3,800 sources for health-related projects and institutions and over 12,000 grant descriptions. **Price:** $150. **Order from:** The Foundation Center (see above).

National Guide to Funding in Higher Education, 5th edition (June 1998)
Over 3,900 sources of funding for higher education projects and institutions and over fifteen thousand grant descriptions are included. **Price:** $145. **Order from:** The Foundation Center (see above).

Other National Guides from the Foundation Center
These are available in the following areas and for the indicated price:

> *Aging* (1995), $95
> *Children, Youth and Families* (1997), $150
> *Community Development* (1998), $135
> *Information Technology* (1997), $115
> *Libraries and Information Services* (1997), $95
> *Religion* (1997), $140
> *Substance Abuse* (1998), $95
> *Women and Girls* (1997), $115

Who Gets Grants, 5th edition (February 1998)
This book features over sixty-six thousand grants recently awarded to more than twenty-two thousand nonprofits in the United States and abroad. **Price:** $135. **Order from:** The Foundation Center (see above).

Private Foundation IRS Tax Returns
The Internal Revenue Service requires private foundations to file income tax returns each year. Form 990-PF provides fiscal details on receipts and expenditures, compensation of officers, capital gains or losses, and other financial matters. Form 990-AR provides information on foundation managers, assets, and grants paid or committed for future payment.

The IRS makes this information available on aperture (microfiche) cards that may be viewed for free at the reference collections operated by the Foundation Center (New York, San Francisco, Washington, DC, Cleveland, and Atlanta) or at the Center's regional cooperating collections. You may also obtain this information by writing to the Ogden IRS Service Center, P.O. Box 9953, Mail Stop 6734, Ogden, UT 84409, fax (801) 775-4839.

Enclose as much information about the foundation as possible, including its full name, street address with city, state, and zip code, employer identification number (EIN, which appears in Foundation Center directories and Infotax, a CD-ROM database), and the year or years for which returns are requested. It generally takes four to six weeks for the IRS to respond and it will bill you for all charges: $1 for the first page and fifteen cents for each additional page or $1 for the first aperture card and eighteen cents for each additional card.

Try websites www.irs.ustreas.gov, www.guidestar.org, and www.non-profits.org to obtain information on these organizations from the 1990s. For historical information on a private foundation contact Indiana University/Purdue University Indianapolis University Library at (317) 278-2329. It has 990-PFs dating from the late 1960s donated by the Foundation Center.

State and Local Grantmakers

Visit the Foundation Center cooperating collection closest to you to determine what directories are available for your state and surrounding region. The following three regional guides are available through the Foundation Center:

Guide to Greater Washington D.C. Grantmakers (3rd edition, July 1998), $60
New York State Foundations (5th edition, June 1997), $180
Directory of Missouri Grantmakers (2nd edition, June 1997), $75

Visit the Rural Information Center on the Internet at www.nal.usda.gov/ric/ricpubs/funding/funding1.htm for a comprehensive listing of available state directories. Note that some directories are updated regularly, but many are not.

Corporate Grant Resources

Corporate Contributions in 1997

Sponsored by the Conference Board and the Council for Financial Aid to Education, this annual survey includes a detailed analysis of beneficiaries of corporate support but does not list individual firms and specific recipients. **Price:** $25 for associates, $100 for nonassociates. **Order from:** The Conference Board, 845 Third Avenue, New York, NY 10022, (212) 759-0900.

Corporate Giving Watch

This newsletter reports on corporate giving developments. **Price:** $149 for sixteen issues. **Order from:** Gale Group, P.O. Box 9187, Farmington Hills, MI 48333-9187, (800) 877-8238.

Directory of Corporate Affiliations (1999)

This five-volume directory lists divisions, subsidaries, and affiliates of thousands of companies with addresses, telephone numbers, key persons, employees, and the like. **Price:** $1,059 plus shipping and handling. **Order from:** Reed Elsevier New Providence, P.O. Box 31, New Providence, NJ 07974, (800) 323-6772.

Dun and Bradstreet's Million Dollar Directory (five volumes)

These list the name, address, employees, sales volume, and other pertinent data for 140,000 of the largest businesses in the United States. **Price:** $1,525 print copy; $9,975 Internet database. **Order from:** Dun and Bradstreet Information Services, 3 Sylvan Way, Parsippany, NJ 07054, (800) 526-0651.

The National Directory of Corporate Giving, 5th edition (October 1997)

Information on over 1,905 corporate foundations, plus an additional nine hundred direct-giving programs, is provided. An extensive bibliography and seven indexes are included to help you target funding prospects. **Price:** $225. **Order from:** The Foundation Center, 79 Fifth Avenue Dept. FJ, New York, NY 10003-3076, (800) 424-9836, in New York State (212) 807-3690, fax (212) 807-3677, www.fdncenter.org

Standard and Poor's Register of Corporations, Directors and Executives (three volumes)

This annual register (volume 1, *Corporations*; volume 2, *Directors and Executives*; volume 3, *Indexes*) can only be leased. The volumes provide up-to-date rosters of over five hundred thousand executives of the seventy-five thousand nationally known corporations they represent, along with their names, titles, and business affiliations. **Price:** $795 per year for print, $1,095 for CD-ROM or Internet; both include quarterly updates. **Order from:** Standard and Poor, Attn: Sales, 65 Broadway 8th Floor, New York, NY 10006-2503, (212) 770-4412.

North American Industry Classification System Manual

Developed for use in the classification of establishments by type of activity in which they are engaged. **Price:** printed version $28.50 softcover, $32.50 hardcover; CD-ROM version $45 single user, $120 for five or fewer concurrent network users, $240 unlimited concurrent network users. **Order from:** National Technical Information Service, Springfield, VA 22161, (800) 553-6847, www.ntis.gov

Taft Corporate Giving Directory (1999)

This provides detailed entries on a thousand company-sponsored foundations. Included are nine indexes. **Price:** $440 plus postage and handling.

Order from: Gale Group, P.O. Box 9187, Farmington Hills, MI 48333-9187, (800) 877-8238.

Who's Who in America 1998/1999, 53rd edition
Known for its life and career data on noteworthy individuals. Two volumes. **Price:** $525. **Order from:** Reed Elsevier New Providence, P.O. Box 31, New Providence, NJ 07974, (800) 236-6772.

Government, Foundation, and Corporate Grant Resources

Many of the following research aids can be purchased from Jossey-Bass, 350 Sansome Street, San Francisco, CA 94104, (800) 956-7739, fax (800) 605-2665, www.josseybass.com

Winning Grants Step by Step
Support Centers of America's workbook for planning, developing, and writing proposals. **Price:** $25.95. **Order from:** Jossey-Bass.

The Teacher's Guide to Winning Grants
A systematic guide to grantseeking skills that work for classroom leaders. **Price:** $24.95. Order from: Jossey-Bass.

The Principal's Guide to Winning Grants
Strategies principals can apply to support grantseeking at their schools. **Price:** $24.95. **Order from:** Jossey-Bass.

The Complete Grants Sourcebook for Higher Education, 2nd edition
Four hundred sixty-five pages of research on funding sources for higher education. **Price:** $85. **Order from:** Oryx Press, 4041 N. Central Avenue Suite 700, Phoenix, AZ 85012-3397, (800) 279-6799, fax (800) 279-4663.

The Complete Grants Sourcebook for Nursing and Health
A practical guide that includes an in-depth analysis of three hundred funding sources for nursing and health. **Price:** $75. **Order from:** Oryx Press, 4041 N. Central Avenue Suite 700, Phoenix, AZ 85012-3397, (800) 279-6799, fax (800) 279-4663.

Directory of Biomedical and Health Care Grants
This provides information on biomedical and health care–related programs sponsored by the federal government, corporations, professional associations, special interest groups, and state and local governments. Published annually. **Price:** $84.50. **Order from:** Oryx Press, 4041 N. Central Avenue Suite 700, Phoenix, AZ 85012-3397, (800) 279-6799, fax (800) 279-4663.

Directory of Building and Equipment Grants, 5th edition
Aimed at aiding in the search for building and equipment grants, this directory profiles more than eight hundred foundations. **Price:** $59.50.

Order from: Research Grant Guides, P.O. Box 1214, Loxahatchee, FL 33470, (561) 795-6129 (no credit card or phone orders accepted), fax (561) 795-7794.

Directory of Computer and High Technology Grants, 3rd edition
This directory provides five hundred foundation profiles to help organizations obtain software and computer and high-tech equipment. **Price:** $59.50. **Order from:** Research Grant Guides, P.O. Box 1214, Loxahatchee, FL 33470, (561) 795-6129 (no credit card or phone orders accepted), fax (561) 795-7794.

Directory of Funding Sources for Community Development
Description of programs that offer funding opportunities for quality-of-life projects at the community level are included. Funding programs sponsored by both local and national sources are listed, including state, local, and federal government sources, nonprofit and corporate sponsors, foundations, and advocacy groups. Published annually. **Price:** $64.95. **Order from:** Oryx Press, 4041 N. Central Avenue Suite 700, Phoenix, AZ 85012-3397, (800) 279-6799, fax (800) 279-4663.

Directory of Grants for Organizations Serving People with Disabilities, 10th edition
Profiles on more than eight hundred foundations that have a history of serving people with disabilities are included. **Price:** $59.50. **Order from:** Research Grant Guides, P.O. Box 1214, Loxahatchee, FL 33470, (561) 795-6129 (no credit card or phone orders accepted), fax (561) 795-7794.

Directory of Research Grants
Information on government, corporate, organizational, and private funding sources supporting research programs in academic, scientific, and technological subjects is included. Published annually. **Price:** $135. **Order from:** Oryx Press, 4041 N. Central Avenue Suite 700, Phoenix, AZ 85012-3397, (800) 279-6799, fax (800) 279-4663.

Giving USA 98
Annual report on philanthropy for the year 1997. **Price:** $49.95 plus $25 for each newsletter. **Order from:** AAFRC Trust for Philanthropy, 25 W. 43rd Street Suite 820, New York, NY 10037, (212) 354-5799 ext. 3001 (customer service).

Computer Research Services

Community of Science (COS) Funding Opportunities
Included with fee-based membership in the Community of Scholars. Other institutions may purchase access for a fixed annual fee. **Price:** depends on the amount of external research funding your institution manages. To receive more information about rates, subscriptions, or free

trials, contact Edwin Van Dusen, VP-Information Products, 1629 Thames Street Suite 200, Baltimore, MD 21231, (410) 563-5382 ext. 225, fax (410) 563-5389, evd@cos.com

Congressional Information Service Index (CIS Index)
CIS covers congressional publications and legislation from 1970 to date. Hearings, committee prints, House and Senate reports and documents, special publications, Senate executive reports and documents, and public laws are indexed. Includes monthly abstracts and index volumes. Hard copies of grant-related materials are also available from *CIS*, including *CIS Federal Register Index*, which covers announcements from the *Federal Register* weekly. **Price:** $1,460 hardcover (1998 edition); monthly service (including hardbound annual edition) is on a sliding scale depending on your library's annual book, periodical, and microform budget. Order from: Congressional Information Services Inc., 4520 East-West Highway Suite 800, Bethesda, MD 20814, (800) 638-8380.

DIALOG On-Disc Grants Database
This lists approximately 8,900 grants offered by federal, state, and local governments; commercial organizations; professional associations; and private and community foundations. Each entry includes a description, qualifications, money available, and renewability. Full name, address, and telephone number for each sponsoring organization are included as available. **Price:** $850, which includes a bimonthly updated CD-ROM. **Order from:** DIALOG Corporation, 11000 Regency Parkway Suite 10, Cary, NC 27511, (800) 334-2564, fax (919) 468-9890, www.dialog.com

Federal Assistance Program Retrieval System (FAPRS)
This provides access to federal domestic assistance program information. All states have FAPRS services available through state, county, and local agencies as well as through federal extension services. For further information, call (202) 708-5126 or FAPRS toll-free answering service at (800) 669-8331, or write to your congressperson's office; he or she can request a search for you, in some cases at no charge. **For more information contact:** Federal Domestic Assistance Catalog Staff (MVS), General Services Administration, 300 Seventh Street SW, Reporters Building Room 101, Washington, DC 20407.

FEDIX
FEDIX (Federal Info Exchange) is a free on-line database of federal grant and research opportunities for educators and researchers. Participating federal agencies use FEDIX as an outreach tool to enhance communications with colleges, universities, and other educational and research organizations. **For more information:** (800) 875-2562 or www.fie.com

Foundation Center Databases

The Foundation Center offers two on-line computer databases—one providing information on grantmakers, the other on the grants they distribute. Both are available on-line through DIALOG. **For more information:** DIALOG Corporation, 11000 Regency Parkway Suite 10, Cary, NC 27511, (800) 334-2564, fax (919) 468-9890, www.dialog.com

GrantScape CFDA

This is an electronic edition of the *Catalog of Federal Domestic Assistance*, including the full text of all federal grant programs included in the CFDA. **Price:** $175. **Order from:** Aspen Publishers Inc., 7201 McKinney Circle, Frederick, MD 21704, (800) 638-8437.

GrantSelect

This database is available on the Web and provides information on more than 9,400 funding programs available from over 3,400 nonprofit organizations, foundations, private sources, and federal, state, and local agencies in the United States and Canada. Grantseekers can subscribe to the full database or to any one of five special segments offered: children and youth, health care and biomedical, arts and humanities, K–12 schools, or adult basic education and community development. An e-mail alert service that notifies grantseekers of new funding opportunities is also available. **Price:** Yearly subscription to full database, $1,000; e-mail alert service only, $1,000; full database plus e-mail alert service, $1,500; single database segment, $350; single-segment e-mail alert service only, $350; single-segment plus e-mail alert service, $500. Prices are for one campus or institution only; add 25 percent for each additional campus. A 25 percent discount is available for two-year subscriptions, and consortia pricing available on request. **Order from:** Oryx Press, 4041 N. Central Suite 700, Phoenix, AZ 85012-3397, (800) 279-6799, fax (800) 279-4663, www.higheredconnect.com/grantselect

Illinois Researcher Information Service (IRIS)

The IRIS database contains records on over 7,700 federal and nonfederal funding opportunities in the sciences, social sciences, arts, and humanities. It is updated daily and is available in WWW and Telnet versions. **Price:** IRIS is a subscription service available to colleges and universities for an annual fee. **For more information** on the subscription policy and/or an IRIS trial period, contact University of Illinois at Urbana-Champaign, 128 Observatory, 901 South Mathews Avenue, Urbana, IL 61801, (217) 333-0284, fax (217) 333-7011, rso@uiuc.edu

KR OnDisc: Federal Register

This is a CD-ROM version of the *Federal Register*. **Price:** Depends on whether your organization subscribes to other DIALOG services. **For**

more information or to order, contact DIALOG Corporation, 11000 Regency Parkway Suite 10, Cary, NC 27511, (800) 334-2564, fax (919) 468-9890, www.dialog.com

The Sponsored Programs Information Network (SPIN)

This is a database of federal and private funding sources. **Price:** from $1,000 to $6,000 depending on the institution's level of research and development expenditures. **Order from:** InfoEd, 2301 Western Avenue, Guilderland, NY 12084, (800) 727-6427, fax (518) 464-0695, www.infoed.org/products.stm